The Killing Zone

MY LIFE IN THE VIETNAM WAR

The Killing Zone

MY LIFE IN THE VIETNAM WAR

FREDERICK DOWNS

W·W·NORTON & COMPANY
New York   London

To the men of Delta One-six,
and to our commander,
Captain Harold Sells

Copyright © 2007, 1978 by Frederick Downs

For information about permission to reproduce selections from this book,
write to Permissions, W. W. Norton & Company, Inc.,
500 Fifth Avenue, New York, NY 10110

Manufacturing by LSC Harrisonburg
Book design by Jacques Chazaud
Production manager: Devon Zahn

Library of Congress Cataloging-in-Publication Data

Downs, Frederick.
The killing zone.
1. Vietnamese conflict, 1961–1975—Personal narratives, American. 2. Downs,
Frederick. I. Title.
ISBN 0-393-07531-1
DS559.5.D69
959.704'38

78-17032

ISBN 978-0-393-31089-4 pbk.

W. W. Norton & Company, Inc.
500 Fifth Avenue, New York, N.Y. 10110
www.wwnorton.com

W. W. Norton & Company Ltd.
15 Carlisle Street, London W1D 3BS

1

ACKNOWLEDGEMENTS

I want to thank all of my friends who have listened for so long to my war stories. A deeply felt appreciation is extended to: Virginia Kenney, typist extraordinary, who patiently translated my handwriting into typed pages; Sheila Dunne, who typed on short notice; and Virginia Shively, who cheerfully transformed Dictaphone ramblings into coherent sentences.

A note of recognition to those unpaid critics who read the manuscript and gave me valuable comments: David and Susan Walls, Ray and Emma Smith, Kathleen Leone, Melissa Allen, Alan Bow, and John and Mary Spangler. You all had opinions and did not keep them to yourselves.

Thanks to Leona Schecter and Ed Barber for taking a chance on an unknown, and Joel Swerdlow for offering invaluable advice, not all of which I have taken.

To my wife, Mary Boston Downs, a special thanks; you always knew I could do it.

CONTENTS

CONTENTS

PREFACE

In the fall of 1968, as I stopped at a traffic light on my walk to class across the campus of the University of Denver, a man stepped up to me and said, "Hi."

Without waiting for my reply to his greeting, he pointed to the hook sticking out of my left sleeve. "Get that in Vietnam?"

I said, "Yeah, up near Tam Ky in I Corps."

"Serves you right."

As the man walked away, I stood rooted, too confused with hurt, shame, and anger to react.

Ten years have passed. The hurt, shame, and anger still flood over me with the memory. But of one thing I am certain—none of the men I knew who served in Vietnam deserved to die or to be maimed, either physically or mentally.

I think it is necessary now to give another view of Vietnam, that of the day-to-day life of an infantryman on the ground.

I have always been asked what I thought about Vietnam, but never what it was like to fight in Vietnam.

This is the way it was for us, the platoon of Delta One-six.

SECTION 1

The Bridges

8 September 1967

At 2330 hours the Continental "Big Bird with the Golden Tail" DC–8 dropped through the night sky into the landing pattern over the black landscape of Vietnam. Twenty-three hours earlier 165 of us had been crammed aboard the commercial jet at the airport near San Francisco.

I looked around the cabin at the officers and enlisted men who had come from all over the United States to catch this flight from San Francisco.

How would they return? How would I return?

I had graduated six months earlier from the U.S. Army's OCS program at Fort Benning, Georgia, and now I was soon to be leading men into combat. I was twenty-three years old and I had been trained to lead. Physically, I thought I was ready. Mentally, I was as confident of myself as any young officer could be, but underneath my confidence were the ever-present questions, worry, and curiosity about war and my role in it.

I was eagerly looking forward to finding answers. I would not have long to wait.

I was surprised at the number of lights below. I had always thought that a war zone would be blacked out, yet the jewels of lights spread haphazardly through the dark. I expected tracers to rip the night as the enemy tried to shoot us down, but the landing at Tan Son Nhut was uneventful.

We exited the aircraft in a long khaki line to stand apprehensively under a series of large open-sided tents with tables lined up under them. The oppressive heat and humidity was filled with the smells of dust, machinery, and rotting vegetation.

Everything was lit up. I wondered when the mortars would start dropping in. How could the enemy miss a target as tempting as that plane and all of these men?

The plane was being refueled for takeoff. Opposite our naive line stood another line of soldiers, waiting to go home. The soldiers hooted disparaging remarks at us.

"It's a lick, motherfucker!"

"You'll be sorrryyy!"

"New cannon fodder!"

"You guys short yet? Only 365 days to go? Shiiiit!"

We had no comeback to those veterans. After all, hadn't they just completed a tour of war duty? We suffered our ignominy in silence.

We were checked through rapidly. As we were directed to the buses that would take us to the disbursement center, I looked back. Spotlights shone on the airplane that had brought us here. Pretty stewardesses in pert uniforms smiled and chatted with the boarding soldiers. The crew was inspecting the underside of the plane in a preflight check.

I turned around to stare into the blackness in front of me. What was there?

We walked to the convoy of buses sitting in the darkness with their motors running. The windows were fogged from the air conditioning which the drivers had turned up full blast. As we got close, one driver opened his door, releasing a blast of cool air and the sounds of the country and western music his radio was getting on the armed forces station. Man! I wasn't expecting this cushy treatment. This wasn't anything like a war zone.

After a short ride through some checkpoints (this was more like it), we were unloaded and told to hit the sack. Barrack-like tents, with wood sides halfway up and canvas for the rest of the wall and roof, were our first homes. After our twenty-three-hour flight, we plopped down to sleep on the cots lined up along both walls.

There was a crowd around the bulletin board the next morning. Men were laughing or bitching as they discovered their new units. I pushed through the crowd to look for my name and found it with "4th Division" next to it.

"Fourth Division! Hey! Anybody ever heard of the Fourth Division? Where is it operating? I never heard of it."

A grizzled career sergeant was standing next to me.

"That's a good outfit, lieutenant. They're stationed out at Pleiku, up in the Central Highlands."

"I never read about them anywhere in the papers back home. Are they doing much fighting up there? I don't want an outfit that's not in action."

The sergeant turned to look at me. "They're spread out in I Corps and II Corps in the Central Highlands, like I said. Not everybody doing the fighting is in the newspapers. You'll never ever see a reporter up there. It's too rough for them." He looked at my youth. "You'll get a belly full of fighting up there, son, if that's what you want."

"Thanks, sergeant," I mumbled as I pushed to the back of the crowd to return to my tent.

I didn't care whether I seemed anxious or not. I was waiting beside the road with my duffle bag and flight bag long before transportation arrived to take us to the airport.

A C-130 leapfrogged north from one airfield to another on its journey to Pleiku. The procedure was the same each time we took off and landed. We sat in rows on the bare floor of the airplane. Long canvas straps hooked from one side of the plane to the other supposedly acted as a buffer against bumps and jolts. Actually, the straps were worthless for protection but the colorfully dressed crew chief always made certain they were fastened each time new passengers walked up the tail for loading.

I was interested in the crew chief's uniform. He was wearing a tiger-striped jungle fatigue outfit. He had a pistol on one hip and a knife on the other. He even had a knife strapped to his leg. Maybe he never did any fighting, but he sure looked the part.

Sitting on the floor of the military aircraft was just one stretch of a pain in the ass. I exited the C-130 at Pleiku, glad to have it over with.

We loaded aboard deuce-and-a-halfs to ride across town to the camp, a huge sprawling base on the highland plains from which the war in that zone was run.

Vietnamese were everywhere, on the roads and in the camp. They were in places I thought would be taboo on a military base. As the driver navigated between the neat military tents, he explained that Americans used the gooks for all the dirty jobs. The lucky ones were the hootch maids, who had the plush job of making the beds and cleaning up the tents.

"You mean every soldier has a maid regardless of his rank?" I asked.

"Yep, sir! They work real cheap, thirty to thirty-five piasters or 'P' a day, about twenty-eight cents. It's easy living for us. At evening they have to be outside the gate, but the next morning they're lined up ready to come in again. Of course, they have to have a card to get in. Security, you know."

I didn't know. From everything I had been taught about the enemy, that would be a perfect way to get information. A camp this size must employ hundreds of Vietnamese. It would be impossible to check them all. I decided not to question that line of reasoning further and asked him something I was curious about.

"I noticed you called them gooks. I thought that would be what we called the enemy. Does everybody call them gooks?"

"We do around here, sir." He was enjoying his status as teacher. "Different units got different names for them, but it don't make no difference what you call them, you know. Friendly or not, they're all called the same. Look at them. They don't even know what good living is. They're ignorant as owl shit, you know?" He blasted his horn at a group of Vietnamese to get them out of the way.

"Wait till you get to Sin City. Of course, you're an officer and they aren't allowed in, but you can take your rank off, it won't make no difference, you know?"

"What's Sin City?"

"That's a little town outside the camp near Pleiku. The army tries to control prostitution and V.D. by keeping an area over there where you can go and fuck your eyeballs out if you're an enlisted man, or, being an officer, can sneak in. It's guarded by MPs and everything. The American doctors check the whores three times a week for V.D., but you got to be standing first in line after they get through to be sure you don't get the clap, you know?"

I was beginning to think I didn't know anything.

"You mean the army supports something like that?"

"Sure. They know they can't stick your ass over here for a year and not expect you to fuck something, so they must have decided that since they couldn't stop it, the least they could do was control it, you know? They even make sure the whores don't overcharge you!

"Here you are, sir. Just report in at the building over there," he pointed.

"Thanks." I pulled my bags out of the back of the truck and carried them over to the doorway he had indicated.

There might not be much fighting around here, I thought, *but there seems to be plenty of action.*

I reported to the sergeant, who told me to report to the supply sergeant for my equipment. The supply sergeant gave me two sets of jungle fatigues, olive-drab underwear, towel, M-16 rifle with magazines. He told me to stuff all of my other junk into my duffle bag, gave me a card to fill out to attach to it, and told me he would store it there while I was in country. He gave me a rucksack to carry all of my things in from that point on.

"What unit will I be attached to?"

"I don't know. You got to attend a three-day training class before you get assigned to the field."

"I've been in training for a year and now I have to go to more classes?"

"Yeah, that's SOP in this division. It used to be five days, but they cut it back to three because they need you guys out in the field."

I was upset. More training. I had been training long enough. I wanted to get out with a company in the field, not jack around in some stupid base camp, but orders were orders. But first, I had to go through an endless line of company clerks asking their questions and banging the answers out on forms in their typewriters. The clerks double-checked to make sure we had turned in all American money for Military Payment Certificates, MPCs.

For the next three days I was with a group of other men new-in-country as we endured the now-familiar routine of firing our weapons, throwing grenades, attending classes on tactics, and playing hearts at every break.

I learned the camp was well protected. Watchtowers were placed at regular intervals around the entire perimeter. Bunkers were spread in between for fire support and defense. Three concentric rings separated by barbed wire surrounded the camp. Each ring held land mines and a nasty little item called Foo Gas. Foo Gas was fifty-gallon drums filled with explosives and napalm and buried at strategic places in the perimeter. They were triggered by a blasting cap hooked up to a hand detonator. When they were set off, there was hell to pay as the flaming liquid was thrown a radius of fifty meters in all directions. It was guaranteed to break up a ground attack.

On the fourth day, I was loaded into a C-130 for a bumpy ride to a place further north called Duc Pho, home of the Third Brigade of the Fourth Division. They were operating in the field on search-and-destroy missions.

Duc Pho straddled Highway 1 about a kilometer from the South China Sea, separated from it by a solitary mountain a hundred fifty meters high. Once only a peaceful hill surrounded by rice paddies, the mountain had been developed into a base camp a couple of months before. An airstrip was laid out on the flat ground at the base of the mountain on its western side. A perimeter had been built around the entire mountain to enclose it within the protective confines of the American camp. The mountain was only a little over a half of a kilometer long at its base, making it a perfect defensive location amid all the flat ground around it. We called it Montezuma Mountain.

The camp was fully developed to the west. As more units were assigned to the camp, they were assigned areas in a steadily encroaching circle around to the east side, toward the sea. The First Battalion of the Fourteenth Infantry was around on the east side. That was to be my unit. I caught a ride in a jeep from the airstrip around the mountain to my new home.

The battalion street was laid out at an angle from the mountain's base. The battalion commander's headquarters was located closest to the mountain, with the companies spread out in a neat line leading toward the rice paddies. The company headquarters of Alpha, Bravo, Charlie, and Delta were lined up on one side of the street. A latrine for the enlisted men was located at the end closest to the perimeter. The latrine, a four-holer, closed off the company area. Behind each company headquarters was the supply room for that company. Off to the side, farther behind the company headquarters, were the large half-wood, half-tent barracks to house the men when they returned from operations for a standdown. The company headquarters buildings were the same type of construction, but they were divided by mosquito netting into an orderly room and individual cubicles for the officers. Between the supply room and the back of the company headquarters was a garbage-can shower for the officers.

Behind the battalion commander's headquarters was a two-holer for the officers. Spread throughout the area were piss tubes for everybody. These were constructed by digging a small hole in the ground near a discreet place like a bush, sticking a packing tube used for rockets—about three feet long and four inches in diameter—into the hole so that two feet of it stuck out of the earth at an angle, and pouring rocks in the hole around the tube to hold it in place and to act as a drain. As a finishing touch, a wire screen would be fastened across the end. These tubes were very convenient and, lest anyone had trouble figuring out what they were, there was always a sign next to them with "Piss Tube" written on it.

Across the area to the side of the battalion headquarters was a large mess hall shaped like a "T" and constructed out of the half-wood, half-tent buildings. These buildings were used for every purpose. They were built up off the ground, had wood floors, and were mostly dry.

An old airplane wing tank across the company street served as the enlisted men's shower.

A landing pad with room for one helicopter was marked out in front of the mess hall.

The company area was "L" shaped. Out beyond the top of the "L" were the bunkers and the barbed wire. Beyond that, rice paddies ran to the low sand dunes along the ocean.

That evening I wandered into headquarters company looking for company and information. The company clerks were only too happy to tell the lieutenant new-in-country all about the best damn outfit in Nam.

It was SOP to salute in the company area but not in the field. When an enlisted man saluted, he would say "Golden Dragon, sir!" The officer would return the salute with "Right-of-the-line." I asked about this.

They told me that the First of the Fourteenth was an old infantry regiment steeped in tradition. During the Boxer Rebellion in China the unit had fought bravely. Afterward they had adopted the symbol of a Golden Dragon. The other part of the salute came from some battle in the Civil War. Right before a large battle a staff officer asked a general where to put the First of the Fourteenth. The general had roared back, "Put them to the right of the line, where they belong." The right of the line is where a leader traditionally puts his best men and units. This comes down through military history because, when a man fought with shield and sword, the right arm or sword arm was unprotected. The best fighter was put to the right to protect the sword arm of the man on his left. Only the most trusted and the best fighters held the position to the right.

A radio call broke up our discussion. I listened to the companies calling in their action report for that day. Two men had been killed, a number of others wounded.

After the radio call, under the harsh lightbulbs I watched the clerks struggle with the ever-changing figures of the most important document in the military, the Morning Report, DA Form 1. With this report the army kept tabs on every man under its command. Everyone from the AWOLs to those killed in action. I was familiar with the report, but now a new dimension was added. "Killed in Action" or "Wounded in Action" were things I had only heard of; tomorrow I would be a candidate for both categories. I dismissed the thought of ever dying. A slight wound for my career maybe, but nothing worse.

I walked back up the company street toward battalion headquarters. The night was full of strange sounds made more awesome by the fact that I was in an actual war zone. The distant rumble of a tank engine, vehicles moving, voices of men drifting in from different directions, and uncountable insect noises formed the acoustic backdrop of war.

Across the barbed wire, just meters away, was territory that belonged to the enemy. I had been warned many times already that we only controlled what was within our barbed-wire perimeters, no matter where we were in Vietnam.

All of this—the area where I stood, the night sounds, the barbed wire, the alien land—had yet to make a believer of me. Less than a week ago I had been drinking beer in San Francisco. The year and a half of infantry training had been against make-believe enemies who had died make-believe deaths.

The XO pointed out the cots the other lieutenant and I were to use. I decided to sleep fully clothed, but to remove my boots for comfort. That was the last time in Vietnam I removed my boots to sleep. If anything happened at night in the field, we didn't have time to fumble with boot laces.

Too pent up to sleep, I lay on the cot staring through the screened upper half of the hootch at the dark sky. Suddenly, an artillery gun fired from somewhere close above me. It must have been from the top of the mountain. A flare lit the sky as a four-deuce mortar fired an illumination round. I sat up in the cot, then walked to the doorway to look at the eerie flickering landscape around me and out beyond the barbed wire.

I knew I shouldn't, but I glanced at the flare. Smoke left a corkscrew in the air behind the slowly spiraling burning phosphorus. I could hear the hissing of the burning. The light reflected slightly against the miniature parachute supporting the flare and against the bottom of the stretched-out spring of smoke which marked its descent. I followed the corkscrew of smoke upward, but it disappeared in the darkness far above the flare.

I pulled my eyes away, squeezed them shut for a second, and opened them to stare out again over the area. Deep shadows moved in elongated orbits over the ground in concert with the spiraling swinging of the flare. The shadows grew longer as the flare dropped lower.

The open area not covered by the deep, dark shadows seemed harshly bright by comparison. The flickering light was strange because it did not allow for colors but made everything a contrast of light and dark, of shadow and substance. The scene presented itself to the eyes like a movie film not quite running up to the proper speed. A flickering of seeing and not seeing, with each new flare showing a little different picture than the one before.

As my brain acclimated to the images my eyes were recording, the flare floated to the ground to lay there hidden by the short rice shoots in a mixture of burning light and rising smoke.

For the briefest of seconds everything was pitch black until my night vision started to come back. I lay down again, still unable to sleep because of the sounds of mortars, 105 recoiless rifle, and artillery guns occasionally firing a round. There was no pattern to any of it. Maybe we were being attacked.

Very soon I learned that this nighttime display was known as "H and I fire," harassment and interdictory fire. This was a procedure followed by the Americans, intended to confuse and demoralize the enemy.

The idea was based on the fact that there were no friendlies outside the perimeters at night in this part of Vietnam except American patrols and ambushes and allies, all of whom were carefully marked on the commander's maps. Anyone else moving in Zones I and II at night was considered to be the enemy. With a little luck, one of those shells would surprise the enemy by dropping unexpectedly on the trail or clearing at the same time he was there.

H and I fire seemed a good idea to me. A little wasteful perhaps, but a hell of a good thing for our morale.

I finally allowed my mind to become adjusted to the different sounds and intermittent light, and fell asleep.

13 September 1967

This morning the XO hustled me into a helicopter that was flying out to the battalion located in the field. I jumped aboard with my rifle, web gear, and rucksack, and sat in one of the canvas seats in the middle of the helicopter. It was a style called a Huey, or a slick. It was called a slick because it didn't have any weapons fastened on the outside of the fuselage. It only had two door gunners, one on each side, armed with M-60 machine guns mounted on a swivel. The slick was used for transport of supplies and men. It had a pilot, co-pilot, crew chief, and the two door gunners. This allowed the slick to carry six fully equipped infantrymen into an LZ. The two side doors were always fastened open or removed.

It was rumored that any enemy soldier who shot any aircraft down was promoted on the spot. If so, the helicopters helped quite a few enemy soldiers along in their careers.

To supplement the firepower of ground troops and protect the slicks, the gunship was developed. This was a slick converted to a weapons carrier by adding multiple rockets launchers and machine guns. They all carried plenty of firepower and were excellent in ground support, but they were still only converted slicks.

The Cobra, another fire-support helicopter, had recently arrived in Vietnam. It had a narrow three-foot-wide fuselage, was a faster fighting machine, and carried a weapons system classified as light, medium, or heavy. All three weapons systems consisted of various amounts of multiple rocket launchers and machine guns. Some Cobras had multiple-feed M-79 grenade launchers mounted in the nose. There were only two crewmen, one seated above and behind the other in the narrow cockpit. The Cobra was half again as fast as the Huey, and a formidable weapon.

The pilot landed on one of a group of small hills that marked the boundary line between the flat rice paddies that spread to the sea and the mountains that were the beginning of the ranges that covered the interior leading to the Central Highlands.

The battalion had set up a firebase on one low hill from which the battalion commander directed the operation. The major introduced me to the colonel who walked out of his CP. The colonel welcomed me and told me that I would be assigned to Delta Company as an observer so that I would have a chance to become familiar with how the company worked in the field. He would send me out in a chopper later that afternoon.

I wandered around the firebase observing the men in their different activities. I particularly noticed the four-deuce mortars set up in the middle to provide fire support. Each tube was surrounded by sandbags. An ammo supply was next to each tube. Men lounged around their guns, smoking cigarettes and joking with each other. Most of them were stripped to the waist in the hot sun. Mud was everywhere.

I stood on a rock to get a better view of the rice paddies to the east. Below me, the edge of the lush green paddies gave way to irregular flat areas of bright green, spreading as far as I could see. Clumps of trees stood out like little islands in a sea of green. Every once in a while a HE (high explosive) shell would be fired from the tubes behind me, to explode among the trees.

Off to the north, thin columns of white smoke marked the leading edge of the company's movement through the rugged foothills. Each column of smoke represented a hootch on fire. I could see small groups of black-pajama-clad people moving out of the hills. They were loaded down with belongings carried on their backs or across their shoulders, balanced on the long bamboo poles so prevalent in the Orient. Several pushed heavily loaded bicycles. The people streamed out of the foothills from the direction of the rising columns of smoke, following paths along the edges of the rice fields, making their way across the large open areas toward a destination on one of the large islands barely seen across the immense sea of green. They avoided the small islands within range of our mortars, as explosions warned them of the indiscriminate death being dealt from our low hilltop.

When the chopper was finally ready, I grabbed my pack and jumped aboard. I sat in a side seat instead of on the floor with my feet on the landing skid. I wasn't quite ready to sit on the edge of that chopper with one or two thousand feet of empty space between me and the ground.

We flew north along the foothills until the chopper started circling. Far below me I could see purple smoke marking the landing spot for the pilot. The chopper pilot lowered the aircraft to within a few feet of the ground and then settled in. I jumped off as a group of disheveled-looking soldiers stepped out of the thick brush. I ran in a crouch out from under the rapidly turning rotor blades as the crewmen threw out some cases of C rations and ammo.

Bugs swarmed around my face. I swatted and looked at the men, who looked right back at me. It was my first view of American GIs who had spent several days in the jungle. I stood there in sparkling crisp fatigues, brand-new boots, new rifle, clean shaven, fresh haircut. I even smelled clean. My helmet camouflage cover didn't have a mark on it, nor did I.

The two men opposite me were filthy. Their fatigues were torn, and they had scratches all over their skin, two or three days' growth of beard, and dark circles under their eyes. They looked tired, and they smelled to high heaven.

One of them introduced himself as Sergeant Schaldenbrand; his radio operator (RTO) was named Mann. Schaldenbrand was about my size; Mann was taller and thinner. Some other men were hauling away the supplies as the chopper lifted up out of the small landing zone.

Schaldenbrand told me to follow him, as the company was located on the small hill behind him. The other men called over to say they were ready. I followed Schaldenbrand and Mann into the brush. We wound and twisted and the sweat started pouring off me. The sun was beating down; the humidity must have been close to a hundred percent. The brush wasn't much taller than we were, so it provided no protection. The bugs started to bite in earnest. The aftershave lotion I had used that morning was an obvious lure to every mosquito within a hundred meters. They all homed on me, trying to suck out my blood before I reached the top of the hill.

Halfway up the hill, we pushed through tall elephant grass whose sharp edges cut my exposed skin. I couldn't tell how far we had to go. My pack straps were cutting into my shoulders; my fatigues were wet with sweat. Where was the company?

A voice next to me said hi. I jumped from the sound of a voice speaking out of the elephant grass. Right next to me were a couple of men barely visible in their position at the edge of the company perimeter. They were so close. I swallowed hard and returned the greeting.

Schaldenbrand led me through more elephant grass to the small inner circle of the perimeter where the CP was located. He introduced me to the individual who would be a dominant figure in my life for the rest of my tour in Vietnam, Captain Harold Sells.

Captain Sells was an ROTC officer, twenty-six years old, the son of a father killed in Korea. He was my size, about five feet ten inches tall, and medium built. He had light-brown hair and a no-nonsense air about him.

He introduced me around to the company CP group and then assigned me to the First Platoon, led by Lieutenant Smart. Lieutenant Smart was a tall, red-haired guy who had brought the company over from the States with Captain Sells when the battalion had been transported en masse by boat. He and the captain were good friends and he expected to be the XO for the company as soon as I was ready to take over his platoon.

Captain Sells pointed out the location of the other company in the area, on the next low hill to the north of us. By stretching up on my toes I could see across the top of the elephant grass to the other hill, a twin to the one we were on and also covered with elephant grass. The hill was only a couple of hundred meters away. Charlie Company was there.

The enemy, I was told, was all around us. Not in great force, but in small units of snipers and attack groups. It was hard for me to take seriously. It was still like an OCS exercise.

Lieutenant Smart said I could share his and Schaldenbrand's hootch that night. Smitty and Snodgrass, the CP RTOs, showed me how to fill my canteen when it rained, as it surely would later. The sun cooked us during the day but it seemed to rain every night. Since we never knew when we would be able to get water, we collected the runoff from the slick sides of our hootches.

The hootches looked dirty as hell to me. I made sure I had my iodine tablets ready to sterilize the water in the morning.

After the RTOs were satisfied that my canteen was set up properly, I went over to Captain Sells to find out what our mission would be the next day. He explained the mission to me as he and the men warmed their C rations for the evening meal. He informed me that his radio signal was Delta Six. Lieutenant Smart, the First Platoon leader, was Delta One-six; the Second Platoon leader was Delta Two-six, etc. Sixes were the commanders of their units. Their seconds in command were known as fives. For instance, Delta One-five was the First Platoon's platoon sergeant.

Sells asked me about my family. I explained that I had a wife and two little girls back in Illinois, right across the state line from Indiana where my family lived and where I had grown up on a farm in Kingman.

I was telling him about the latest news in the States when automatic rifle fire shattered the stillness of the early evening air. The men around me instantly threw themselves into defensive positions, their eyes searching outward in an attempt to pierce the elephant grass. All of them clutched their weapons. Spilled cans of C rations lay next to the burning Alka-Seltzer-size heating tablets of compressed solid fuel used to heat our food.

Delta Six grabbed the horn from one of the RTOs. He called Charlie Six to ask what had happened. Delta Six had a "bitch box" on the back of the CP's radio to amplify any incoming calls, which allowed us to listen.

We all heard the excited, tense voice of Charlie Six's RTO report. A dink had fired a BAR into the hilltop, firing blindly through the elephant grass. The unexpected burst had shattered the face and lower jaw of one of the sergeants. The same burst of bullets had passed through the sergeant hitting a lieutenant, who was standing behind him, across the shoulders. Charlie Six thought the lieutenant might live but the sergeant was in a bad way. They had to get a dustoff in quick if they were to save him.

I was stunned. Not two hundred meters away from me a group of men had been doing what we had been doing and now two of them were badly wounded. Jesus! That Vietcong could have fired into our hilltop!

I asked one of the men next to me how they could tell that it was a BAR that had been fired. He answered that every weapon had a distinctive sound. After a while I would be able to pick out the weapon like everyone else. Once I had been shot at with a particular weapon, I would never forget it, he casually remarked.

Delta Six passed the word not to give away our position unless we had a positive target.

We heard the dustoff coming. Everyone tensed. The chopper would offer a perfect target. I spotted it coming from the south, a blot against the now cloudy gray sky. It would be dark in a few minutes. I wondered what would have happened had it been pitch dark. Could they still land?

For the first time I felt the odd sensation of willing my soul upward to assist the chopper crew coming for my fellow soldiers. My body strained as if I could leap upward to the chopper to add my strength to its survival. I prodded the chopper with my thoughts. *Come on, hurry up, you men, just hold out a little longer. Come on. God, I hope the chopper doesn't take fire. Isn't it ever going to get here?*

The dustoff pilots were very, very good. They often had to land in almost impossible landing zones or hover above the growth as the wounded were winched up to safety. The dustoff choppers were ordinary Hueys modified to carry litters. They had little, if any, firepower. The crew was often just a pilot, co-pilot, and medic, sometimes a gunner. The Red Cross painted on both doors, the nose, and belly meant nothing to the enemy. They shot them down as they would any other aircraft.

The chopper circled once to identify smoke, then dropped rapidly downward. In seconds it lifted and tilted forward in that particular tail-up altitude of a chopper pouring on the coals.

The lieutenant survived. The sergeant died.

Apprehensive, we settled down to finish our meal. I sat listening to the men talk. A brilliant flash, a tremendous crack and explosion ripped the air near us. With only reflexes guiding me, I slithered across the ground only to note that the men had not even moved from their positions. They were still squatting over their C rations and chuckling at me.

"What the hell was that?"

Only lightning and thunder, said the captain. The lightning had struck the hill we were on, drawn by the metal of our equipment. I didn't think it was as funny as they did. A guy could get killed around here.

Darkness quickly engulfed us. My hootchmates watched in astonishment as I pulled out mosquito netting and spread it over my poncho liner and air mattress. They were aghast that I carried so much extra weight. "No," I answered, "this is all good stuff." Their amazement grew as I revealed three changes of underwear and fatigue clothes.

Wait until the next day, they scoffed, when the sun and heavy pack would drag me down. The jungle would exact a toll for every ounce I carried. "We'll see," I answered.

Lieutenant Smart said, "Yeah, you'll see. You'll see that the only change of clothes you'll carry will be an extra pair of socks. You'll learn to live in one set of jungle fatigues until they rot off you or are ripped too badly to wear."

It rained steadily all night long and quit right before daybreak. I retrieved my canteen from the corner of the hootch and dropped two iodine tablets in it, hoping to kill all the germs. After a few minutes I tasted it. Blah! Undrinkable, gritty as hell. One of the men handed me a half-package of Kool-Aid to pour into the canteen. It tasted better.

My first days on combat patrol introduced me to the vicissitudes of war: ten-foot-deep punji pits; wait-a-minute vines that collected around the feet and legs until their combined strength stopped you and you had to say "wait-a-minute" while you untangled or cut yourself loose; the hot sun beating down on us as we marched with seventy-pound packs, the sweat pouring off us; bugs so thick around our faces that we sometimes inhaled them; and the physical agony of forcing tired muscles to keep on going.

It was a search-and-destroy mission, which meant we searched all the hootches we found and then burned them down. Whether a single farmer's hootch or a whole village—all were burnt. The few Vietnamese we found in the area were women, children, and old men who had been left behind. When we started to burn their particular hootch, they would start wailing, crying, and pulling at our clothes. We didn't harm the people, but the orders were to destroy all the dwellings, so we did.

The first time I saw a Vietnamese family go into hysterics when their hootch was set on fire I was unsure of whether burning down their home would accomplish our mission. The mission was to deny the enemy the use of the hootches, to destroy any food we found, and to teach the people a lesson about supporting the enemy. But I quickly got used to it and accepted that this was one way to win the war.

I was fired at by a sniper shortly after we had swept through one small hamlet. I always thought the sniper was firing at us becaue we had just set fire to his hootch and, unfortunately, he picked me as a target. I was more surprised than scared as I huddled on the ground and bullets thudded into the earth next to my legs.

Schaldenbrand took the opportunity later that day to explain that in this unit everyone called the enemy, and ultimately all outsiders, "dinks." It turned out that the enemy started calling us "dinks" first, because it was an insulting or demeaning term that meant "hairy man from the jungle." We had just turned the word around and started calling them dinks. At least, that was the story.

I learned to refill my canteen by dragging it through rice paddy water while making an on-line assault into a burning village that had been "prepped" by air strikes and artillary fire.

I saw the face of the enemy for the first time. He had been machine-gunned by one of our gun crews. The powerful weapon had thrown a hail of bullets into the brush where we had spotted him. When we got to his position I saw for the first time the death of a soldier. The machine gun crew had done a good job. The young soldier's green combat-uniformed body was riddled with bullets. He was sprawled across his bicycle with his face toward the sky. At last I had before me the enemy I had been trained to destroy. He was a young man for whom the war and life had ended.

One evening a jet was returning to base and needed a target to get rid of his unexpended bomb load. The captain called the forward air controller and gave him the coordinates of a sniper three hundred meters away who had been pestering us on and off for three days. As the jet pulled up after dropping napalm on the sniper's position we could hear the "pop, pop" of the sniper firing at the jet. The men talked about the gall of that sniper as I watched the napalm burn itself out. I wondered what would drive a man to stand up to death in so remarkable a manner.

I saw bravery on our side, too.

19 September 1967

Early morning. More of the search-and-destroy mission.

The Third Platoon was moving diagonally across a small hill seventy meters to the south of us, a long ragged line of men with misshapen backs bowed by rucksacks, inching toward the top of a small ridge. An occasional curse drifted across to us as a man stumbled on the hillside.

I was watching the point man approach the top when a cloud of dirty gray smoke enveloped the three men on point. The sharp "rumpf" of an explosion broke the beauty of the morning. Screams pierced the air.

Four or five men in line behind the point dropped to the earth in a reflex motion, then jumped up to run forward. I watched as they bent over the wounded men. Across the seventy meters of open space between our two units a small drama of war unfolded.

Captain Sells radioed the platoon leader for a report on the condition of the men. Meanwhile, some of our men had run forward to the edge of our hill. They yelled to ask if anyone had been killed. One of the men bending over the wounded raised his head. He yelled back that no one was dead but three men were pretty badly wounded.

Captain Sells had received the same information over the horn from Three-six and had told his other RTO to call in a dustoff.

In the gully between us was a small dry rice paddy. It was surrounded by tall, thin palm trees, but the paddy was just large enough to allow a helicopter to set down. Captain Sells sent two men down to the paddy to pop smoke when the dustoff arrived. They would guide the chopper in.

The platoon across the way was carrying the wounded men down to the paddy. They reached the edge of the paddy as the sound of a chopper's rotor blades came toward us from the south. One of the men in the paddy popped a smoke grenade to guide the pilot's attention to our proposed LZ. The man stood with his legs spraddled, holding his M-16 horizontally above his head with both hands. The yellow smoke from the grenade curled around the clear air of the paddy, turning the outline of the man into a surrealistic vision as the sun's rays broke into lines through the smoke across the small amphitheater.

The pilot circled our position to orient himself on the guide-on man. The man would be facing the direction he wanted the pilot to come in from. He was facing a narrow gap that seemed large enough to admit the helicopter on its sharp guide path.

We held our breath as the pilot skillfully slid his craft between the dangerous sentinels of trees. He settled the chopper to the ground, the rotor wash causing the thin trees and bushes to whip violently back and forth. We were on a level with the rapidly turning rotor and could feel a slight movement of the disturbed air.

An olive-drab clump of men rushed their wounded comrades aboard the dustoff. They ran back and waved to the pilot, who increased the speed of his rotors. The ungainly looking craft rose slowly upward a few feet as the pilot pivoted the chopper to weave out through the same gap he had come through. The heavy laboring of the motors reverberated through our bodies as the pilot moved forward. We held our breath, but to no avail.

A misjudgement of air currents caused the craft to drift sideways a few feet. A terrible whop and crack of a blade striking the tree on the right side of the craft grabbed our attention. A section of the blade and wood chips flew in all directions.

The chopper rocked and shuttered violently as the pilot fought to maintain control. For a brief instant the chopper slid sideways.

"Look out, he's going to crash!" someone yelled.

The men around the paddy ran in all directions, frantically trying to escape the impending doom above their heads.

With a supreme effort of flying ability and adjustment of his controls, the pilot regained control as he fought to gain altitude. There was no place to bring it down. He had to make it fly.

The uneven distribution of weight in the two rotor blades shook the helicopter unmercifully as the twin forces of physics and fate were overcome by the pilot's determination to fly the stricken craft. And fly he did, south in a cacophony of tortured machinery.

We waited to hear on the horn if the pilot made it back. Finally the call came. The pilot had landed safely with a two-foot section sheared from his rotor blade.

24 September 1967

My letters home for this day were filled with the activities of my unit being lifted out of the operations area and flown back to the base camp at Montezuma Mountain.

During the short period of standdown the battalion was patched up with resupplies of equipment and men. I was assigned as platoon leader of the First Platoon of Delta Company, the same platoon I had been with as an observer on the operation.

After sixteen days "in-country," I had finally sifted down through the various army units and reached the slot where the army needed me. My complete address was a historical trek which every replacement soldier must make and is always his record of travel. Mine was:

> 2nd Lt. Frederick Downs, Jr.
> 1st Platoon
> Delta Company
> 1st Battalion of the 14th Infantry
> 3rd Brigade
> 4th Infantry Division

Lieutenant Smart called the platoon over to introduce me as their new commander. Schaldenbrand, my platoon sergeant, was officially not high enough in rank to hold that job, but there being no experienced sergeant around, he was acting. Schaldenbrand had only been in the army a year or so. He was about twenty-two, from Philadelphia, a typical big-city type who had been drafted and didn't like the army, but nevertheless possessed a natural ability to get men to do what he told them.

Schaldenbrand had two unusual idiosyncrasies—a consumming passion for checkers and a frequent desire to brush his teeth. He had a tin checkerboard about a foot square that he always carried strapped to the outside of his rucksack. During rest breaks he would lay out the board and pieces (some were rocks and buttons) and whoever was closest would have to play. Schaldenbrand would hunch over the board, a toothbrush in his mouth to sort of chew on and worry with. Any stress brought his toothbrush out of his shirt pocket and into his mouth, like a big toothpick. Schaldenbrand would roll it around his mouth with his tongue as he used his hands to hold onto his map or whatever else he was working with.

Schaldenbrand was worth his weight in gold to me in running that platoon. He even introduced me to the platoon motto, IT'S A LICK.

"A lick is a lick on a young man's ass, lieutenant. You remember when you were a kid and you did something wrong or something got fucked up that you got the blame for, the old man would give you a licking with a switch or a belt?"

"Yeah, I sure remember getting lickings."

"Well, when something goes wrong, it's a lick on you, see? Anything that goes wrong will give you a lick, and over here you'll get plenty of licks."

My RTO was the other most important man to the platoon. His job was to carry the radio and stick to me like a shadow. The radio was our link with literally everything outside our platoon, from supplies to survival. Without a working radio and a good RTO, a platoon leader and the platoon were as good as lost in this war.

My RTO, Mann, a skinny kid five feet eleven inches tall, was next to perfect for the job. He loved to know what was going on and his job was akin to the central switchboard operators. Mann was so good that he would often call in dustoffs or reach other people for me even before I had a chance to tell him what I needed. All of the RTOs in the company net had their own gossip society and they kept each other informed of what was happening in the company. No better grapevine in the world existed than those RTOs.

RTOs had a high mortality rate because the radio they carried made them a prime target. The radio antenna sticking up above their heads allowed the enemy to pick out the two most important elements in a platoon—the RTO and the man in front of him, the lieutenant —because wherever the lieutenant was, the RTO had to be right next to him. In a firefight both of these men were constantly moving, directing the fight.

Mann's idiosyncrasy, besides the fact that he didn't mind carrying the extra twenty-five pounds of radio, was that he made coffee at the strangest times. If I stopped moving in the middle of a firefight, even for two or three minutes, I would be sure to notice Mann heating up a B-3 C ration can of water to make coffee. The first time this happened I was surprised that anyone could calmly heat up water for coffee with bullets flying all around us. "What the hell are you doing that for?" I asked. "Coffee helps my nerves," Mann replied, handing me my cup. I was probably the only lieutenant in Vietnam who got hot coffee served him in the prone position. Many times Mann would no sooner have the coffee made than we changed positions on the run, forcing him to leave it behind. But that never stopped Mann from pulling out the "makings" and starting another cup at the earliest opportunity.

My squad leaders were: First Squad—Delk, a tall cowboy type from Wyoming; Second Squad—Porter, a slightly built black from East St. Louis; Third Squad, Jose, a skinny, short, swarthy Puerto Rican; Fourth Squad, Gallagher, a medium-built redhead from the New England states. And, of course, there was the platoon medic (everybody called him "Doc," regardless of his name).

The platoon makeup was whites, blacks, Puerto Ricans, Mexican-Americans, an Indian, and a Japanese-American, all of them from eighteen to twenty-one years old. In a combat platoon we were evaluated by our peers on our ability to help the platoon survive and not on our racial backgrounds. A combat platoon "pulled" together and was "tight" with each other, with no room for the soldier who wouldn't do his share.

25 September 1967

My first orders were to take my platoon south on Highway 1 about three kilometers to a mountain and to climb it, clearing a trail through the mines and booby traps for the rest of the company. The mountain belonged to the enemy but the Americans were going to take it and make another base camp from which to operate.

Since this was my first command, the captain eliminated the chance I would miss the mountain by pointing across the rice paddies to a large hump. Even a Second lieutenant couldn't miss it.

Two deuce-and-a-halfs and a three-quarter-ton truck were laid on to carry us south to the mountain. Everyone had been resupplied with new jungle fatigues, a new issue of ammo, and C rations.

We traveled out the front gate, onto the highway leading through Duc Pho. Duc Pho was typical of the villages I was to become familiar with along the fringes of the American army. It consisted of scroungy mud, straw, and cheap tin hootches located on both sides of the highway. Vietnamese of all sizes and descriptions moved incessantly along the muddy road through the village. On a tin roof I saw the only cat I was ever to see in Vietnam. He looked tough and wily, crouching on the edge of the roof, watching. ARVN and American soldiers were spread through the crowd, their distinct OD uniforms marking them as different.

My three-quarter-ton truck was the lead vehicle. Like the captain of a ship watching a pilot take his vessel into a narrow harbor, I nervously watched the experienced driver weave through the shoals of people and vehicles.

Duc Pho was not very large and we were out of the village in a few minutes. I noticed a sign on the right side of the road proclaiming this section as the Sea Horse Highway, compliments of the American army's Nineteenth Engineer Battalion.

The old narrow French highway ran straight as a die into a small cut through a ridge half a kilometer ahead of us. The open rice paddies spread out on both sides of the road made me feel relatively safe against the chance of an ambush.

I thought of land mines, however. My feet rested on the layer of sandbags covering the floor of the little truck. They would offer some protection from a small mine the vehicle might run over. I scrunched up in the seat, sucking in my abdomen and pulling my balls in a little closer to my body.

Guiltily, I glanced over to the driver to see if he had noticed. He seemed to be holding his breath, too.

As we approached the cut, I forgot about the sandbags and began to worry about the high sides along the road through the cut. I had read a lot about the French being ambushed in narrow passes such as this one. I stuck the barrel of my M-16 out the window just in case.

We made it through safely. Was I taking this short trip too seriously? After all, everything looked normal enough. Vietnamese were walking insouciantly along the road and occasional vehicles passed us. Still, I continued to worry.

Little kids would hear us coming and run to the side of the road to give us the finger. I had seen this before and at first I had thought, *The nerve of those little bastards, giving us the bird.* But they were just copying the Americans, I learned. Americans gave each other and the Vietnamese the finger so much that the children thought it was a form of friendly greeting and would line the roads smiling and waving both hands, middle fingers extended.

The American soldier was claimed to be many things in Vietnam, but he was like any other soldier when it came to kids. Through the rearview mirror I could see candy bars and cigarettes being thrown out of the sides of the trucks. Like schools of fish moving in unison, the kids would sweep toward the nearest thing thrown to them.

We arrived at the west base of the mountain. My small truck and the two deuce-and-a-halfs pulled off the road and the men piled out.

The mountain was covered with short, knee-high scrubby bushes and occasional clumps of grass. It was composed of sharp lava rock on which only the hardiest vegetation could survive. The hot sun beat down, accenting the dried-out bushes trying to exist on the rocky surface of the three-hundred-meter-high mountain.

We spent the rest of the morning and part of the afternoon slowly searching out and marking a path up the side. There were numerous booby traps spread around. Each one had to be marked with a flag for the engineers who would destroy them when they followed along later.

It was dangerous, hot, tedious work. Sweat dripped from us during the slow climb up the hot mountain. I was struck by the contrast between the dangerous work we were doing and the innocence of the rugged quiet beauty around us. In the haphazardly laid out paddies below us, farmers and their families were working industriously in their fields, trying to produce a crop while seeming to ignore the war swirling around them. I had thought the country through which we moved would be vacant of people except those in groups barricaded in their villages. Instead, the Vietnamese were going about their everyday duties, singly or in groups, ignoring us as if we weren't really there, and only taking notice when we passed too close for them to ignore.

We reached the top in midafternoon. Just in time, too, for I could see the convoy bringing the rest of the company down the road.

A strong breeze was blowing in from the ocean. We looked over the edge facing the ocean. The mountain dropped steeply down to the rice paddies which ran to the wide beaches. On either side of us, ridges sloped gradually down to parallel the road. Fishing boats were along the shore; to the west were the mountains.

I assigned the squads in a perimeter around the top and set my hootch up on the highest point, a wind-swept rock. I sent a few men down to lead Captain Sells up through the safe path.

After he had directed the platoon leaders to their positions, Captain Sells looked over the edge and asked me what I thought about the danger of attack from that side. I replied that it was pretty steep and it should be safe enough until it was swept by a platoon of men.

My platoon rested as the rest of the company dug in. Other sections of the battalion began to show up: the engineers to clear the booby traps, the four-deuce mortar platoon, the battalion CP group, the medics and other essential elements of a battalion moved around marking off the areas for their equipment.

The view from the top was terrific. We could see for kilometers in all directions. The mountain would be easy to defend and would make a good observation point. We named it Thunder Mountain.

That night we were treated to the spectacle of hundreds of fishing boats up and down the shore as far as we could see. Each boat was allowed to fish if it hung a lantern from the mast at night. From our vantage point, they looked like a line of slowly undulating, illuminated pearls as they bobbed up and down in the waves.

26 September 1967

This morning Captain Sells called his lieutenants to a meeting. It was the last half of September, and back in the world the first cold winds of fall were blowing across the plains of my home state, Indiana. But here in Nam it was the dry season and hot as hell. Our uniforms were soaked with sweat. Our equipment straps cut into our skin as my fellow lieutenants and I stood around Captain Sells, receiving our orders.

My platoon, the First Platoon, was to guard three bridges, 101, 102, and 103, separated from each other by a couple of hundred meters and a half kilometer respectively. The Second and Third Platoons were assigned bridges, and the Fourth Platoon was to be a guard for Headquarters Company. Headquarters would consist of the captain and his RTOs and the company medic. The Fourth Platoon was a weapons platoon. They were in charge of the 82-mm mortars which could be set up on a defensive location such as a mountain, but were too cumbersome and ineffective to carry in the jungle. A weapons platoon would also normally be in charge of antitank weapons (90-mm recoilless rifles) but in Vietnam they were never issued. They had been replaced by the LAW (light antitank weapon) that each infantryman could carry. Therefore, because of reduced duties the Fourth Platoon was always assigned to Captain Sells's headquarters unit.

Walking back to the edge of the mountain where my platoon was stationed, I sat down with Schaldenbrand and my squad leaders to inform them of our new mission. Distributing the maps, one to each squad leader and one to Schaldenbrand, I gave them the orders, codes, and other information concerning radio procedure, food, ammo, clothes, and any other gear that would be needed.

"We'll be moving out at 1200 hours. Have the men down by the captain's CP at 1130 hours and we'll move down to the road to load onto the trucks," I stated.

I had divided my platoon into three groups. I would be in charge of the middle bridge with nine men, Schaldenbrand would have the north bridge with eight men, and Jose would be in command of the south bridge with nine men.

Each of us carried what we owned in our rucksacks, so in short order all of my men were lounging around, resting against their packs, smoking, writing letters, reading paperbacks, playing cards, or just bullshitting, waiting for the order to move out. C rations and ammo were distributed and we were ready.

Many thoughts rushed through my mind as I chain-smoked Pall-Malls. The bridges were only three or four klicks down the road, but it would be my first time in command; I was responsible. I had joined the company out in the field as an observer so I knew most of the men. I had been under fire, but I had not been responsible for anyone but myself. Now, at twenty-three, I was in charge of thousands of dollars worth of equipment and the lives of my men.

After a year and a half of training at Fort Leonard Wood, Fort Jackson, Fort Benning, and Fort Gordon, I knew all the tactics and the weapons. I had the knowledge picked up from conversations with sergeants and officers who had been to Nam. I was as primed as a green lieutenant could be.

There were other schools—Ranger, Airborne, Jungle Training—that I could have gone to, but it was 1967 and the United States Army needed infantry officers fast. There just wasn't time to attend those schools. I didn't know what the life expectancy of an infantry lieutenant was in Vietnam, but I knew the army couldn't get enough of them.

But, what the hell! Nothing would happen to me. It was always the other fellow that got zapped. Now I would find out what it was all about. Would I react under fire? Could I stand up to the fear of death, the responsibility of command? Would my men have faith in me and take pride in my leadership? Could I make the right decisions under fire? Would I fail them and myself? All of the training in the world could not answer those questions.

"Lieutenant, are your men ready?" Captain Sells yelled at me.

"Yes, sir!" I replied.

"The trucks will be down at the road any minute. Load your men immediately when they arrive."

"Here they come!" someone yelled. The squad leaders ran around making sure their men were ready.

Riding in the cab of the deuce-and-a-half, I again studied the terrain and the people. Farmers were out in the paddies working in the hot sun. Evidence of the war was everywhere in the form of bombed-out hootches, craters in the earth, and blasted trees. The road had only been opened in this section of Vietnam for five months. It only belonged to us during the day. At night it belonged to the dinks, and no one moved on it if he wanted to stay alive. Even the area around the bridges was surrounded by concertina wire.

Bridge 103 was coming up. "Stop on the other side," I motioned to the driver as I opened the door and jumped out. As Schaldenbrand's truck drove up, I waved at him to halt and looked the bridge over. It wasn't much, just a short span across a stream that could be waded. However, the banks were high so the bridge was the only way across.

"Well, this is all yours, Schaldenbrand. Set your men up and I'll be back to check you later." There was a track vehicle sitting alongside a sandbagged bunker.

The men who had been guarding the bridge were packed up and ready to go. Schaldenbrand and I spent some time with the man in charge of the bridge as he pointed out the best lines of fire, where to expect the dinks to take potshots from, and gave some advice about the villagers down the road. There were villages all around the area. As my men got off, the unit we were relieving got on the trucks and we drove down to my bridge, 102. The lieutenant in charge was glad to see me. His men were ready and he walked around showing me his old positions, the dangerous areas, and telling about the villages down the road twenty-five meters. There was one track and a tank at this bridge. "Jesus," I said to him, "don't tell me you have trouble with all that firepower sitting there?"

"Don't let that fool you," he replied. "The dinks hit us a week ago with a coordinated infantry and rocket attack. They hit the front of the tank that was here before this one. The rocket exploded on the front slope, sending the force of the blast upward. The driver got most of his head blown off and the tank lost the use of its main gun and xenon searchlight. They just about overran us. Also, you'll notice this is a Bailey bridge. The unit before us did get overrun and the old bridge was blown up. That's it over in the field." He pointed to a pile of twisted wreckage.

"Thanks for the warning," I murmured. My respect for the Vietcong went up a few more notches.

"Have fun," the lieutenant said as he swung up into the cab.

"Yeah, sure, thanks. Hey! Set my men up on that last bridge, will you?"

"Sure, be glad to," he said as he lit up a cigarette. "It's only a culvert, though."

"Hey, Jose," I yelled. "Go on with this other lieutenant and get set up. I'll be down later to check up on your position."

"Okay, lieutenant. I'll call you on the radio when we get set in," he answered.

"Roger."

Schaldenbrand also had a radio, so all three bridges would be in communication with each other.

I surveyed my new command as the trucks moved on down the road. The tank commander came over and introduced himself.

"How are you doing, lieutenant? I'm Lieutenant Knutson and we'll be staying on. Those are my tracks on the other two bridges so coordination will be easier. We were assigned here a week ago after the other tank outfit got zapped."

I introduced myself and my men; he did likewise. He had been in Vietnam almost two years and was up for captain. While I was new in the country, he certainly was not and looked on us with a critical eye. Track units provided the firepower but they needed the infantry to protect them, especially in static positions. Undoubtedly, he was wondering how good a job of protecting them we would do.

From my point of view, I certainly welcomed all that armor and firepower. On the other hand, the armor always made a wonderful target. Dinks would be drawn to this bridge like bees to honey.

Lieutenant Knutson had a first sergeant who had been in the army a long time and had his own ideas about how things should be. Infantry and armor soldiers are clannish and tend to look on the other as something to be put up with. The track units on the other two bridges got along well with my men, but on our bridge we were together but not close. We were to coexist only from necessity, and no friendships grew on our bridge between track crews and infantrymen.

The next morning, Captain Sells called me as I was eating Cs.

"Delta One-six, this is Delta Six, over."

"This is One-six, over."

"This is Delta Six. The weather reports from Dragon Six show a storm moving into this area by tonight. Be prepared for it. Also, One-six, the area you occupied last night was attacked by three Vietcong who crawled up the side of the mountain. They threw grenades into your old location and zapped two men. Before one of the men died he was able to kill two of the dinks. You're lucky, One-six. Out."

A shiver passed through me at the thought of how close I had been to death. One more night and I would have been one of those dead men. I had been lulled by the steepness of the mountain.

Thirty meters to the east of the bridge was an old bunker. I decided to make that my command post. It was located close to the barbed wire that ringed the eastern side of the perimeter and commanded a reasonable field of fire. There was a low parapet on the other side of the stream twenty meters away, but it could be covered by the bunker located at the south end of the bridge in case of attack. It was not an ideal situation, but the parapet could not be destroyed and the tank was located in the bend of the stream as it turned under the bridge.

The track crew sat close to the tank on the sand which had been laid down over the last two or three thousand years. Plenty of firepower on this side, but what about the west side? When the French built Highway 1, they had built a narrow-gauge railroad parallel to the highway. It was only thirty or forty meters away and the built-up rail bed formed a perfect place to launch an attack. With only nine men to guard an area that should have had thirty, I put three men on the old rail bed. If we were attacked they would have to pull back to the highway bridge, but at least they would provide protection against a surprise attack.

27 September 1967

My first day on the bridges. This and the following days would be a maturing time for me.

Mann and I were busy preparing the bunker for defense. My men had just put two claymore mines in front of the barbed wire and had run the detonating wires back to me. Evening thunderstorms were blowing heavy, low clouds in from the sea. The wind increased in intensity, bending the trees at its whim. The atmosphere had a surrealistic quality, imparting a sense of impending doom to the fields and rice paddies around us. I hooked the hand-squeezed detonators to the claymore wires and laid them on the sandbags next to me. Three of the track crew lugged concertina wire past us to reinforce the concertina wire already in place. They carried it beyond the existing wire with the intention of laying a row further out from the first. I glanced over my shoulder and asked what they were doing, since I thought we had enough of a defensive line. Shrugging my shoulders, I turned my attention back to the map and radio codes that Mann and I were going over.

An explosion ripped the air behind me, followed immediately by a scream. My body instinctively threw itself against the sandbags as my mind shouted *mortar attack*. My eyes registered the scene of men frozen in shocked wonderment, their eyes staring behind me. Mann was directly in front of me and the track men were in the background, crouching where they were when the explosion went off. Quickly turning around, my eyes swept in the awful catastrophe.

One of the claymores had gone off, shattering forever the lives of the three men in front of it.

"Jesus Christ!"

"Was it a mortar?"

"No, one of our claymores went off."

"Get those men, quick."

"No! No! Wait! There's another claymore out there!"

"What the fuck set it off? What about the other one?"

The detonators were still lying on the sandbags, the safeties on. The track men and my soldiers were grouped around me, straining to rush forward to help the three men in front of the wire.

One man was lying dead still, sprawled on his back, his head a bloody mess. One was on his knees with one arm dangling, the other hand clutching his neck and shoulder, blood streaming down the front of his fatigue shirt. The third man was standing, bleeding, in a shocked daze aware of the danger still existing in the other claymore.

"Shit, it's the static electricity in the air that set it off," I exclaimed. The charge used to set off the blasting cap on the claymore was generated by squeezing the fist-size detonator. The electricity in the air around us could certainly be capable of setting off the blasting cap.

What a helluva dilemma! The three wounded men needed help fast. But first, the other claymore had to be disarmed. To do that, one of us would have to unscrew the plug holding the blasting cap in the claymore. Simple enough, except that the storm was building in intensity. Tremendous bolts of lightning cracked through the clouds and into the ground. The air was charged with electricity. Explosion of the other claymore could be imminent, resulting in death to the men in front of it. If it went off while someone was crouched over it unscrewing the cap, he could be blown apart.

Only a few seconds had passed since the explosion. One of my men and I dashed to the claymore, frantically fumbling, unscrewing the plug holding the blasting cap, throwing it away from the claymore. Then I rushed back to the radio. Two men were applying first aid. The other positions were covered by the men assigned to them; they had stayed in place during the action.

Good training, I thought, as I fumbled with my map. It was folded in the plastic radio battery bag all of us used to carry maps in.

"Delta Six, this is One-six, over."

"One-six, this is Delta Six, over."

"This is One-six. I need a dustoff. There's been an accident resulting in three peanuts, over." We tried to say nothing over the radio that could be understood by the enemy. Thus, we used code words for certain things. A "Kool-Aid" was a dead soldier and a "peanut" was a wounded soldier.

"This is Delta Six. What the hell happened? Over."

"This is One-six. Static electricity in the air set off a claymore while three track men were putting out barbed wire, over."

"This is Delta Six. What's your position? Over."

Now what would he ask me that for? I was on the bridge he had assigned to me. *Let's see . . . we're here so I read right and up . . . real easy . . . just like training all along.* Of course, that was my first responsibility where men had been hurt, so maybe that accounted for what happened next, in spite of training.

"Lieutenant! Lieutenant! You've got to get a dustoff here quick. This man's got a bad head wound," said one soldier as they brought the wounded over by me. Dirty black clouds with lightning crashing around added to the confusion as the wind howled from all directions. Huge raindrops spattered down.

"This is One-six. I'm at coordinates 298028, over." I read them out.

"This is Delta Six. Are you sure of that? Over."

"This is One-six. Uhhh, let's see, yeah, that's it alright, over."

"One-six, you'd better check that again. According to what you gave me, you're in the South China Sea, over."

Ooooh, did he sound mad! Goddamn! I've done this a million times, the thought ran through my mind as sweat broke out.

The wounded were groaning, the storm was reaching gigantic proportions, and the track sergeant was demanding to know where the fuck that dustoff was. "Concentrate, Fred, concentrate," I said to myself while staring at the meaningless blob of colors, whirls, and numbers. Suddenly, everything jelled in perfect clarity.

"Delta Six, this is One-six. You're right, my coordinates are 288028. "I need a dustoff fast, over."

"One-six, this is Delta Six. I know where you are, I just wanted to see if you could figure it out. I've already called the dustoff and they've just reported the storms are too dangerous for flying. One pilot tried it but had to come back, over."

"This is One-six. Wait one . . . The dustoff can't make it through the storm. Lieutenant Knutson, can that man with the head wound wait?"

"No way! If he doesn't get help fast, he'll die," Knutson answered.

"We'll put them in a track and run the wounded back to Thunder Mountain on the road," the old sergeant growled.

"Hell, you'll lose that track. It's almost dark. The dinks have that road mined by now," I argued.

"Hell, we'll make it. I'll drive the tank ahead of the track!" the sergeant boasted. "What do *you* think, sir?" The sergeant directed this to Lieutenant Knutson.

Standing with both hands on hips, watching the wounded being given first aid, Lieutenant Knutson turned his head toward us and said, "You're right, sergeant. Load them up and let's go before it gets completely dark."

"I'll radio ahead to let them know you're coming," I told Lieutenant Knutson.

"Delta Six, this is One-six, over."

"This is Delta Six, over."

"The track crew is going to take the wounded back in a track. The tank is going to lead them in, over."

"This is Delta Six. I'll notify the other units on the road and mountain so they won't be blown to bits by any friendlies, out."

The tank was crawling on to the edge of the road, its motor bellowing, its tracks clanking and grinding as they sought purchase. The armored personnel carrier followed behind. At full acceleration, both vehicles roared north toward the mountain and medical help, five kilometers away. Watching from the road until they disappeared around a turn, we wondered if they would beat the dink land mine teams which mined the road almost nightly. As they passed my last bridge, Schaldenbrand reported. I breathed a sigh of relief that they had made it unharmed through my section anyway.

They made it all the way. All of the men lived and two came back to the unit eventually. The man with the head wound was flown back to a MASH unit. We never heard anything else about him.

My first opportunity to show the captain my abilities had been miserable. Two lessons: claymores and thunderstorms do not mix, and reading a map under pressure is not like reading one in a training exercise.

A typhoon brushed against us for three days, flooding the area until only the Bailey bridge we were guarding was above water. The M-60 tank and the APC had backed up on opposite ends of the bridge to escape the torrent. The men on the other two bridges were safe on high ground. We had abandoned our hootches on the third of October and were with the tracks on the bridge.

4 October 1967

God, we were miserable this night. We infantrymen had to stay outside to guard the tracks and bridge. We huddled around the engine and exhaust pipes for a little heat while the wind and rain beat down. It was nearly impossible to sleep with no place to lie down. The damn bridge was trembling, in danger of collapse with the weight of the tracked vehicles and the power of the water rushing around the supports. Our ponchos had been used to make our hootches so there was nothing to shed the rain from our bodies. Constantly wet, we were cold and shivering violently. Finally, around 0500, daybreak, the storm lifted, the rain slacked off, and the water level started dropping. Our jungle fatigues began drying as we prepared a C-ration breakfast with coffee or cocoa. It was a relief to be able to see, unhampered by rain and darkness, and to be dry. We razzed each other, especially the track crew who had spent the whole storm inside those dry, warm behemoths. We worked the kinks out of our cold, cramped muscles, fed ourselves, and watched the water go down as the morning wore on.

About 1000 hours, someone let out a shout. We all became immediately alert as we saw old mamma-san from the village pop up on the railroad embankment. Her hootch was twenty or thirty meters from my hootch on the railroad bridge, and damn it, if she wasn't heading for my hootch. I don't know where she had survived the storm, but it was obvious to her that with all of us stranded on the highway bridge, she could steal everything on the rail bridge. We had run her off a couple of times but she was a persistent old cuss. Now she had me beat.

Dinks know that Americans hate to and often refuse to harm them without provocation. The old mamma-san was pretty sure that no one would shoot her just for stealing, so she had decided to gamble on it. We were yelling and raising hell, but she kept heading for my hootch in that hunched-over way, her black pajamas flip-flopping against each other. She would glance over at us just fifty meters away, her betel-nut-stained mouth in a smile as if to say "gotcha."

It didn't seem serious; after all, we knew which hootch she lived in and Mann and I didn't have much except food and odds and ends in our hootch. But all of a sudden the situation became very complex and passed from semicomical to deadly serious. She grabbed hold of the case of grenades we had had to leave behind. Gripping the case by its rope handles, she started back down the track. My God! My men looked at me for an answer. We didn't think she knew that it was a case of grenades she was making off with, but this area was heavily Vietcong. The villages all around us were known sympathizers and we were hit on a regular basis. If she disappeared over the railroad bridge with that case and gave it to the guerrillas, had it stolen from her, or hid it and told us it was stolen, all I could do would be to turn her in, but hell, that would do no good. The hand grenades would be gone and I would be responsible for American deaths somewhere. On the other hand, if I shot and killed her, she was after all an old lady and I wasn't sure she knew what she was stealing. No way to know.

I exchanged magazines in the M-16, replacing regular ammunition with one of the tracer magazines I always carried. The men were watching the old lady intently and a few started to raise their rifles. The track men were excited, very interested in the outcome of this drama. Yelling at everyone to hold fire, I squeezed off a tracer right past her nose and yelled *"Dung lui."* She didn't stop so I started firing at the rope handles she was carrying the case by. I was an excellent shot and there was a good chance one of the bullets would hit the handle, cutting the rope. I fired seven or eight shots, but with her hobbling and bouncing around my tracers were zinging all around her hands but not hitting anything. If one of those high-velocity bullets hit that case of grenades, her problems would be over but mine would just be beginning.

Success! One of the tracers slammed into the left rope handle and/

or mamma-san's hand and she stumbled over the case as it fell to her feet. She picked herself up, yelling what I am sure were obscenities at me while she sucked her fingers. I fired a few more rounds close to her body and near her feet to speed her on her way. If it can be said that she moved reluctantly but like a shot, that is what she did, running over the edge of the railway bank and disappearing forever. We never saw her again.

5 October 1967

Finally the water receded, allowing our group to go about making camp and settling into a semiroutine of bridge guarding. Delta Six was anxious for me to get patrols out and I was eager to become acquainted with the area after the storm and to shake up any dinks who might have moved in during the storm. Sergeant Schaldenbrand and I decided the streams were fordable and drew up plans for a short patrol, no longer than five hours.

The foothills behind us to the west were full of trails, disembarkation points, caves, old streambeds, plus a host of other delectable items agreeable to the guerrilla movement in our area. The guerrillas had relatives in the many villages around us from which they received their supplies of food, guns, ammo, and explosives, brought in by sea on bogus fishing boats. Our failure to patrol during the storm would have allowed them to reequip and to visit home. We intended to stop that by patrols and ambushes. Those hills would be first.

The road was usually cleared by the engineer battalion by 0900. Therefore, each of the other two bridges would send four or five men to join us as soon as the road was cleared. From B-102 we would move out in a southwesterly direction until we found a place to ford west across the stream. Checking the various trails and points of interest, we would swing to the south half a kilometer and connect up with the road to end our patrol. Using my bridge as a base, I drew up a cloverleaf on the map and intended to cover a leaf a day, or a reasonable facsimile thereof. Early in the morning, two days after the storm, we grouped at B-102. The mine-clearing team had swept by from the north with Schaldenbrand, Doc, and three riflemen following along behind. Shortly thereafter, Jose brought his section up from the south as the mine-clearing crew passed his bridge. Porter, with a squad from my bridge, completed the patrol unit. We were ready.

The sky was gray and dirty and a light rain fell in the midmorning. Everyone was in the process of getting sorted out in proper squad order, point squad, flank, and rear. We were wearing only our web gear for this patrol, consisting of wide canvas belts around our waists supported by shoulder suspenders. Our ammo containers hung from our belts, with grenades hanging from them. We also had two canteens and one or two first-aid packages. From the suspenders hung smoke grenades, another first-aid bandage, plus we all wore two bandoliers of ammo crisscrossed over the chest, a few M-79 rounds, and an occasional belt of M-60 ammo. A very formidable picture, I'm sure.

I gave the order to move out. The men, many of whom were old-timers with more experience than me, automatically spread out like an accordian as the point element threaded its way through the west edge of the village and headed into the rice paddies. I always traveled with the point so as to have better control in case of trouble. My sergeant always took his station in the rear so that our snake would have two heads. There was water in all the paddies so we walked on the small dams separating the paddies, zigzagging to a curve in the stream two hundred to two hundred fifty meters away. The village was behind us, there were farmers out in their fields, and I must admit, none of us expected trouble so close to the beginning of our patrol. The point had just reached the stream where I called a halt while they looked for a place to cross. An old man in the usual peasant garb of black top and trousers was hoeing viciously in the paddy next to the dam we were standing on. My men were smoking, keeping an eye out as we waited for the point to cross.

I decided to question the old man while we were waiting. "Come on, Mann," I said to my RTO, "let's question this old dink and see if he has seen any other dinks in this area." We waded the twenty or so feet over to the old man. As soon as we started toward him, he stopped hoeing and glanced at us apprehensively. He straightened up as much as his stooped shoulders would allow as we stopped in front of him. Neither of us spoke the other's language, but since he lived so close to the highway, perhaps he had picked up some pidgin English. Mann offered him a cigarette to help allay his fear of us. *"Chao ong,* papa-san, do you know where Vietcong are?" He was holding his cigarette a few inches from his mouth looking vaguely back and forth between Mann and me. *Well,* I thought to myself, *these old cats don't lower themselves to speak to soldiers on the road like the young ones who are always trying to con GIs do, so I'll have to try pantomine with him.* Hell, if he didn't catch on to "papa-san," he wasn't going to know any pidgin English. I would act out my questions. I held my M-16 up and pointed to it, then pointed toward the hills. "Weapons! Weapons! Same-same." I spoke louder and slower as most people do in a foreign country, mistakenly thinking I would be easier to understand. I then crouched down acting like I was sneaking up on the unwary American soldiers standing on the dike, pointing to the weapon and the hills and shooting the soldiers. All the time, I was yelling in pidgin English. Well, I doubt if that old farmer standing barefoot in that field with his pants rolled up, holding a hoe in one hand and a cigarette in the other, had ever been to a play in his life, but I provided enough entertainment that day to last him the rest of his life. I often wondered what he was thinking, watching this crazy American acting like he was having a fit.

"Goddamn it, Mann!" I said in disgust, "let's get out of here. He doesn't know anything, and even if he does, he won't tell us." I stomped back through the dirty paddy water over to the dam, then to the edge of the stream.

The point element had found a ford which they were crossing. Two men had crossed over, the water coming up to their chests. Three more were in the water. I was standing on the bank when all hell broke loose. Six dinks came bursting out of a hootch fifty feet on the other side of the stream crossing, obviously as surprised as we were. Everyone opened up, including the men who were spread out behind me in a sort of half crescent. Their firing endangered the men in front, especially those on the other side of the bank, which was a little higher and in the line of fire. I yelled for the rear to stop firing, told Schaldenbrand to take command of the rear half of the platoon, and took the front part of the platoon on across the stream as fast as I could. How can I properly explain my feelings at that moment? My first real combat command, first contact patrol, and already we had flushed six dinks. I rushed up the opposite bank, dripping water, trying desperately to keep the dinks in sight as they bounded across the rice paddies, dodging in and out of the hedgerows as they frantically sought the security of the steeply rising hills a few hundred meters away. By this time, eight or ten of us had reached the far bank and were firing at the fleeing black-pajama-clad dinks. Our firing was intense and we delayed only a few seconds to allow a few men behind us to hold our beachhead before running after the enemy.

Spagg, Mann, Porter, McCovey, and I followed the left wing of the escaping dinks. Hunter, Iding, Jose, Villasenor, Collins, and others spread out to the right. The frantic scrambling to escape had split the six dinks up. They were disappearing into the brush-covered old creek bed, behind hedgerows, and were crawling through the grass at the base of the hill in front of us. Our blood was up as our quarry bounded, jumped, dodged, and ran like hell for their lives amid a torrent of bullets. *Damn! With all that firing why aren't they falling?* I thought. Only two dinks were in sight on my side of the firing line as the rice paddy water splashed beneath our hurrying feet. I had to keep control but I wanted to kill at least one dink. I stopped and my men stopped with me as I yelled to aim and fire instead of just blasting away. My M-16 contained a magazine of tracers. I steadied my M-16's sights on the fleeing figure a couple of hundred meters away. The black-clad running figure rested for a split second in the sights as I pulled the trigger. The red line of death reached for his life, intersected with his body, and he went down. I got him!!! Unbelievably, he jumped up and ran with a listing, jerking movement. I fired desperately trying to hit him again. After five or six shots, he went down from my bullets or someone else's, I didn't know.

We ran forward, Spagg firing the M-60 machine gun from his hip. "Stop that, Spagg," I barked out as we ran to the spot where the dink had gone down. "You can't hit anything firing that thing like John Wayne. Wait till we get to that dam and use it for a base."

The firing on my side had pretty well stopped because no dinks were in sight. Heavy firing was taking place on the right with an occasional head or body briefly coming into view as the right side moved up. They were a hundred or so meters to our right, pushing up the hill we had just reached. *"Where the fuck is that dink I shot?"* I wondered as we frantically beat the small bushes and grass for his body. Torrey found a blood trail and a couple of Ho Chi Minh slippers where I had first shot him, but we couldn't find anything else. The edge of the hill was mostly grass twelve to eighteen inches high, and these two-foot-high bushes didn't look thick enough for anybody to hide in.

As we crossed the stream, I had radioed Delta Six to inform him of what we had run into. Knowing he would be raising hell wondering why I hadn't contacted him since, it was time to make another call. Just then I heard an explosion over on the right and a scream, then the dreaded call "Medic, medic!" Running quickly along the base of the hill, I burst through a hedgerow to see one of my men, a young man of eighteen by the name of Williams, lying on the wet ground, his right knee shattered.

The scene is frozen in my mind. In a split second my eyes and ears recorded on my brain the horrible consequences of command. Rain was lightly falling, sprinkling the small pools of water lying in a small forty- to sixty-foot field surrounded by small hedgerows. Williams was lying on his side, clutching his knee as his blood stained the water he was lying in. His helmet was lying about ten feet away, upside-down, with his letters from home tucked up under the webbing. I ran over to him, knelt down, and lifted his head out of the mud and water. The medic started working on his knee as I cradled Williams's head in my lap. The pain and shock were causing tears to run down his face as he bit his lip to keep from crying out.

"Did I get him, sir? Did I get him?"

"I don't know, someone is checking now, Williams. What happened?"

"I was chasing this dink and he ducked into the hedgerow. As I ran across this open area, he popped up and threw a grenade at me. I fired a seventy-nine round at him at the same time. That fucking grenade went off and blew me down." His body jerked and he cried out as the medic wrapped his knee to stop the bleeding. "I think I got him though, sir."

"Good job, soldier," I said as I felt my own tears well up at the impact of seeing one of my men, a man I was responsible for, hurt and bleeding. I couldn't keep my eyes from glancing at the water turning red around us.

"Where the fuck is that dustoff?" I shouted.

"He's on his way, sir," Mann answered back. "Delta Six wants to talk to you, quick."

"Okay, okay, I'm coming. Hold on, Williams, the dustoff is coming. I've got to leave you now."

"Okay, sir, I'll make it," Williams replied. I laid him down and ran over to Mann, standing a little way off with the big ten-foot antenna sticking up out of the radio.

"Delta Six, this is One-six, over."

"This is Delta Six. What the hell is going on down there? Over."

"This is One-six. We surprised six dinks in a hootch and were chasing them. One of my men is hit but not bad, over."

"This is Delta Six. Did you get any of the dinks? And I can't hear you, you're fading, over."

"This is One-six. I think we got two, over."

(Static) ". . . Delta Six. I can't hear you, One-six, over" (static).

"Fuck, we've lost contact. Call the track units and we'll relay through them, Mann."

Everyone was wanting to know what happened: Delta Six, the tracks anxiously waiting on the road, and the battalion commander. I had lost contact with headquarters thanks to the weather and the high ridge between us. Jesus, what a time to lose contact! The dustoff would be coming in and Delta Six couldn't tell them where we were because I couldn't tell Delta Six where we were. Meanwhile, the firefight was still going on. "Mann, you got those tracks yet?"

"Yes, sir."

"Have them call Delta Six and tell him there's a ridge between us so we can't talk. Also, tell them to radio our position for the dustoff." As Mann was doing that, I turned to my men and told them to watch out for the right side, still advancing up the hill. I bellowed at the top of my lungs for the right side to stop and hold until we got straightened out and got the dustoff in and out.

"When that dustoff gets here, be ready for dink fire," I yelled. Meanwhile, I heard Delta Six still trying to call us, madder than hell because we wouldn't answer. Over on the road the tracks were pacing back and forth, anxious to do battle.

Lieutenant Knutson, the track commander, relayed the situation to Delta Six, who in turn relayed to me the dustoff's frequency and Delta Six's recommendation that we search the area until we found the dinks. A nice open area, flat, perfect for the dustoff to land, was right next to where Williams lay. My smoke grenade was in my hand, the men were searching around, and the rain was lightly falling as I nervously awaited the dustoff. Damn, where was that chopper? Williams wasn't going to die, but he was in pain. Besides, every minute we delayed those dinks were getting further away.

"Lieutenant," Mann called over, "the dustoff's coming in and wants us to pop smoke."

"Okay." I gave a frantic pull on the pin and threw it out where I wanted him to land. The throbbing sound of the chopper signaled his arrival through the light rain as he circled, checking us and looking for the smoke.

"What the hell? The smoke isn't working!" Mann exclaimed. My hand still clasped the reason the grenade wasn't working. The pull ring was in my hand, but its cheap metal had straightened out, slipping out of the pin instead of pulling the pin out. "Quick, who's got smoke?" I asked. The medic then threw one out. It didn't go off either. Christ, the chopper was asking for smoke and no one around me had any left. I ran out, picking up one of the grenades. If I straightened the pin, it would slide out easier. I quickly straightened the pin with my fingers, jabbing the hell out of them, and then like a Grade-B movie hero, attempted to grip the pin with my teeth to pull it out. "Goddamn, that hurts. I'll chip my teeth on that motherfucker," I said to Mann who had came up beside me. "If that dustoff has us in sight, tell him we don't have any smoke, so come on in."

"He's doing just that," Mann replied.

"Ah, I got it!" I had been fiddling with the pin and had worked it out with a piece of equipment. Flinging it away from me, I raised my M-16 above my head with both arms to guide the chopper in. As the chopper settled in, purple smoke from the grenade whipped from the downblast, curling back up the outside of the rotor tips. The crew jumped off to assist the men carrying Williams. The crewmen reached him, unfolded a stretcher, hurriedly laid him on it, and rushed back to the chopper whose rotors were rapidly turning, anticipating a quick return to its element. The last crewman jumped aboard just at the moment the dustoff pilot poured the coals to the engine, causing the chopper to surge up and forward. The pilot pivoted the chopper quickly before it passed over our heads and headed toward the road and relative safety from ground fire.

There were now three tracks on the road, armored personnel carriers. The tank was guarding the bridge, and they were constantly asking us if we wanted any help. No, we didn't want any help, but they were so raring to fire their weapons the commander said he was bringing his three APCs across to us. I picked up the horn and told him it was softer than hell—those APCs would sink out of sight. Also, there was a pretty deep stream between us and the road. No matter! He would make it.

"Shit, they're gonna get stuck," Mann told me.

"Yeah, and we'll have to guard their ass while they dig out," I complained as a couple of men headed toward me. "Hey, Schaldenbrand! What did you find?"

"Look at this, lieutenant. A medical kit full of penicillin, bandages, and other supplies," Schaldenbrand said, "and here's a deck of cards they were playing with. There were six hands around the table in that hootch. We scared them so bad they left their cards laying perfectly, except one hand which was scattered over the floor."

We were all struck with the wonder of the dinks playing cards. It almost seemed like something we would do.

The track vehicles caught our attention, their growling engines rising angrily as they fought the sinking fields, their commanders searching in a zigzag route for a path to where we were. None of us felt they would make it across the wet fields and the stream. Our attention turned back to the business at hand, digging out the dinks if they were still in the area. We lined up in two fire teams and started up the hill, firing and covering for each other. The dinks opened up on us with sporadic gunfire, their bullets zipping around us. The challenge of battle in conflict with the will to survive drove us on. We would stop and fire while the right side rushed forward a few feet and dropped to provide us with covering fire. As we rushed forward, I noticed one of my men had stayed behind, hidden by a rock.

This young man had had his mother write a number of letters to his senator to investigate the army's cruel treatment of him. He was a constant malingerer and had no friends in the platoon. Combat platoons pulled together with no sympathy for the soldier who did not pull his share. Now, the son-of-a-bitch was hiding behind a rock! I hollered at my men to hold their place until I got that malingering coward up with the rest of us. In a running crouch, I dashed back to the man hiding behind the lava rock. Dink bullets continued to fly haphazardly around all of us.

"What the fuck are you doing, you motherfucker? Get your ass up on line. Now!" His eyes were wide with fear. His body was crouched low behind the rock, his hands gripping his M-16 as he glanced from me to the men on the hill ahead of us.

"I'm scared," he quivered.

"Fuck, we're all scared but we have to stick together. You're endangering the lives of the other men. Now get your ass in gear."

"I don't care about them. Let them die. I don't like this fuckin' war anyway."

"Listen, you chickenshit son-of-a-bitch, none of those guys likes the war either but they're not hiding behind some rock, letting someone else die for them. Now get up there on line."

I was frantic. Sweat was pouring off me from the heat, bullets zinging by me. My men were crouched or lying down, firing up the hill; one of my men had been hit; the captain was raising hell on the radio because I couldn't answer him and he wanted to know what was going on; the tracks were roaring around a couple of hundred meters behind me, demanding on the radio that we help them get across the stream so they could get into the firefight; and, as if I didn't have enough problems, this soldier had given up.

I had a responsibility to my platoon to keep them alive, and I had the mission to attack. Since this one man was no good to me, the whole was more important. I struck him on the shoulder with the rifle stock of my M-16, knocking him into the dirt. Pointing my rifle within a few inches of his face, I told him (my face undoubtedly contorted in rage), "You move now, motherfucker, or I'll shoot you through the head!" The shock of being hit plus the actual belief that I might kill him caused his muscles to force his body up and forward. I followed closely behind and to the side, shouting at my men to attack.

We finished the assault, but the dinks had pulled back and disappeared, leaving us an empty ridge line. Plodding uneasily back down the hill, we passed the evidence of their occupation—spider holes, straw-lined caves, paths, trash. The tracks were waiting at the bottom, and because they were so eager I had them fire a few belts of fifty-caliber into the ridge to scare any dinks still left. After the order to march, we headed back for the road. Wait a minute! One of the tracks had gotten stuck. We knew that was going to happen. The men and I grouped around the tracks to watch what would turn into great entertainment, we were sure.

The track men always lorded it over the infantry because the track men rode everywhere, carried plentiful C rations, ice coolers filled with ice and beer they bought from the dinks, slept inside their tracks when it rained, and generally led a life of Riley. It was with great satisfaction that we observed man's helplessness over ten tons of machinery stuck in the mud.

Just one track was stuck. The driver was trying to rock it out, but once the topsoil was broken the battle was lost. The APC was resting on its belly, its tracks spinning uselessly, unable to grip the dirt. One of the other tracks pulled up to hook its cable to the stuck one. As it pulled, its own tracks broke through the tenuous topsoil.

"Stop! Stop!" one of the track men yelled. "If both of these get stuck, we're dead!" We agreed with that. It was the middle of the afternoon and if those tracks weren't free and back on the road by nightfall, we, the infantry, would have to form a perimeter around the tracks to protect them.

None of us cared to spend the night guarding some dink's promotion. Being stuck out in the middle of that rice paddy with hedgerows all around us would be a sure ticket to a killing. The dinks could slip up to within thirty or forty meters to fire an RPG right into one or both of the tracks. With only a handful of men to protect the tracks, possibly all of us would be wiped out. The track crew had spades out and were digging frantically to free both machines. The third track had crept carefully up to the edge of the paddy and its crew had hooked its cable to the second partially stuck track. Finally, all three were hooked together like railroad engines, with only one having a certain purchase to earth. The other two were vice versa, as the earth had purchase on them. The digging was finished with all manner of rocks, shrubs, and tree limbs thrown under the tracks and along the probable route to freedom.

The crews, muddy, stripped to the waist, backed out of the way as the drivers of each vehicle revved up their engines. The track on solid ground brought up the tension on the cable as it visibly hunkered closer to the earth under the strain. The middle track slowly rotated its drive mechanism trying to retain what slim purchase it had, to gain a bigger bite of solidarity. The third track, buried to the belly, could only rev its engines, in hope of gaining freedom. As the strain increased on both cables, the third track slowly rotated its tracks. As the track moved, the crews threw rocks, shrubs, anything, under the tracks to form a base. Everyone tried to keep free of the area that would be wiped clean if a cable broke, but it was nearly impossible since it took close work to throw items under the tracks.

At a signal, all tracks kicked into gear and pulled like hell. Slowly, the vehicles moved up and out. In one mighty surge, all three shot out of the paddy. The crews quickly unhooked and wound up the cables, jumped into their tracks, and headed back to the road and relative safety. We looked around at the torn earth as dusk settled down. The assholes had taken off with not so much as an offer of a ride back.

Oh, well! I ordered the point to get going. If we hurried, we would be back before dark.

7 October 1967

Today I took another patrol composed of men from all three
bridges on a sweep toward the sprawling village northeast of us, next
to the ocean.

The sun was hot by 1000 hours, warning us of another sweltering
day. I could never figure out whether we were in the dry season or
the rainy season. The mixture of alternating rain and sun made me
wonder if the distinction was a figment of someone's imagination.

The point man followed the edge of the stream toward our destination, the sweat was pouring off all of us. Some of the men draped
dull-green towels around their necks to wipe off the constant stream
of perspiration. The point found an old booby trap near one of the
hootches. This put us on edge. It was destroyed with a hand grenade
and we moved on.

Generally we never found anything on our short patrols, but this
time it looked like we had finally hit paydirt. One of the hootches we
searched yielded a large binder notebook full of diagrams of the road,
bridges, and boundaries of the land area. An old man with a scraggly
white beard yelled at us and tried to take the book back. I ordered
one of the men to tie the old man's hands behind his back so we could
turn him and his book in at the end of the patrol. Although we
couldn't read the writing, the diagrams could easily be something the
Vietcong had drawn to locate our positions and the locations of mines
in the road.

In the next cluster of hootches was more good hunting—a military-
age young man was loafing around. Since all young Vietnamese males
were supposed to be in the army, any strays in the area had to be
Vietcong. Again, amid much yelling and protest from the accused, we
tied his hands behind his back and brought him along also. I was
pleased so far with the success of this patrol. One of the men ripped
the man's shirt away from his shoulders to check for marks on his
back from carrying a pack. This would be a sure sign that he was a
Cong. We all knew the Cong transported rice and ammo on their

backs. I was never sure this was a good idea. We also carried packs
and we never had any marks from them—but we always checked
anyway. You never could tell . . .

The two men were put in the middle of our patrol and went from
village to village with us. When the villagers spotted them, they would
start talking very fast and some of the women would start wailing. The
old man would calm them down by saying something in Vietnamese,
after which the villagers would leave us alone and just watch us as we
moved from hootch to hootch in our search.

During the two or three hours our prisoners were with us we gave
them cigarettes and let them have water that the villagers brought
them at each place we stopped. We began to think that maybe they
were not Vietcong, but we still had an obligation to take them in so
they could be questioned by the "Rough Puffs," the local police force.

I had informed Delta Six that we had taken prisoners and he had
told me that a unit of ARVN or Rough Puffs would meet us at the
bridge for a pickup at the end of our patrol.

We completed our sweep in the middle of the afternoon and
trudged back to the bridge, thankful that we could finally stop moving
in the hot sun.

We walked down the road to the bridge where the men filtered over
to their hootches to plop down for a rest. I had a couple of the men
guard the two prisoners, squatting in the sand by the track crews. The
damn ARVNs had not arrived, so the two men guarding the prisoners
gave them cigarettes which they puffed while squatting with their
hands still tied behind them.

I was looking through the binder trying to figure out what all of
those reference points meant when I heard a growl from inside the
APC. The old tank sergeant had been drinking beer in the hot sun all
day and had gone inside the APC to escape the heat. Everyone back
at the bridges had heard over the radio that we had taken prisoners
and I found out later the tank sergeant couldn't wait until we brought
them back. The growl had come from him as he rushed out of the
APC to run down the ramp over to where the prisoners were waiting.

The old man and the young man stood up as the heavily built
sergeant came up to them.

"Sooo, you're the fuckers that zapped my buddies in the tank," the old gray-haired sergeant snarled.

Without warning, he swung a heavy fist into the face of the old man, knocking him down. The other fist swung into the face of the younger man, knocking him down beside the old man. The sergeant was screaming and bellowing as he pummeled the two men on the sand. They rolled into balls for protection, but were hampered by their tied hands.

I ran from the road, yelling to my two men to pull the sergeant off the prisoners. They grabbed him by the shoulders as he fought them to get back to the Vietnamese. He lashed out with his foot at the prisoners, catching one of them in the side.

"What the hell are you doing, sergeant? Those men are my prisoners!" I exclaimed. His face was red with fury as he yelled back at me.

"You had no right to take these stinking Cong prisoners." His breath smelled of the beer he had drunk. "You should have killed those motherfuckers like they killed that other tank crew!"

"Fuck! These men are tied up. We don't know who they are!" I yelled back.

I was saved by the sound of Lieutenant Knutson's voice breaking over the argument. "Calm down, sergeant. Go back to your tank! What's going on here, lieutenant?"

I explained what had happened. While Lieutenant Knutson and I were talking, the ARVNs drove up and loaded the prisoners on their three-quarter-ton truck. They didn't treat the prisoners much better than the sergeant had. We all cooled off, but the sergeant never really forgave me for bringing those prisoners back alive.

That night we were shot at by a sniper. He didn't hit anything, but we were nervous and jumpy all night long.

The next day I was surprised to see the two men we had taken prisoner the day before standing in a group of men. As they told their story, the village men kept glancing in our direction. I called the captain to find out the status of those two men. He told me that the old man had been the records keeper in the area for the land boundaries, sort of a county clerk. The young man had been on leave from his ARVN unit.

All the villagers, from the women going to market in the morning to the kids harassing us during the day, started to avoid us. *It's a hell of a thing,* I thought, *to try to fight a war with all these goddamn civilians around.* Who was the enemy and who was not?

9–10 October 1967

Engineers in all the AOs were busy working on the road, strengthening the road bed and widening it in preparation for someday paving the whole damn thing clear to the DMZ. Someone in some headquarters thought the road would be harder to mine if it were paved. We infantry soldiers didn't think it would make much difference since the dinks would just burrow under from the side, but no one asked our opinion. Besides, it might help a little bit. The road would be able to carry traffic more safely and, more importantly to us, it would keep the dust down.

To the south of us past Bridge 100 the road bent around an outcropping of rock. A group of engineers were working to widen the road at that point by blasting the rock from the cliff edge.

One evening, after I had finished my bath in the stream, I was standing on the railroad bridge next to my hootch when all of us had our attention drawn to an unnatural sight. A small convoy of vehicles was coming toward us from the south with their headlights on. We couldn't believe anyone would be dumb enough to travel the road at night.

The twilight was just ready to give way to the full darkness of night. I ran across between the two bridges to the Bailey bridge to stand with my men who were watching through their gunsights the convoy coming toward them. It could be a trick.

The first vehicle was a three-quarter-ton truck, followed by a deuce-and-a-half, a payloader, and a tanker-like vehicle used to haul paving tar. I waved at the convoy to stop and asked who was in charge. A second lieutenant opened the door of the three-quarter-ton and said that he was.

"What the hell do you think you're doing? Don't you know the dinks mine this road all the time? You'll get the shit blowed out of you!"

"Yeah, well, we're engineers working on widening the road and we just worked a little late to try to make up some lost time," the lieutenant answered.

"Well, you'll just have to stay here tonight. It's too fucking dangerous on this road. You'll never make it back to Thunder."

"Bullshit! We're going on. The dinks haven't had time to mine this road. We got to get back and get something to eat."

"This is my AO and I say it's too dangerous. Besides, we got food right here."

"Ahhh, lieutenant, get out of the way. We're going on. I'll run my operation and you can run yours. Get out of the way. Move it, driver."

"You stupid fucker," I yelled at him as he drove into the darkness, "you'll get zapped for sure!"

The convoy ignored me as it drove on up the road, their headlights blazing just like it was Route 41 back in Indiana.

"Dumb, dumb," I muttered, and I called Schaldenbrand so he would know who was coming. Then I called Delta Six to tell him about the nut who was ignoring my warning. He said I had done all I could and that he would tell the battalion commander.

I listened intently until the sounds of the convoy faded in the night. Delta six called me later to tell me they had made it.

The next day the M-60 tank let out a large crack and settled abruptly onto its tracks. After much deliberation the tank crew decided a suspension bar had broken. They ordered a new one and began the herculean chore of taking their sixty-ton tank apart so they could replace the broken piece when it arrived.

The infantrymen gleefully lined up on the bridge to watch the track assholes strip down to their waists and sweat mightily as they dismantled the crippled machine.

That evening we heard the convoy coming up the road, again with lights blazing.

"That goddamn dummy is just aching to get himself killed," Porter said in disgust.

"That's no shit," I answered. "Those dummies are going to get zapped."

"It's even later than it was last night," Torrey remarked to me.

I ran over to the Bailey bridge again; I was really perturbed this time.

"Goddamn it, lieutenant, I warned you last night about this shit!" I hollered.

The convoy didn't even stop, it just slowed down to cross the narrow bridge.

"What the goddamn hell do you think you're doing driving down the middle of this fucking road in the middle of the night?" I shouted above the sound of the motors.

"Don't be an old grandma," he yelled back. "We made it last night, didn't we? Besides, the mine sweepers don't open the road until 0930 in the fucking morning and we have to make up that lost time!"

These last words were spoken as he yelled them from his three-quarter-ton as it moved down the road.

"It's a lick on him, sir," Porter remarked.

We stood there watching the taillights fade into the darkness. Taillights, for Christ's sake.

"This country fools a guy. It looks so peaceful with all these people," Bell remarked. "It just doesn't seem like there could be any danger."

His words were punctuated by a huge explosion. A dark column of smoke rushed into the night sky, silhouetted against the lighter heavens.

I ran to the radio to call Schaldenbrand at the north bridge. His RTO said that Schaldenbrand and some of the men were running toward the convoy which had hit a mine at the bend in the road.

Delta six had heard the explosion from his location on the mountain and called to ask what had happened. I told him I was unsure but it looked like that convoy's luck had run out.

After a while, Schaldenbrand came on the horn to tell Delta Six a dustoff was needed. Two men on the payloader had been killed. Schaldenbrand told us over the radio what had evidently happened. He thought the mine must have been planted just at dark. It must have been a command-detonated mine because the dink had let two vehicles cross over it before blowing up the payloader. Schaldenbrand couldn't understand why the dink had blown up the payloader instead of the other vehicles, which were better targets militarily, unless the dink had thought the weird shape of the payloader made it a more important vehicle. If he had blown the tanker-type truck with the paving material, he really would have gotten some fireworks.

Schaldenbrand said the dustoff was coming and that he would call us back. He had to change frequencies to bring in the chopper. We saw the brilliant landing light flash on in the distance as the chopper looked for a place to land on the road. The muted sound of its motor carried to us through the quiet air. We prepared ourselves to hear the dreaded sound of gunfire directed at the chopper, but none came. With a surge of power, the chopper lifted its load of bodies back to the firebase.

Schaldenbrand came back on the horn to report that the two men had been blown to smithereens, killed instantly. It turned out that the one man should not have been on the payloader at all, but he had jumped on at the last minute because his friend was driving it.

The following day the engineers came out to retrieve what was left of the payloader. From that point on no engineers traveled the road after dark. It bothered me a little that I had failed to make the lieutenant realize that in the first place.

12 October 1967

An evening or so after we had built two bunkers around the bridges, Porter and I were standing in the road smoking cigarettes and looking north toward the bend where the convoy had been blown up. There was still enough light that we thought we saw movement on the road.

Porter remarked that it was probably dinks setting another mine, but the light was so bad we could have been seeing things. I raised my M-16 and fired a round down the road just for the hell of it.

Not really expecting anything, we were both shocked when the road erupted in a tremendous explosion. A mushroom-shaped cloud rushed into the sky. The shock wave hit us as we saw clouds of dirt falling into the rice paddies with little splashes of water and onto the road with little wisps of dust.

As the last clouds of dirt fell, Mann yelled to me that Delta Six was on the horn and wanted to know what the hell that was. I explained that I wasn't sure, but I thought I had startled a dink land-mine team and they had blown themselves up.

Delta Six told me to take a team down there before first light to see what had happened.

By 0400 hours we were ready to move out. I was determined to move up the road in the best tactical maneuver possible. If we were attacked, I wanted us as spread out as possible so one volley wouldn't wipe us out, and yet close enough together to launch a successful counterattack.

I split my unit into two elements and put one unit on each side of the road. At my signal we moved slowly forward through the ditches.

Schaldenbrand radioed from his bridge that he would wait until my signal before he moved his men forward since they were so much closer. We thought it was important that we arrive at the same time so that we could provide mutual support in case of a firefight.

At the halfway point I radioed Schaldenbrand to move out. I also moved the unit on the other side of the road back to my side because of the terrain.

Enough light was available to allow us to see the bend as we approached. We could see nothing out of the ordinary from where we were. I was disappointed.

Schaldenbrand and his men approached on the road itself. Suddenly his point man stopped and dropped to one knee, the men behind him following his movement. We continued forward in a crouch.

Schaldenbrand saw it first and cried out that he had found it. Still maintaining caution, we spread in a line across the road down into the paddy on the other side and continued to move up. The light was better now. We could see what Schaldenbrand was excited about.

A large crater had been blasted in the road, reaching from one side to the other about twenty feet wide and about three or four feet deep. We were puzzled as to what type of explosion it had been.

If it was a land mine, what had happened? Had the dinks set it and gone away and had it gone off by itself or had my shot startled someone messing with it when it exploded?

One of the men let out a squawk. He found the sole of a foot complete with toes. We ran over to look at it. The sight of a human foot lying upside down on the dirt in the ditch was weird. There must be other parts around.

I had the men form a circle around the crater. We fanned out like the spokes of a wheel, searching for more evidence of a human body. Exclamations from the men indicated their success. As each part was found, the men would pick the piece up to bring it back and pile it on the edge of the crater.

The men fanned out for about a hundred to a hundred fifty feet, stopped, then formed a circle perimeter around the area while Schaldenbrand and I looked over the small pile of flesh. There were three penises, two complete faces, which looked like masks they were so complete, five soles of feet, three hands, and a few other parts. The largest body part was a section of a rib cage with parts of four rib bones connected to a small section of the shoulder.

The bodies had disintegrated from the force of the blast. We figured from the parts that three men had been leaning over a land mine of approximately thirty pounds of explosives. My shot must have startled one of them, causing him to brush two wires, making an electrical contact and setting off the mine.

We examined the pieces of what had been two M-16 rifles, serial numbers still intact. I radioed the numbers to Captain Sells, who would hand them in to S-2 who would track down the last known owners of the two rifles.

All of us were happy over the turn of events, pleased that the dinks had messed up. Except for the rib and arm parts, there was only enough left of three men to fill a two-gallon bucket. Better them than us.

One of the men took one of the dink's hands that had been severed at the wrist and stuck it upright in the soft dirt at the edge of the crater. He then put a cigarette between two of the fingers. It looked great. It looked like someone lying underground had paused in the motion of moving his cigarette from his mouth to his side. Everyone took pictures of this bizarre construction. We never thought it was ghoulish. The hand with the cigarette was just our way of releasing emotion against an elusive enemy finally caught.

Every morning the engineer battalion commander hedgehopped along the road in his chopper to check it out before his mine-sweeping crew started their sweep. Our attention this morning was drawn to the sound of his low-flying chopper coming from the north. We waved our arms as the pilot passed a few feet over our heads. The pilot flew a hundred meters further before swinging around to see what all the commotion was about. Evidently the engineer battalion commander was unaware of the explosion the night before. The chopper circled us. We could see the men in the chopper watching us from the open side door.

I ordered a smoke grenade to be thrown so the pilot would land. I reported to the colonel what the situation was. He was very, very pleased, because this sector of the road had been mined constantly and was a constant pain in the neck to him. He sent word by radio for the engineers to send a bulldozer down to fill in the hole which made the road impassable, and he congratulated us on a job well done. He and his crew then climbed aboard the chopper to continue their aerial sweep.

The prime intelligence find had been a mangled but still legible identification card. Delta Six had ordered me to turn it over to the ARVN S-2 when they arrived.

While we were waiting for the mine-sweeping team and the S-2 following them, I ordered the men to go into the village to the east of us and bring back some villagers. I wanted the villagers to bury what was left of the Vietcong as a lesson to what happens to folks who messed with Americans.

We kicked the hand and other parts into the crater and took the villagers off to the side about fifty feet away where the ribs were located. The farmers gathered around the small pile of remains with their hoes and rakes, unsure of what we expected of them.

With pantomime we let them know they were to scrape out a shallow hole to push in the remains. They looked at the pitifully small pile of flesh and began to scrape frantically at the dirt. It only took a small hole. After a few minutes the hole was big enough and one of the old men hooked his hoe over the ribs to drag them into the small depression.

The job done, the villagers walked home, glancing over their shoulders at us as we returned to our bridges, feeling smug.

We need not have felt smug. The next morning Schaldenbrand called to tell me the mine-sweeping crew had just cleared his bridge. A few minutes later we heard an explosion from the bend.

In retaliation, the dinks had set up a command-detonated mine next to the road. When the three men with the mine sweepers crossed a certain spot in the road, the dinks set off a claymore-like device sending a spray of shrapnel across the road. The dink must have been nervous though, because he set it off before the three men were in the killing zone. The three men were hit by the edge of the shrapnel field instead of taking the full load. They were stunned and shook up, but their injuries were slight—only a few shrapnel wounds.

The relief crew opened up with their rifles at the dinks, who disappeared without leaving a blood trail. No one in the sweeping crew felt inclined to chase after them.

A dustoff carried out the wounded. The relief crew was so nervous and cautious that the road wasn't cleared until 1100 hours. The traffic built up behind them but the crew didn't care. They were not going to be hurried now. Every irregular buzz in their headphones would bring them to an immediate halt until the suspect area was cleared.

In a few days their confidence returned, proven by the fast walking speed they maintained in their sweep.

Mines continued to be laid in the road at irregular intervals. It was a fact of life, but the terror of an explosion never failed to send a shiver through our guts no matter how many times we heard them. Whatever we were doing, our heads would jerk around. It was terrifying to hear the explosion, see the ugly gray and black cloud as it ripped into the air, see dark pieces of metal, canvas, machinery, and human beings flying in a blossom of death out from the center of destruction.

A week later a deuce-and-a-half loaded with artillery shells and with two men in the cab stopped at our bridge to shoot the breeze.

They started the truck with a grinding of gears, heading north toward Thunder. Shortly after they crossed Schaldenbrand's bridge there was a terrible explosion. I stood in the bright sunshine watching the black cloud.

Schaldenbrand reported what had happened. About two hundred meters north of his bridge a land mine had exploded right under the cab of the truck. The cab was completely demolished as the heavy truck was blown in two. The top of the deuce-and-a-half was made of canvas. The passenger was thrown through the canvas top fifty or sixty feet out into a rice paddy. One of his legs was blown off at mid-thigh, but he was still alive when the dustoff arrived. The driver took the full force of the blast. He was completely mutilated, his body intertwined in the mangled, twisted wreckage of the cab. He was killed instantly.

The artillery shells lay scattered in a rough circle around the smoking wreckage. By some miracle they had not gone off.

I approached the twisted wreck. It was very disheartening to see the smoking wreck which had once been the carrier of human beings. There were wisps of smoke drifting upward from the hulk. As we approached closer, we saw parts of the driver's body mangled beyond recognition in the cab and on the ground. The main portion of the driver was only recognizable because we knew that was what it was supposed to be.

My men ran toward the still-living being huddled in the rice paddy mewling over and over that his leg was gone.

The scene of desolation brought about the true impact of the Vietnam War to me. There was no enemy to fire at, there was noting to retaliate against. At a distance, the traffic of vehicles and Vietnamese watched.

All that remained was the messy job of cleaning up while thinking that this could happen to us. A small part of our mind tried to retain its sanity by reminding itself over and over that it would never happen to us. It can happen to everyone else, but it would not happen to me.

With that in mind, we started scraping up what was left, preparing it for the plastic body bag. We completed the gruesome details of loading the wounded and dead onto the dustoff, calling the engineers to come haul the truck away and patch up the road so that in a few hours, when someone crossed that way again, unless they looked very carefully they wouldn't see anything to signify the horror and destruction that had taken place there earlier. Maybe a blackened place in the road, a few pieces of metal, but other than that, nothing.

14 October 1967

Early this morning Delta Six called to say that a couple of members of the local police force were going to set up a checkpoint at my bridge to check IDs of people passing by.

We thought this would be great because each day we either checked some IDs or we traveled out from the bridge on patrols, searching through the heavily populated area for evidence of the enemy. However, we traveled in a vacuum of understanding among the villagers and farmers because neither we nor they understood the other's language. Whenever we found a booby trap in or near a village full of people, we were powerless to question anyone or do anything about it. We couldn't take the whole village prisoner, so we were forced to vent our anger by destroying the hootch closest to the booby trap.

With the police coming out to check IDs it would be a matter of countryman questioning countryman, which seemed to us a hell of a lot more effective than what we did.

Since the area was mostly controlled by the Vietcong or was supported by Vietcong sympathizers, we thought the appearance of the police on the road could mean trouble. So when the police arrived on their Honda 50, we were dressed in full combat web gear with each man assigned to his guard post.

After an hour and half, the Vietnamese were lined up on both sides of the road as the police methodically checked the IDs which everyone in Vietnam was supposed to carry. We were not supposed to assist in this action, which was just as well because we were having enough trouble just keeping all the kids from carrying away everything we owned.

About noon the hot sun seemed to have slowed the police down even more and traffic continued to back up. About that time a burst of automatic rifle fire from an AK-47 shattered the air as puffs of dust flew up from the road around the police and the civilians.

The effect was much the same as throwing a snake in the middle of a flock of chickens. Vietnamese men, women, and children ran in all directions, yelling, screaming, and waving their arms, abandoning their Honda 50s, Labretters, trucks, produce, and whatever else they were carrying. The two policemen dived behind their Honda 50, then crawled into the ditch.

We were surprised but prepared. We turned in our positions toward the ridge behind us to the west and returned a blistering wave of fire toward the area where the shot came from. Another burst of AK-47 fire swept the road, but still no one was hit.

A small squad of my men who had already been assigned this duty ran toward the ridge. No more shots rang out as the squad maneuvered up the ridge.

I reported the episode to Captain Sells. While he and I were talking on the horn, a motorcycle engine started up behind me. The men had just reached the top of the ridge when I turned to yell at whoever started the cycle that it still was not safe to move. I was surprised to see the two police officers leaning over their Honda 50 as they frantically weaved in between the belongings and vehicles on the road in a frenzied effort to escape the area. They looked pathetic.

Mann yelled at them, "Chickenshit sons-of-bitches!"

The civilians slowly returned from their hiding places to recover their belongings. In a few minutes they were gone and traffic on the road returned to normal.

We never heard of the police conducting an ID check in the area again.

16 October 1967

It was another blazing hot afternoon. Distinct figures bent over in the fields to the east. I was leaning on my elbow against the bridge railing when one of the dogs from the village started chasing something in and out of our barbed wire. He quickly became a nuisance as he tripped first one flare then another. The trip flares were strung through the wire to discourage the Vietcong from trying to slip through. The concertina wire had gaps from numerous explosions and floods tearing it apart, but that didn't deter us from setting trip flares in the wire and the gaps between.

We hollered at the dog but he continued to bark and chase whatever he was after until I decided that if we didn't stop him, we wouldn't have anything left. Other dogs had bothered us in the past for different reasons and the solution was the same. We would use the opportunity for a little target practice. The only requirement after killing the dog was that whoever did the shooting had to do the burying.

This would be my dog. I carefully lined up the M-16's sights on the dog and squeezed the trigger. It was an easy shot of fifty meters.

I nailed him with the first shot, pumped a few more rounds in him just for the hell of it, then followed my own instructions by picking up an entrenching tool and calling for Mann to come along to guard while I dug.

While I was digging, a group of women came out of the village talking excitedly. Mann called my attention to them. I straightened up as they approached and wondered what the hell I had done wrong. Probably shot a holy dog or the village chief's dog or something.

The women gathered around us making pantomine expressions that they wanted the dog. I was only too happy to let them have it, as it released me from the chore of digging a hole for it. They hauled it back to the village, chattering and laughing, while Mann and I returned to the bridge.

I never gave it any more thought until the village chief's son, whom we called William, arrived a few hours later to invite me to supper. I was astonished. Never had the Vietnamese extended an offer of this nature before. I was not sure what to do, but I didn't want to offend the village chief, and after all, we were supposed to win their hearts and minds. I could hardly turn the invitation down.

As evening approached I put together a packet of C rations as a gift to the chief. The Vietnamese loved army C rations so I knew the Cs would make an excellent gift. I told Yoder, one of my riflemen, to accompany me to stand guard outside the chief's hootch. I wasn't about to go by myself into a Vietnamese village at night, no matter how close it was to my bridge.

We approached the chief's hootch with trepidation, not knowing what to expect. The chief, his family and guests were waiting for us. I left Yoder outside as I entered the murkily lit hut.

It was like every hootch I had ever entered in Vietnam. It smelled of humans, animals, old food, and rotting vegetation, all smoothed over with the smell of dirt. The floor was packed dirt, the walls were a mixture of mud and grass, and the roof was a series of overlapping grass tied in bunches.

Next to a wall I saw two women turning the dog on a spit.

Oh, oh, I thought, *what have I gotten myself in for?* It was too late to back out, but I didn't like the looks of that dog.

The chief entered the hootch behind me and indicated I should sit on the ground in front of the dog. I began to think that maybe I was not the one to win the hearts and minds of the people as I graciously handed the chief my little gift packet of C rations. He seemed pleased with the gift and gave it to one of the women who secreted it in the back of the hootch. The others, perhaps twenty, seated themselves in a rough circle in front of the cooking dog.

"Yoder! You still out there?"

"Yes, sir! What's going on?"

"I'm not sure. You just hang in there. I think it's a lick on me! They expect me to eat that dog I shot this afternoon!"

"Shit! Good luck, sir!" Yoder laughed.

I kept nodding and smiling to the Vietnamese crowded around me to show them I was enjoying myself. They nodded and smiled right back to let me know they were enjoying themselves, too.

I was served a piece of the dog meat along with some rice and vegetables with parts of fish in it. I looked at it as portions were served to the other people in the hootch. Food was very precious to the farm people. It would be a great offense if I refused to eat it. I decided to wait until someone else stuck the food in his mouth so I would not be the first one poisoned.

They passed around a little bowl containing evil-smelling nuc-mam to spread over the rice. Nuc-mam was made by putting out a layer of fish, then spreading salt over it and repeating this until there were about ten layers of fish and salt. This was allowed to rot in the sun for three weeks as a greasy, oily liquid ran off into bowls. We could smell it downwind for three klicks. I hadn't been sure that the people really ate it.

I put one or two drops on my food then passed the bowl to the next person, William, who I thought was our friend. He was grinning like I was his long-lost brother.

The whole meal turned out to be pretty good. Candles threw distorted shadows against the walls as everyone talked or laughed during the course of the meal.

Afterward I stood up to offer a small speech as to how gratified I was that I had been welcomed into their house. I hoped that we were doing a good job of freeing their country from communism. They did not understand anything I said, but they seemed to enjoyed it anyhow. And the village chief gave a little speech to which I nodded ignorantly. He could have been saying that now that they had fattened the American pig, everyone could stab him to death.

Still, I was pleased with the whole evening. The people had been very friendly. I had responded in kind. I left after shaking everyone's hand. I couldn't help but notice that one of the women was wearing a new blouse of parachute silk made from our artillary flares. I touched the material, nodding my approval. They all got a kick out of that.

They could have been anything, including Vietcong, but that night was one of the few times I ever saw friendly Vietnamese faces.

The next day I got the shits. You can't win!

23 October 1967

We hit the village to the west of our position in a predawn raid that had been well planned the day before. We moved in early-morning blackness from my bridge to Jose's bridge, where we would link up to move out on the village. (I hated moving at night, especially toward another position, but I had called the track crew before we left our position to warn them we were coming and not to shoot us.)

I walked the point, my imagination conjuring up all sorts of boogy men and sounds from the pitch blackness around me. *Damn this night work anyway,* I thought. *We could be walking into an ambush ourselves.*

I walked as quietly as possible, but each crunch of the flint rocks beneath my boots sounded like an avalanche. The soft crunch of the men behind told me that we were moving much quieter than my imagination thought.

I caught myself cringing as my mind pictured bullets flying out of the darkness into my body.

There was a thump on the ground in front of me and an explosion went off. I heard pieces of shrapnel rip by my face and body as I saw dots of light dancing crazily in front of my startled eyes.

I froze, terrified of moving one way or the other. The thought flashed through my mind that whoever was on guard duty had followed SOP for hearing enemy activity in the night. He had thrown a hand grenade so he wouldn't give away his position. I knew with dread certainty that either an M-16 on full automatic or an M-60 machine gun was pointed right at me. The only reason he hadn't fired was because he was waiting for some sound to fire at.

The grenade had landed practically at my feet, but miraculously we had not been hit. Everyone behind me was deathly still, thinking the same thoughts I was. I couldn't understand why the man didn't fire at the sound of my heart, it was thumping away so loudly inside my chest.

I pictured the man crouched over his weapon, ready to spray the area immediately in front of him. I remained frozen, my mind running through possibilities of what I should do.

I was going to die by the guns of my own men.

A voice behind me bellowed out, "Who the fuck threw that grenade? You stupid son-of-a-bitch, it's us out here, you crazy motherfucker!" My RTO angrily spelled out all of our sentiments. I tried to make myself as small a target as possible at the first sound of Mann's voice.

"Who is that?" We recognized Jose's voice. "Is that you, Mann? Lieutenant?"

"Who the fuck did you think it was? Jesus Christ?" Mann started yelling at the darkness.

"Okay, Mann, hold it down, hold it down! We don't want to wake the dead, for Pete's sake!" I slowly walked up to Jose's position. Other men had rushed from their positions to find out what was going on. Jose stood up when he saw me.

"What the goddamn hell do you think you're doing, throwing that grenade? Didn't you know we were coming?"

When Jose was excited, he started talking rapidly in Spanish mixed with English. He was able to get enough English out to tell us he knew nothing of our plans.

I stormed to the back of the APC where I raised holy hell with the track men and the squad leader.

"Goddamn, I must have called down here five times to make sure everyone knew we were coming. Who the fuck dropped the ball here?" I was pissed off. I chewed everybody's asses out, to relieve my fear more than for anything else.

It turned out that Jose was going to pull guard duty on the last watch, so he had gone to sleep early when he got back from sick call. Everyone had assumed he knew about the plans. So everyone knew we were coming but Jose, and he had the guard duty at that crucial time. The track man had received my call before we started out, but he had just woke up one of the men to ask him if everyone knew we were coming. He had assumed that the positive answer included the present guard, so he had reported everything was ready.

The attack was unsuccessful. The VC escaped the village before our unit was properly set up. Shots were exchanged, but there were no casualties. I called Delta Six to report we had failed and were heading back.

Outside the east end of the village we found a graveyard. Like all of the Vietnamese graveyards that we had seen, each grave had a long hump of dirt over it. Little containers for holding burning incense were at the head of each grave. The older ones had grass growing on them.

Our attention was drawn to a fresh mound of dirt. We had heard of missing American soldiers in the area and we had heard that the Vietcong sometimes hid weapons in false graves. We decided to dig this one up to find out what was in it. I sent some of the men back into the village to bring back some diggers.

They brought back a couple of middle-aged women and one young girl who looked to be eighteen or nineteen. She was good-looking for a Vietnamese.

"These the best grave diggers you could find, for Christ's sake?"

"Everybody else has disappeared, lieutenant."

We sent them to work digging up the grave. Some of the men took turns helping.

The atmosphere around the grave was strange. It was like a holiday, with all of us laughing, shooting the bull, and smoking cigarettes. The strangest of all was the attitude of the women. They seemed to be enjoying the digging and holiday atmosphere right along with us. We kept them supplied with cigarettes, which they thoroughly enjoyed.

I began to think there might really be something down in that hole. Otherwise, why would the women act so happy about digging up a body? I couldn't figure out their attitude unless there was no a Vietnamese body there. I had thought of calling the whole thing off, but the women's attitude made me decide we would keep digging.

After a while one of the shovels hit wood. The digging became more intensified until all the dirt had been cleared from the coffin. One of the men leaned over to pry the lid off. We gathered around the coffin with anticipation as the lid was pried up.

A body was lying inside, all wrapped up like a mummy with white strips of cloth. For the first time the women became uneasy, which surprised us after their attitude before. Surely they knew it was a grave they were digging up. The fact that it had a body in it should not be a surprise.

We used a hoe to pull off the strips from the head so we could identify the body as to whether it was an American or not.

The women dropped to their knees, wailing, crying, and moaning. We couldn't figure that.

Before we unwrapped the head completely, we hooked a couple of hoes under the body to see if there were any weapons under it; there were not. When we pulled off the bandages from around the head we were struck with the powerful stench of rotting flesh. It was not an American.

We threw the top back on the casket and motioned to the women to cover it back up. They ignored us as they continued to wail and wave their arms in the air.

We were in a hurry to return to the bridges because we hadn't eaten, so we tossed the hoes next to the women and marched back across the paddies. We found an onion patch on the way back not too far from the south bridge and we all pulled a few to spice our C rations with. There was nothing left when we departed. It wasn't often we found fresh food, so we took advantage of it.

I thought afterward that we were all becoming pretty callous to life. The thought was a small one and soon left me.

2 November 1967

Our battalion had been ordered into the mountains west of the highway. We were to be relieved today by the 198th Brigade, fresh from the States. Bridge duty was relatively easy and it was thought that the green troops, "new" to Vietnam, should be broken in on the bridges before becoming bloodied in the jungles. The procedure for relieving us would be the same as before, only now, some weeks later, I would be the critical old-timer, scrutinizing the soldiers new to Vietnam.

But with one night remaining for us, there was time for a last mission. The platoon relieving us in the afternoon would allow me to use my complete platoon in an operation Captain Sells and I had been planning for days.

Intelligence had word that the village directly to the east about half a klick had nightly visits from the Cong, coming to see their families and draft new recruits. My platoon would work a coordinated attack by closing the village off on three sides after midnight. The east side, which abutted a large lake, would be covered by gunships in case any of the guerrillas tried to escape by boat. The frosting on the operation would be an MI (Military Intelligence) team, with a Chou-Hoi. The team would fly in at daybreak with an intelligence expert whom I would get to know in the future on other jobs. The man with him would be a dink named Fouel. Fouel had been a guerrilla for many years but, for unknown reasons, he had become a Chou-Hoi. A Chou-Hoi was an enemy who turned himself, and hopefully his weapons, into the hands of the ARVNs or the Americans.

Our air force dropped millions of yellow leaflets urging the enemy to give up by waving the yellow papers at us. When the distraught enemy soldier gave himself up, he would be welcomed by smiling South Vietnamese soldiers into the fold. At least, the Chou-Hoi leaflets showed smiling South Vietnam soldiers welcoming the enemy soldier. Somewhere there are records which show how many Chou-Hois came in. I was always skeptical of their effectiveness, but they did work to some extent. If the enemy were getting beat pretty bad, they were more likely to turn themselves in. We never wholly trusted the Chou-Hois. There were many rumors circulating among the American soldiers stating that many Chou-Hois came in only to get information for their commanders in the field. After gaining the trust of the ARVNs or Americans, they would be issued an M-16 and assigned to a unit. When the fighting started, they would bug out back to their side with their new weapons, plenty of ammo, and good intelligence as to what kind, how many, and the disposition of the troops they had just left. True or not, we never trusted Chou-Hois.

Around 1400 hours the platoon relieving us arrived on deuce-and-a-halfs. I quickly briefed Lieutenant Lorbieki, the platoon leader, and went back to planning my operation. The skies were heavily overcast, boding a wet, miserable night; with luck, the rain would hold off. The operation would start from my bridge after dark.

I stood on the bridge facing east toward the village we would attack, seven hundred meters away. The villagers were coming home from their everyday chores. I thought of the many patrols we had conducted through that village in the last two to three weeks; we had found nothing. At night, we took fire from the direction of all the villages and I was slightly wounded.

We gave our equipment a last check. This operation called for web gear only. It meant we would carry only weapons, ammo, canteen, and first-aid packets. All the men had been briefed. The platoon would leave after dark in single file, going directly across the open rice paddies toward the village. Fifty meters from the village, one squad with Spagg's machine gun would go around to the north and spread itself in a line to the lake, cutting escape to the north. I would stay at the west end with one squad spread in a line across the west end of the village, preventing escape. The third squad, with Indian's M-60, would spread to the south in a line to the lake. We would lie in wait all night until dawn, when the MI team would land by chopper to take us into the village. There was only one blind spot that was not covered, but it couldn't be helped. Starting at the edge of the lake, coming straight out into the rice paddies for two hundred meters, was a string of hills no more than fifty meters high. The village was built along the north side, out to where the hills ended. Some of the villagers had built up into the hills, which were heavily grown over. My squad on the south had those hills between them and the village. We believed the guerrillas would hide in the hills, but since the hills were small we would sweep them out fairly easily.

Lt. Lorbieki's platoon had completed taking over our old positions on the three bridges. My platoon had all gathered at my bridge (now Lorbieki's bridge), where the relief men would guard our packs until we returned the next day.

It was dark. Lorbieki wished me luck.

"Saddle up!" I called. Then I gave the order to the point to move out and we filed into the darkness. The point was zigzagging through the paddies, following the small paddy dikes so we could stay in the dry paddies.

The flare was totally unexpected. One second we were dark ghosts drifting through the night; the next second our bodies stood out in stark relief, our shadows sifted into the knee-deep rice. "Down," our voices rasped to each other, needlessly. Our bodies had responded the instant the light flared into existence. I was terrified that we had triggered an ambush. My body and mind prepared to respond to the sound of bullets and explosions. In the next second, however, I realized the light was coming from the sky to the south. We all lay hidden in the rice fields watching the pyrotechnic show. *Puff is working,* we suddenly realized, as two solid red lines reached from the sky to etch the earth. This explained the flares. Above Puff was a flare ship. They were far enough away so their sound didn't carry to us, only the sight of flares and the red lines of tracers. We didn't dare move because the flares would point us out to the guerrillas in the village, who were undoubtedly also watching the show. The RTO had gotten the captain for me and handed the receiver over.

"This is One-six. What the hell is going on? We were caught out in the middle of this rice paddy and almost gave ourselves away! Over."

"This is Delta-Six. Dragon Six said that one of the new units is being attacked by a battalion of dinks. I don't believe it, but their Dragon Six got Puff called in anyway. Just lie low until the show is over, then get into position before any of those guerrillas escape, out."

"Those assholes down the road there are going to get us killed," I whispered to the men around me. The word was passed to let the men know what was happening. I informed the point to move out as soon as the flares quit and those flyboys went home. "Puff the Magic Dragon" was a C-47 loaded with thousands of rounds of ammo with mini-guns or gatling guns bolted into the side door. It was said that a ten-second burst would cover every square foot of a football field. The twin red lines we saw were tracer rounds, every fifth round in a belt of machine gun ammo. Puff was firing so fast that the tracers were two solid lines in the sky. It was a pretty sight, but hardly conducive to our plans.

The flares finally died and darkness returned. Our night sight was also gone, but it would come back. Unfortunately, as we moved forward, Puff also came back. As the first flare lit the sky, we hit the dirt.

"Son-of-a-bitch," I remarked. "If that lieutenant down south isn't being attacked by the dinks, I'll go down there and kill him myself."

The action finally ended and we moved into position fifty meters from the village. The north squad radioed in that they were further away from the village, about a hundred meters. The south squad radioed that they were right next to the small hills separating them from the village. The men with me were lying prone, heads resting on a small dike, bodies for once lying in a dry paddy. We could hear the villagers talking and a few girls giggling.

"Goddamn! Charlie is having a good time, having a family reunion, while we're out here lying in rice paddy shit," Mann mumbled to me.

"He'd better enjoy it while he can because it'll be the last reunion he'll ever have on this planet," Doc whispered over.

"Yeah, when that MI chopper lands and the dinks start deciding to move, I don't want one fucking dink to get away," I stated.

The inevitable rain started falling about 0200 hours. Not a hard, driving rain but a good, steady, ass-soaking rain that the gods unleash on soldiers to remind them who is really in charge. Off to the north the rain-muted sound of a machine gun, ours by the sound of it, muttered a few seconds then quit.

"What the hell? Mann, call Schaldenbrand and find out what happened!!"

"Yes, sir. Here's Schaldenbrand."

"One-five, this is One-six. What was that firing all about? Over."

"This is One-five. A dink was trotting down the rice paddy dike out of the village right toward the Mike-60. Spagg opened up on him when he was only a few feet from us. He's deader than hell. His left arm is ripped almost off, out."

The rain stopped about the time the sky started to lighten in the east. All of us were crouched, wary of any movement in the village, ready to move as soon as MI arrived.

The villagers were becoming more active as they prepared for the day. As their movements increased, our tension mounted. Where was that chopper with the MI and his turncoat dink?

The chop-chop of rotor blades beat the early morning air. This was it! Suddenly the chopper came into view. The noise within the village became excited and the dinks started moving faster. The hell with them! My men could hold them. I would set the chopper down. The funny burbling voice of the chopper pilot came over the radio.

"Delta One-six, this is Early Bird with Hawk. Pop smoke, over."

"This is One-six. Affirmative, out."

The man who had popped smoke stood facing the direction the chopper would come from, holding his rifle in a horizontal position with his hands over his head. The pilot would read on the man holding the rifle. As the pilot drew closer, he would watch the rifle to correspond the altitude of his chopper with the altitude of the rifle. Since the man on the ground would be aware of hidden rocks, holes, or obstructions the pilot couldn't see, it was the soldier's duty to act as a guide-in. As the chopper approached the exact spot on which he should land, the soldier would begin to lower the rifle straight out in front of his body. When the set-down spot was reached by the chopper, right in front of the soldier, the soldier would crouch down, bending both elbows together, and act as though he was laying the rifle down at his feet. The pilot would then settle in.

As the chopper landed, the field agent and Fouel jumped out. The pilot immediately headed back to base. I shook hands with the agent and he introduced me to Fouel. Fouel was a typically built Vietnamese, five feet tall and starving. He was wearing black pajamas and carrying an M-2 carbine. He looked just like a Cong in that outfit.

I called the other two squads to warn them not to shoot our own man. One of my men yelled and pointed toward the village with all the activity. It looked like someone had kicked an anthill. Hot damn! There were dinks in there for sure.

We moved on line through the west edge of the village. The villagers stood in groups. This was not going to be just another patrol designed to show strength. This time we had something definite in mind.

A man went into each hootch, ripping apart the rooms and belongings, looking for guns, ammo, anything which the dinks used for weapons or war. The Chou-Hoi, Fouel, was a fanatic. He knew the people in this village personally and he was grabbing certain men and talking to them very rapidly, pointing his gun at their heads, waving his arms, and just generally stomping around.

Action! The squad on the north side had intercepted about ten or more dinks trying to escape. The dinks had run back into the village on the side facing the lake. The squad stayed on line, causing them to move slower. They called on the radio to say they could see the dinks piling into boats.

I yelled to no one in particular, "Where are those motherfucking gunships? If those dinks get away across that lake . . ."

We couldn't see to the east end of the village but I could hear the firing going on. The right side of the squad on the north could now be seen. Good! Good! The south squad was holding its position on the other side of the hill. When my squad reached the lake, we would swing around and sweep the hills.

I grabbed the radio. "Those gunships show up yet? One-five, what the hell's going on? Over."

"One-six, this is One-five. Those dinks took off in their boats but we shot one boat up pretty bad. Six dinks were on board; all of them had Thompsons [submachine guns]. We zapped five of them and have captured one. Here come the gunships! It's a fucking lick! They have two boats trapped out in the middle of the lake. I'll get back to you, out."

The sound of the gunships was clearly audible. We could catch occasional glimpses as they rose up after completing a firing run. They didn't have to make many passes. The dinks in the boats only fired a few rounds before they were chopped to pieces. My squad had almost reached the edge of the lake and the village and had not run into anything but the hostile stares of the villagers. They wouldn't say anything to Fouel, no matter how much he berated them.

I called again. "One-five, where are you? I've reached the lake, over."

"This is One-five. We're right north of you. We have you in sight. This rain is screwing up visibility." (It had started again.) "We're diving in the lake where the boat flipped over; we want to get some of those Thompsons, over."

"Okay, just don't let that prisoner loose. Have a couple of men bring him over and we'll question him. Out."

My squad had found a clear spot on the side of the hill a little higher than the main village area. The trees formed a kind of shelter and we were sitting in a circle taking a smoke break. I was preparing the plans for the sweep of the hill behind us when two of my men arrived with our prisoner. He was the healthiest dink I had seen up to then, about five feet three inches, very muscular, and well fed. His shirt was khaki, but it was pretty much in shreds. He had on shorts which were common among the lake people.

"Here, sir, we found this on him." My man handed me a billfold and some papers. I couldn't read the papers, but in the billfold was a very clear photograph of a Vietcong squad, complete with weapons. The prisoner was one of the men in the photograph. Paydirt! This man could lead us to weapons and perhaps other members of the squad. I pointed him out in the picture and pointed to him. He just looked defiant and stuck out his jaw. I tried to get some information out of him, but he could not or would not understand what I was saying. One of the guys gave him a smoke.

The Vietcong squatted down on his haunches with his arms wrapped around his legs, smoking our American cigarettes, waiting for us to take him in. Here was a live enemy squatting there smoking, seemingly unconcerned with us or the fact we had captured him. I wished I could speak his language. I didn't understand why he seemed so unconcerned. Probably because he didn't fear us now. He knew the Americans turn their prisoners over to the ARVNs at which time he would have plenty to worry about. The field agent and Fouel had been nosing around somewhere in the village when the prisoner had been brought to me. Fouel and the agent suddenly burst into the circle of soldiers. Upon spying our prisoner, Fouel yelled a few short words in Vietnamese toward the prisoner. The guerrilla's expression turned from a cool disinterest to one of terror. He obviously knew his adversary.

Fouel ran across the short distance of the circle and kicked the guerrilla as he was rising from his crouch. The guerrilla rolled backward and drew his body up into the fetal position, covering his head with his hands to protect himself from the kicks and slaps which Fouel battered him with. Fouel was screaming the whole time. He would stick his head down and yell what was obviously a question. No response from the guerrilla brought a good kick in the ribs from Fouel. The guerrilla would roll on his other side and Fouel would kick that side for a while. This shock treatment went on for a few minutes to loosen him up. Then Fouel got down to business.

The First Squad had given up diving for the Thompsons and had joined my squad. We all formed a ring around the activities. Fouel grabbed what was left of the guerrilla's shirt to drag him to the center of our ring. The shirt came off as Fouel was dragging him. Fouel immediately whipped the dink with the rag before throwing it to the ground. Fouel made the guerrilla sit up. Fouel's voice had dropped to a serious businesslike manner as he began to question the guerrilla. The black pajamas Fouel was wearing made the scene look eerie, as if one Vietcong were questioning another Vietcong. The only difference was the ring of soldiers, American instead of Oriental. In fact, it was Vietcong questioning Vietcong. Fouel had come from their ranks and obviously knew this man. Fouel had made his hand into a fist, developing a steady, rhythmic beat between the guerrilla's eyes with his knuckles. I had seen the dinks use this on other prisoners. The actual contact of the knuckles against the skull between the eyes was not a swinging blow but delivered from six or eight inches with a smart rap in a continuous manner. We had tried it on each other enough to know it quickly became a painful and irritating process. After a few minutes, Fouel changed tactics by abruptly lashing out with his foot, kicking the guerrilla in the head. The guerrilla let out a howl as he clasped his head and rolled on the ground. Fouel was methodically hitting the guerrilla with the butt of his rifle. Knee, back, kidneys, head, chest, arms, legs—it didn't make any difference. The field agent finally noticed we were taking pictures and ran out into the middle of the circle yelling, "Hey, no pictures, no pictures of this!" He thrust his hands up in front of a few lenses. We put our cameras away with no squawk. What the hell? We could understand his not wanting pictures to go back home showing an MI interrogation team working over a prisoner. We continued to watch the prisoner. After having a few rounds fired at us in the past—perhaps he had planted the land mines—we didn't care if Fouel killed him. My concern was in information that he could give us.

Eventually Fouel ripped his clothes off him and he was naked. Not much blood was on him, but quite a few knots were rising up on his body. He was muddy, bruised, tired, scared, and he started talking. Every time he slowed down, Fouel would rap him between the eyes.

Translated, his story was this: He had been recruited into the Vietcong in 1960 from this area. The picture he carried was his squad, the members who lived in this and surrounding villages. When time permitted, they would cross the road at night between our bridges to visit in the villages, recruit members, visit their relatives, and develop propaganda against the Americans and the current government of South Vietnam. A year ago he had been picked to go north to a special guerrilla training school near Hanoi. This training lasted about six months. The training involved propaganda procedures, weapons use, both theirs and ours, and recruiting techniques. He had seen some American prisoners in or near Hanoi. After coming back, he had been busy increasing the guerrilla activity in all aspects for this area. After the confession, he sullenly picked up what was left of his shirt and shorts, and got dressed. His hands were then tied behind him. I had kept in contact with Captain Sells during the whole operation. He was particularly happy with the news that we had gotten information from our prisoner. We would finish the operation and bring the prisoner in.

The two squads of men formed a line from the edge of the village at the base of the small hill up to the top. The lake was at our back as we began a sweep back to the west determined to flush out any more dinks hiding on the hill. The south squad was still holding firm at the bottom on the other side. I glanced in both directions to observe that the line was fairly even, cautiously moving forward, halting whenever a hootch or cave opening had to be inspected. The jungle growth of thick bushes, trees, and grass broke us up and also provided an infinite number of hiding places for the dinks.

Woods, a black man who was an excellent shot, held up his hand. Our section of the line stopped, the anticipation of action guiding our every movement. Woods moved stealthily forward from his position on my left. After advancing about five meters, he stared intently to his front. We stared forward, trying to penetrate the thick growth to see what was in front of him. Suddenly he whirled to his left, bringing his rifle up and firing in one motion. Two meters to his left a dink flopped backward, a bullet through his head. Woods cautiously approached the dink and reached down to search the body. Woods stayed alive by being cautious.

"Jesus-fucking-Christ, Woods, how did you see that son-of-a-bitch? I thought there was something in front of you, not sitting in your left side pocket."

"Yeah, that's what that motherfucker was thinking, too. That motherfucker figured if he kept quiet, I'd pass him by since I was staring in another direction. Out of the corner of my eye I saw that mother watching me so I zapped him before he could think about it."

"Hey! Look at this! Look! It's a picture just like the one that other dink was carrying. Look, it's that dink squad."

Sure enough! It was the same picture of that Vietcong squad.

I held the black and white photo and looked at the dink lying dead on the ground before me, his body twisted in the grotesque frozen dance of death. Yes, there he was in the photo, smiling with his comrades as they all held their weapons in preparation for being immortalized by the photographer.

Well, you poor motherfucker, I hope your folks have a copy of this picture because you belong to the jungle now, I thought to myself. We passed on into the jungle growth to complete our sweep.

We had reached a little clear area surrounded by a hedgerow-like bush common in that part of Vietnam. Those damn bushes grew everywhere and anywhere. The dinks used them as fences. They were thick and bushy with a little red flower growing from every major leaf, it seemed like. The only way through one of these bushes was where the farmers had made a path over many years.

This little area was a good place to take a break. The agent and Fouel were standing next to me when Fouel let out a yell and jumped into a large growth of tangled bushes next to the trail. We wondered what the hell was going on in that thicket. Fouel was yelling like a madman. All of a sudden he popped out of the growth, prodding another guerrilla.

We were surprised as hell. How did Fouel know he was there? Some of my men grabbed the dink and tied him up. I looked at Fouel just as he let out another yell and jumped back into the brush. More yelling and talking produced another soldier. This one was different. Fouel explained this was an NVA soldier. We looked on in astonishment.

"Shit, sir, this ain't nothing but a fucking kid."

The NVA soldier was a boy about fourteen years old. The only thing he had left was his green NVA soldier's jungle fatigues. His baggy jungle shirt hung on him a few sizes too big. With his young face and baggy clothes, he certainly didn't look dangerous.

I forgot him as I called my radioman over to call Captain Sells.

I looked around the little grass-covered clearing. The men were spread out in little groups, smoking C ration cigarettes or eating a can of C rations. It had been a good operation so far and we were ready to go back to the bridge. Just a little longer.

Smack! A rifle butt streaked by my side into the side of the young NVA soldier who had sidled up to me. Fouel had hit him with his rifle butt and was on top of him swinging his fists. My men and I pulled Fouel off.

"What did you hit that kid for?"

Fouel looked at the agent as someone translated what we had said. Fouel looked at me and for an answer reached down and ripped the kid's jungle fatigue shirt back. Strapped to his stomach were two American hand grenades.

"Jesus! Didn't anybody search him?" I exclaimed.

We thought Fouel had searched him and he figured we were going to do it. It hadn't been done.

Fouel explained that the NVA soldier waited until he figured out who the leader was and that he was going to blow both himself and the leader up. The dink had seen me talking on the radio and was preparing to take me with him.

I looked at the young soldier lying on the ground. He was looking back at me just as intently.

My life on this sweet earth had been within a few seconds of its end. Everything had seemed so peaceful, the sweep was almost over, I was enjoying a smoke and congratulating myself on a good operation— and this dink kid had almost zapped me. Never again would I trust any dinks.

The squad coming up the other side of the hill called me on the radio to say they had found a big tunnel. Leaving our three prisoners with one squad, we went over the crest of the hill to see the other squad below us in a large grassy area on the hill.

Partially covered over with grass was a huge well-like hole, at least five feet in diameter and fifteen feet deep. The hole went straight down. The walls were perfectly smooth and at the bottom we could see the holes of five or six tunnels. Where we were standing was not an entrance. There was no way in or out. This hole was an air hole for the tunnel systems which honeycombed the little hill.

None of us was going to lower himself to the bottom to explore the tunnels, so I called Delta Six to report the find. We were not too concerned since Vietnam must have had a million miles of tunnels under everything. I had only been in-country a short time and already tunnels were a feature of the landscape.

We completed the sweep and prepared to go back to the bridges. We wanted to get out of this miserable rain.

The agent informed me that Fouel had convinced the young boy to lead us to a hidden weapon. It would be a good way to end our operation.

Fouel and the kid took out ahead of us, heading for the village next to the bridge. We hurried to catch up as I was anxious to see where a weapon was hidden around there, we had conducted so many patrols without turning up anything.

The kid led Fouel across the road. I told Schaldenbrand to take most of the men with him back to the road while I took a squad with me.

The kid twisted through the farmers in their fields, crossed the stream, and pointed to a pile of wood that we had passed many times in our patrols.

"That's one of the few woodpiles we never pulled apart," Mann said to me.

"Yeah, we had better be careful of booby traps."

Fouel did the work for us, throwing the wood out from the pile as he dug down. With a yell of discovery, he pulled out a rifle wrapped tightly in plastic and tied with cord. The rifle was unwrapped, revealing a delapidated M-1 carbine and magazines with ammo.

We trudged back to the bridge through the rain with our find, proud of the success of the patrol.

SECTION 2

The Jungle

The
Jungle

October and the bridge duty had fulfilled my romantic notions of war. Almost every day we had gone out from our three bridges on patrol. There had been a few casualties, some death and ugliness, and we had suffered. But the bridges did not move. We had become familiar enough with the area and the villagers to be almost comfortable.

We had gotten used to one way of war. That was to change in November. November would be spent in the jungle of the Central Highlands, where everything seemed impermanent and the only thing of value to either side was survival.

4 November 1967

The beating of the chopper blades against the jungle air heralded our arrival into what we hoped would be a cold LZ, twenty kilometers west of Duc Pho. Three of us sat on both sides of the doorless slick, resting our feet on the landing skids. The ground we had passed over during our flight had been pocked with the explosive pellets of destruction that were hurled into its soft skin.

How many dinks had we killed with all of that instantaneous force? There were thousands and thousands of pockmarks below us. It seemed impossible that anyone could have escaped, if indeed anyone had been there.

This is how it worked. A report would be sent into headquarters with the message that dinks were traveling a trail at a particular time during the night. The coordinates for that location and the time for firing would be relayed to the gun crews. At the specified time, the gun crews would be awakened. Perhaps it would be just after midnight. As the minutes ticked closer to a time set by an unknown intelligence the men would load the artillery pieces, anticipating the release of their impersonal death into a grid square.

The gun commander would give the order to fire and the night would explode with man's lightning and thunder. After the prescribed rounds, the guns would cease, the cleanup would begin, and the men would go back to their bunks. Thinking what?

Within the range of those guns, within a specified area, the Central Highlands had for a brief moment changed from the jungle it had been for thousands of years into the particular insanity of man.

As the gun crews wandered back to their bunkers to settle down for the night, the jungle would also begin settling down for the night to begin healing the new wounds.

If all had gone well, the dinks had been using that particular trail at that particular time and we had blasted them all to hell. If not, well . . .

Suddenly I recognized our LZ. My left hand clutched the door frame and the first adrenalin entered my arteries. My platoon was to be the first in, my chopper the first down. The sky was filled with slicks. A massive swarm of hornets prepared to attack. We circled as the gunships swept in on their runs to prep the LZ. The artillery guns had worked it over while we were en route. Then the gunships took over, firing their rockets and machine guns in a methodical pattern designed to destroy likely enemy positions or to draw fire from those positions.

The ballet of helicopters over an LZ is beautiful. Gunships work in duets, one peeling off as the wing man follows, both firing into the tree line surrounding the small ridge which represents the LZ stage. Other duets of gunships crisscross the LZ. The noise of their rockets and machine guns overpowers the roar of the choppers.

The main players are poised in the wings, circling as the gunships complete their prepping. An order is given and our flight separates to begin the first phase of the ground attack. Six of us, three on each side, stood up on the landing skid so we could jump off as soon as we got close enough to the ground. We made a wide sweep over the mountainous terrain, losing altitude as we went toward the LZ on a heading of about ninety degrees.

We were most vulnerable now. The chopper crews knew it, the soldiers knew it, and the enemy knew it. Our feet were on the skids, our hips resting against the bottom of the door edge, one hand holding onto the soldier in front, the front man holding the doorjamb, our free hands holding our weapons.

The noise was tremendous. The wind from the rotor blades whipped down on us as the speed of the chopper pushed the wind past. Seventy-pound packs, plus extra ammo, canteens, bug juice, cigarettes, miscellaneous crap, and weapons—we balanced it all as the LZ rushed toward us. Suddenly the gunships rushed by on each side, rockets and machine guns roaring into the earth as they made another attempt to help get their comrades down safely. Then the ultimate noise blasted away six feet from us as the door gunner on our chopper opened up. The noise startled us so much the first time we heard it, we practically jumped out of the chopper.

My blood was pounding through my body. Every sense was alert to the action around me. No incoming rounds. Good! We were coming in, the chopper barely slowing down as it hovered five to ten feet from the ground.

"Hey, motherfucker, get lower!" we all screamed, but it was useless and we knew it. The chopper, which had never really stopped moving, was going forward. We jumped, aided by our friendly door gunner who kicked our asses off the skid if we didn't go fast enough.

All the soldiers tumbled to the ground from the first chopper. My RTO, medic, and machine gunner were with me on the first chopper and we all fell into the elephant grass. Jesus Christ! We were higher than we thought. The grass was deep. Regaining my feet, I yelled to the men to spread out and move forward at a run. The rest of the company was coming in behind us. We had to clear the ridge.

The goddamn ridge didn't look anything like I had pictured it. Not only that, the elephant grass hampered my vision. However, I knew the general direction we were supposed to go. The ridge was honeycombed with man-made tunnels and air shafts. Big holes five feet in diameter, ten to fifteen feet deep with tunnels running out in all directions at the bottom. We dodged all of them until I stopped the men at what I thought was a good perimeter line. The choppers kept coming in on the ridge until finally Delta Company had secured the LZ.

The LZ was cold, thank God.

As I surveyed the ridge, which was part of a large mountain to the north of us, the embryo of an American firebase was beginning to grow.

Chinook helicopters sidled in with the 105 artillery guns slung under their mammoth bellies and the ammo slung under the guns. There would be six of these big guns set up in the middle of the firebase for fire support and defense. The big double-bladed choppers slowed their descent as the sling of ammo neared the ground. Working in coordination with a soldier on the ground giving hand signals, the pilot lowered the chopper until the ammo sling touched the ground. The gun itself was next to touch the ground, as the pilot shifted slightly to set it down next to the ammo. The tremendous downdraft from the blades whipped the dirt and grass in all directions as the sling released the chopper back to the sky.

The soldiers busied themselves pushing the guns into place in the middle of the firebase. The guns formed a rough circle with the barrels pointing outward. The nature of this location was such that an attack could come from any direction, and the guns had to be ready to offer the same kind of protection.

The battalion of approximately five hundred fifty men was completely on the ground as the last flight of slicks dropped off their load of soldiers and returned to Duc Pho. Alpha, Bravo, Charlie, and Delta Companies were linked in an uneven circle, with the ridge making a rugged, ragged spine through the middle.

The soldiers were digging holes all around the perimeter and throughout the firebase, preparing their homes for the night. The platoon leaders were placing three men to a position, both for protection and because it takes three ponchos to make a decent hootch. Each man carried a poncho; two ponchos made the tent and the third was used as a ground cover.

Hootch poles were an important facet of a poncho hootch. After building a hootch once or twice, a soldier became an an expert in picking out good ones. Two would be stuck into the ground with one pole tied across them horizontal to the ground. The two ponchos were tied together with shoestrings and thrown across the horizontal pole.

The corners and edges of the ponchos were fastened to the ground with any sticks that were handy. One more pole was needed to lay at a ninety-degree angle across the horizontal pole. The hood of each poncho was fastened to the end of that pole to hold the sides of the tent out straight and to keep the rainwater from running through the hood into the tent.

Each company was assigned a particular section of the perimeter to protect. The company commander would then parcel out a section of his perimeter to each platoon. I had pointed out the section my platoon was to protect to Schaldenbrand. My command post was set up a few meters behind my platoon for better control in case of an attack.

The engineers were in little teams investigating the many tunnel shafts and air holes. As soldiers within the perimeter discovered new holes, they would mark them for the engineer teams. The engineers would police around the entrances checking for booby traps and recent occupation.

I watched as one engineering team threw a rope down an air shaft. A sergeant rappelled down the rope to the bottom but found nothing. After planting C-4 (plastic explosive) in the entrances of the tunnels, the sergeant climbed back up the rope, stringing out the fuse behind him. All through the area cries of "Fire in the Hole" spread. The explosion in the air shaft sent a smoke ring into the misty sky.

The grunting and swearing of the artillery men drew my attention. Each gun crew was stripped to the waist for relief against the muggy air. The objects of their exertion were the big guns that had to be wrestled into position. The area of grass the guns originally sat on had been churned into one large mud hole. The 105s were mounted on two wheels for mobility, but they were still heavy, clumsy pieces of equipment to move by hand.

Silhouetted on the ridge was one gun cocked at an odd angle. One wheel sat in a small hole and the other was chunked up with mud with grass sticking out. Five sweating, muddy, completely frustrated men were leaning almost horizontally into different sections of the gun as they strained mightily to get it to move. Some of the men held the weapon the few inches they had gained while a few of the others ran around to the other side to dig frantically at a path they were trying to get the gun to follow.

One of the men who was leaning his shoulder into the gun while the others dug was obviously near exhaustion. He slowly lowered the side of his head into the mud-caked wheel a few inches in front of his nose. At the same time he let his arms drop, his hands dangling in the mud. The rest of his body was taut as a bowstring as the soldier, grateful to give part of his body a rest, closed his eyes and exhaled, blowing mud from around his lips. Lifting his hands, he lit a cigarette, stuck it in the corner of his mouth away from the mud, and dropped his hands back into the mud.

His body taut, with his shoulder to the wheel and his feet hard in the mud, eyes closed, head lying in the mud on the wheel, a cigarette dangling out of the corner of his mouth, and his arms dangling down into the mud—that is how I will always remember the artillery man in Vietnam.

Off to the side of where the gun crews were working, other soldiers were busy building the battalion command post (CP). A couple of soldiers had been detailed from each platoon to assist in this. The battalion CP group consisted of the battalion commander, who was usually a lieutenant colonel; his staff, composed of a major, a captain, and sometimes a lieutenant or two; a batallion doctor; and other assorted types depending on the mission.

It is said that the outcome of any battle, regardless of strategy or weapons, depends on the individual soldier. If this is true, then the fate of any soldier depends on the vast network of communications available today.

With the radio, we grunts could make use of modern weapons. Without it, everything stayed put. We used the radio to call in artillery, naval gun support if it was close enough, air strikes, gunships, dustoffs, Puff the Magic Dragon, mortars, tanks, APCs and other rifle platoons.

The radio kept us supplied. One day our order went in; the next day the chopper flew out with a delivery. We found each other by using grid coordinates and radioing them back and forth. A pilot knew he had the right location when we popped smoke and he identified it over the radio. By this method, we received C rations, ammo, new weapons, grenades, parts for our equipment, shoes, new clothes, underwear, socks, medicine, personnel replacements, beer, iodine tablets for use in the water, mail, and once in a while even a chaplain.

To complete the cycle, the radio was used to extract us from trouble. Saving a life was often a matter of seconds.

The radio was also a comfort at night. The periodic radio checks assured us that friends and help were always near.

The battalion radio bunker had radios for every contingency. One radio for each company, a radio for the FAC (forward air controller), and a radio for the brigade HQ back at the main base. The top of the bunker so bristled with aerials that the dinks had no trouble determining which bunker was the CP.

Near the 105 gun pit the battalion surgeon was supervising the building of his field hospital. A tent was thrown up in a little depression below the level of the guns. The sides of the tent were staked out level with the roof. This provided a nice airy-looking spot around which sandbags were stacked up to waist level. A surgical table was set up in the center of the tent and around it the surgeon and his assistants distributed their wares on shelves and in drawers of cabinets specifically designed for the battlefield surgeon. Attached to the operating room was the surgeon's hootch, securely built and securely sandbagged.

The CP was nearing completion. The battalion commander's hootch was located nearby, built on the same lines as the surgeon's. It was a nice tent—one could stand up in it—spacious, with a solid line of waist-high sandbags all around the edge. Wood formerly used as braces to hold artillery shells and wood from other types of ammunition crates was used to lay a floor for the commander's and the surgeon's tents. There would be enough wood for everyone in the perimeter if it turned out to be a long operation.

The primary firebase was ready for action. As each day passed, the occupants would add touches with the material at hand to make it more comfortable. But for the approaching night with its danger of attack, defense was all.

I wandered down to my platoon with the sounds of the newborn infant permeating the air around me. The grunts and swearing of men filling sandbags; the scrappling of a trenching tool on the earth; snapping sounds as small trees and bushes were broken down to provide better lines of fire; sucking sounds as boots turned dirt to mud; shrieking sounds emanating from boards as crates were ripped apart for their contents; swishing sounds as legs brushed through the grass; murmerings from small groups of men as they discussed how best to do whatever they were doing; the mechanical clicking and sliding of metal parts as weapons and ammunition of every description were being cleaned, adjusted, and checked for last-minute malfunctions; cries of "Fire-in-the-hole" and explosions as the engineers continued their clearing process; firing from the 105 and the four-deuce mortars as their gunners adjusted the bubbles and arranged the sights so that the shells would go where they were supposed to go; the tweety clatter of voices over radios interrupting the constant static of their electronic musings; staccato sounds of a machine gun firing into the slope to the north; the sound of a helmet hitting the ground; a relaxed sight as a man settled down; the scratching of a match being lit; the scrape cutting of a P-38 opening a C-ration can; cellophane being torn; the sound of my own breathing.

And from the jungle . . . silence.

The night passed uneventfully. The enemy were all around us but in no hurry to attack the firebase. First they would communicate, and organize. As it happened, we had dropped in on what was to them an unimportant piece of ground.

5 November 1967

Dawn brought with it the promise of action from our own commanders. Captain Sells called his lieutenants to an early meeting. We brought our sergeants along as we trudged up the ridge to his CP. Captain Sells had been assigned an area of operations to cover with Delta Company. Two companies would remain behind to form a defensive perimeter around the firebase while the other companies fanned out into their respective areas of operation. Captain Sells showed us the general area Delta had been assigned. The best method for sweeping the greatest area was to divide the company into platoon-size elements. The platoons operated as independent units, separated by distances that could be as much as one kilometer. Since the terrain was very rugged, mountains covered by thick jungle growth, the actual distances meant very little. It could take an entire day to climb up and down a ridge that the map showed to be only five or six hundred meters high.

The theory was that if one platoon ran into anything, the lieutenant could call for assistance over the radio. The platoon would then hold its own until the other platoons had a chance to cut through the jungle to their comrades' aid. The mountainous jungle resisted this type of maneuver, and hours would elapse while the "contact" platoon strived mightily to hold its own.

When the other platoons arrived to form a company and a real battle started to develop, the other companies were diverted from their AOs to assist the "contact company." Meanwhile, artillery and gunships would be brought into action to aid with their superior firepower.

Unfortunately, the dinks were as familiar with our theories as we were. After a platoon had been enveloped in a furious firefight and it was obvious that reinforcements were beginning to arrive, the dinks would break contact.

The majority of the time this was exactly what happened. But woe to the platoon that ran into an enemy unit that was prepared to make a battle of it. The exception to the rule resulted in a bloody fight that would go on for days. The platoon that had initiated the action would take a lot of casualties before it could pull back. The jungle was neither an enemy nor a friend in its attitude toward the opposing forces. It was just there. The secret was in learning how to put it to one's advantage. The enemy always used the jungle to their advantage while we often just cursed it for getting in our way.

We would fight and bleed to take ground that the dinks would pull away from after they had exacted their toll. We always left afterward so they could always come back if they liked that particular place.

The American strategy was to draw them into a fight so we could use our superior firepower to destroy them. To win a battle, we had to kill them. For them to win, all they had to do was survive.

Sergeant Schaldenbrand and I went back down the ridge to inform our squad leaders of the operation and the logistics involved—codes, radio signals, supply, and order of march. The squad leaders would inform the men so everyone would know what the general plan was.

The men broke down their poncho hootches and packed their rucksacks preparatory to receiving the order to "saddle up." Last-minute details were attended to as men rushed to finish letters home. Ammo and three days' worth of C rations were passed out to everyone. Some of the men carried as much M-16 ammo as they could carry, regardless of the weight. One of my men carried the equivalent of fifty magazines of M-16 ammo. Once, right after he had arrived in-country, he had been in a battle that had lasted two days. It had been impossible to resupply his unit, which had sustained the heaviest fighting. Before reinforcements had arrived, he and many others had run out of ammunition. He had resolved it would never happen again.

The order of march remained basically the same my whole tour in Vietnam: the point squad, the flank squad, the tailend-charlie squad. The squads were rotated every day. Because of the thickness of the jungle growth and the steep terrain, the flank squad usually just stayed in single file between the point and end squads.

As soon as everyone was in position, I gave the order to move out. The point element and I checked our compass heading and maps as we entered the thick jungle. I looked back once more at the ridge. Firebase Tempest.

Soon the only sounds were grunts of exertion as the realities of a jungle march made their demands on our bodies. I tried to set a routine of rest breaks on my watch, but the terrain quickly destroyed that idea. The only sane way to march in the jungle was to glance at the watch and gauge the time elapsed against the condition of the men and the area to be covered that day.

Shortly after I had called the third break, Mann suggested I call a leech check.

"A leech check? Hell, we haven't crossed any streams yet," I remarked.

"In this fucking jungle you don't need a stream to have leeches," Mann replied. "It's wet enough that the mothers crawl all over the fucking place."

Whenever I think of leeches, I picture Humphrey Bogart dragging the *African Queen* through a river delta, neck deep in slimy water, with Katherine Hepburn watching apprehensively. Hell, we certainly had not been through anything like that. However, I consented because Mann was an old-timer and knew more than I did.

"Ahgggggggg! There's a motherfucking leech on me," I hoarsely whispered. "Look, look, the fucker's on my wrist. Quick, give me your cigarette. Salt! Salt! Someone give me some salt," I cried, thinking of those boyhood movies and the *African Queen*. I jumped around holding my wrist out. A blood-filled leech dangled, swollen as big as my finger.

Goose bumps ran all over my body and my stomach felt queasy as my eyes took in the ultimate degradation of having a werewolf-like slug sucking my life's blood from my body. Brrrrrr!

"Wait a minute, sir, none of that shit gets leeches off," Mann tried to calm me.

"Here, let me put some of this on it." He took his bottle of bug juice off his helmet and squeezed a few drops on the leech. The leech started withering and dropped off, whereupon Mann put a few more drops on it and watched it die as he squatted down on his haunches to watch its last moments.

"Fucking bug juice doesn't work worth a damn on bugs, but it's hell on leeches," he mused.

Blood continued to run out of my wrist from the hole the little motherfucker had bored in it. I wondered how anything that slimy and creepy had managed to crawl up my body and attach itself to me without my feeling it.

"You better check some more, sir. There may be more on you."

I stripped out of my jungle fatigue jacket so fast, it got hung up on my gun.

"Oh, fuck, fuck, fuck, there's one. Jesus, there's another one," I moaned as I spotted two more leeches sucking on me.

"Oh, Christ! Where's my bug juice? I've got to get these fuckers off me."

The guys around me were nonchalantly looking themselves over and applying bug juice whenever they found a leech. They had already been initiated to leeches in their first operations so it was no big deal to them. Just another uncomfortable part of the jungle to deal with.

"Squirt some of that shit around your fatigue pants where you tie them at the top of your boots," Mann told me as I observed him methodically examining his boot tops. "That way the bug juice acts as a barrier to the little fuckers as they latch onto your boot and try to crawl up to where the meat is. It doesn't stop them all, but it helps a little bit."

I resolved never to let my platoon run out of bug juice. I would order beaucoup on every supply chopper.

We continued on our way, hacking through the jungle when it was impossible to slide through. The rest of the day was an endurance test as our muscles toughened up from their period of languid bridge duty.

Up ridges, down ridges, over ridges, wading through rocky streams, hacking at jungle growth, breathing in and hopefully breathing out some of the constant bugs that continuously swarmed around our heads, watching our skin as it quickly deteriorated from the numerous bites, scrapes, cuts, tears, thorns, and other abuses of the environment that attempted to beat our bodies into submission.

The clothes and boots forming the inanimate part of our body protection were quickly drenched with sweat, dirt, mashed bugs, and the mixed blood and juices from both the bugs' bodies and our own. Covering everything was the smell of slimy, rotting vegetation. Our clothes and our bodies were beginning the rotting process of the jungle. Every scratch was a breeding spot for bacteria which could result in the rapid growth of jungle rot.

This was the essence of a jungle patrol.

Evening was drawing near as we reached a relatively flat top on a ridge which would make a good night location. The only formation for a night position, or any defensive position in the jungle, or an area without definite lines of battle, was a circle on high ground with everyone facing outward. An attack could certainly come from any direction or from many directions at once.

My platoon fluctuated between twenty-three and thirty men. I always put three men in a foxhole so they could build a hootch and set up a proper guard at night. This meant we could have seven to ten positions to form our circle. The medic, radioman, and I represented the hub in the middle of the circle. We were not in the middle for protection but to maintain control. If our position was in the line when an attack started somewhere else, I would have had to pull out to where the fighting was to direct our defensive efforts. My RTO would have to stick with me like a shadow with his radio, and, of course, the medic would be needed when someone was hit. With all three of us out of position there would have been a gap in the line.

My position in the middle provided better control and a roving reserve of two extra rifles to add strength where needed. The medic carried a rifle, but after the first man was hit the medic's firepower was cut as he attended to the wounded.

Every American defensive position in Vietnam was set up on a similar basis, whether it was my small platoon in the middle of the jungle, a battalion firebase, or a main base camp such as the one at Pleiku which was composed of three or four brigades.

The trouble with Nam was that we didn't control anything that we were not standing on at the time. Anything that moved outside our perimeters at night was fair game because the night belonged to the enemy and both sides knew it. The reality of only owning the ground you stood on meant making sure you continued to stay on that ground.

6 November 1967

Muto, a Japanese-American from San Francisco, was on point this day. About two hours after we had started patrol, he reached the top of a small ridge and immediately went to the ground, using a hand signal which meant we were to do the same. The file of men immediately crouched down, roughly every other one facing to the right or left, intensely alert for possible enemy action. I crawled forward to where Muto and his squad leader were kneeling behind a growth of tree roots.

Muto turned to me, his facial expression puckered up into a sound of silence. Pointing forward down the gentle sloping ridge toward a small stream making quiet burbling sounds, he directed my attention to a slight movement in the stream. Suddenly my eyes separated the jumble of growth as a man's figure came into view. He was a dink in uniform, his pants rolled up to his knees, and he was wandering slowly upstream while a female dink strolled next to him holding a towel.

His rifle was leaning against a tree bordering a small ring of camouflaged hootches next to the stream. I gave the signal to the men behind me that dinks had been spotted. Muto, the squad leader, and I raised our rifles. There was a lot of growth between us and the target thirty meters away which might cause the light M-16 bullets to be deflected. Muto, however, was carrying the one M-14, with its heavier shell, in my platoon. I tapped him on the shoulder and indicated he should fire first, aiming at the dink soldier.

"Fire!" I yelled.

Muto fired, hitting the dink high up, spinning him around. The squad leader and I opened up on both the enemy soldier and the girl. The dink soldier was stumbling through the stream on all fours trying to get to his rifle as the girl ran screaming through the jungle on a trail we had not seen from our vantage point. All three of us concentrated on the dink soldier, hitting him a number of times and driving the life from his body. He collapsed short of his rifle.

Leaving the main body of the platoon, the point squad and I ran in a crouch down to the stream. The dink was sprawled out, his body half in the stream. We formed a defensive group as the next squad in line behind the point squad ran down past us and across the stream into the small ring of hootches.

They were empty. The girl had escaped. The rest of the platoon fanned out as it came down the ridge, their weapons ready. We formed a large defensive circle around the area of contact.

Nervousness gave way to relief among the men when it became evident the camp was deserted. We had killed one dink with a weapon without even working up a sweat.

The guys started to smoke and a few started heating water for coffee.

I called the captain to let him know we had had contact.

"Delta Six, this is One-six, over."

"This is Delta Six, over."

"This is One-six. We just ran across a small camp and killed one dink. One dink, a woman got away, over."

"Outstanding, One-six. What are your coordinates and what kind of weapon did you capture? Over."

I told him the coordinates and reported the weapon was a carbine. He asked for the serial number. I called Muto, who was showing his new weapon around to the men, to give me the serial number to read over the air to the captain. Since Muto had made the kill, the dink's weapon was his, as was anything the dink was carrying.

We knew we were looking for an enemy base camp such as this camp could have been. The battalion commander told Captain Sells he was sending a spotter plane over to get the exact coordinates of the deserted camp we had found. Because of the possible inaccuracies of my coordinates with all the twisting, turning, and climbing we had done, he wanted to make sure I was in the place I said I was so he could properly mark his map back at the firebase.

While we were waiting for the spotter plane, we discussed the reasons the dink had been by himself with the girl.

"Look at this, sir. That dink has a bad foot," Marley remarked.

"Yeah," someone chimed in. "I bet that fucker hurt his foot so bad he had to be left behind and that girl dink was his nurse."

Yoder laughed, "That's what the motherfucker gets for malingering. Instead of dink pussy, he got the fuck shot out of him."

It was a great joke and we all laughed.

"Hey, tell everyone to get water while we've got a chance," I told Schaldenbrand. "And upstream from the fucking dink."

The guys were filling their canteens when one of them yelled, "Hey, Doc! What the fuck are you doing, you stupid son-of-a-bitch?"

My medic, upstream from where the men were filling their canteens, was washing his feet.

Doc, an overweight, pimply-faced boy of eighteen from Texas, knew we had no confidence in him and tried to bluster his way out of this situation as he did all situations by swearing right back at us.

"I'm washing my fucking feet, and if you think that's bad, I pissed in this stream a little while ago. I figure you've all drunk piss water by now."

Whereupon a stream of oaths were directed at him by everyone whose canteen was filled. The canteens were abruptly turned upside down and refilled even further upstream. Doc defiantly continued to wash his feet.

The plane was overhead by now. Schaldenbrand's RTO had switched to the plane's channel.

"Foxfire, this is Delta One-six. You're right above us, over."

The pilot was in a twin-engine push-me-pull-me general-aviation-type aircraft.

"This is Foxfire. Pop smoke, over."

One of the men was ready as he received the signal from me.

"This is One-six. Smoke popped, over."

"This is Foxfire. I don't see anything, over."

The jungle canopy was so thick the plane couldn't see the smoke, which had floated up to drift leisurely along at a temperature level under the canopy.

After a few fruitless attempts to get the smoke above the canopy, I had to radio the pilot we just couldn't get it through.

"Foxfire, negative on the smoke. However, you are circling the right spot so radio in your position. That'll have to do, over."

"Roger on that, One-six. Good luck! Out."

The plane droned off with all of us thinking the same thought. What if we really needed that spotter for support or a chopper? How the hell could they get to us to provide air cover when they couldn't see us? They could drop their ordnance on us by mistake.

"Saddle up." Everyone put his rucksack on.

We hadn't marched very far when we ran into evidence of a bombing raid. The jungle had been torn to smithereens by the big bombs. Trees had been ripped from the ground forming an abatis of twisted, interattached splintered branches, vines, and roots that was more impenetrable than the worst the natural jungle had to offer. The point element stopped, looking for a way through.

Muto voiced the seniments of all of us. "Fucking bombing raids! That's the goddamnedest mess I ever did see. We get in there and the dinks hit us, our ass is grass."

"Yeah, but fuck! We can't go around, the damn thing could be a mile long," I remarked.

"Indian, gun up!" I called back. Johnson, an Indian from a reservation in the Dakotas, was the gunner of one of my machine guns.

"Set up for covering fire until we get across this son-of-a-bitch. When Spagg's gun comes along, have Schaldenbrand radio me and we'll cover for you as you come across. Spagg can cover you from this position."

Indian rested his M-60 across a log, the barrel pointing along the path I told him we would try to follow.

The point element and I struggled across the abatis, crawling on hands and knees, sliding on our stomachs over and under logs, the branches and roots snagging us and our equipment. After about the fifth time of being jabbed in the face, I was so mad at the bomber pilots I could have killed them instead of the dinks.

It was slow, extremely hard work to go the hundred or so meters through the blasted area. The machine gunners and radiomen had the extra hindrance of pushing and dragging their heavy equipment along with them.

Finally we were through and I ordered a chow break.

For all of the laborious effort we put into our movements in the jungle, there were never any loud expletives or yelling. Sound was death in the jungle. Combatives often heard each other before they saw each other. All sounds of pain and frustration were soft, limiting their carrying ability. Normal conversation was kept low to maintain the silence needed to survive. That isn't to say there wasn't conversation and plenty of it. A guy could bitch as much as he wanted as long as he didn't get loud about it.

And bitch we did. About the food, the jungle, the bugs, leeches, the heat, dinks, rain, sun, marches—everything, and all the time. We were Vietnam-era soldiers, but some things always remain the same with all soldiers.

While everyone was bitching about the bomber crews, I received a call from Delta-Six to angle back toward the firebase.

A last cup of coffee and cigarette after chow freshened us up. We marched down until we reached the valley floor which marked the spot where we turned toward the firebase. Uphill, naturally.

By late afternoon we reached the last stretch of mountain to be covered before we reached the top, our proposed night location. Elephant grass towered over our heads, but after the jungle we had just exited this would be a snap. How wrong I was.

The elephant grass was too green and thick to go through, so we had to push it down. Elephant grass has razor-sharp saw edges, and a flat blade which when pushed down turns into a slide. As our jungle boots slipped from under us as we struggled uphill, we would instinctively grab at the grass, ripping our fingers to shreds. Wiping the blood off on our jungle fatigues turned us into smorgasbord for every bug within a kilometer. The bugs loved us.

After innumerable falls, I swore. "Goddamn, what what kind of fucking idiot would do this for fun? Those fuckers that go on safari must be nuts."

Porter, a black dude from East St. Louis, gazed up at me, blood and sweat covering him from head to toe. "After you, bwana."

Finally, we broke through near the top of the ridge. A comparatively light growth of trees and shrubs covered the top, a perfect place for a night location. We could see the firebase three hundred meters down the ridge from us.

7 November 1967

We left our night location and skirted the west edge of the firebase down the ridge. The men on the perimeter paused to watch us pass. Word of our brief action the day before had spread to everyone in the battalion. We had drawn first blood early in the game. We were building a reputation.

My line of men glanced up at the men on the perimeter with mixed feelings. We were proud of killing the dink the day before and were anxious to kill more. But to do so meant we had to root them out by traveling in their territory and fighting on their terms. Our risk would be great.

The men in the perimeter, on the other hand, had to wait until the dinks came to them. They were safer, but the firebase's static position limited their ability to kill dinks unless they were attacked.

The perimeter men were on the defense with their dug-in position, stronger manpower, artillery and mortar positions, and good lines of fire. They were relatively in a better position to survive than the platoons searching for the enemy in the surrounding area.

Hence, the mixed feelings. Was it better to be on the offense, looking for dinks to kill while suffering the wearing conditions of the march and placing oneself in extreme danger? Or was it better to be on the defense in comparable comfort waiting for an attack? An actual fight in either situation could result in death.

Regardless of what was on our minds as we brushed by the perimeter, we were powerless to change the reality of our position.

On the large map in the battalion commander's CP in the firebase, we were represented by a small arrow marked "Delta 1–6." The battalion was marked on the brigade map in base camp as "Dragon-6"; the brigade was marked on the division's map in Pleiku headquarters as Third of the Fourth; the Fourth Division was marked as part of the army on the map in the Pentagon as being in Zone I and Zone II of Vietnam; the White House and the Congress had us marked as battles/votes won or lost; the American public had us marked as patriotic soldiers or murderers and fools; our kinsfolk and friends had us marked as alive or dead.

Our personal thoughts meant nothing.

We continued to march.

We rendezvoused with the company at midday. Captain Sells had the platoon spread around a small meadow with a mountain-fed pool at one end. My platoon slipped into its perimeter location and we took turns swimming in the pool while we waited for the resupply chopper.

Captain Sells walked up as I finished getting dressed.

"The battalion surgeon is coming in on the resupply chopper to speak to your medic, Downs. Do you still feel your medic is no good?"

"Yes, sir. The guys haven't trusted him from the time he joined us.

I don't know what kind of shit they fed him down at Fort Sam Houston, but he thinks he doesn't have to listen to anyone but the battalion surgeon. He thinks he doesn't have to do any of the work the rest of us do, and I have enough on my hands without having a smart-ass medic. The son-of-a-bitch has to earn his respect just like the rest of us. Just because he is our 'Doc' doesn't make him God. Besides, the guys, me included, don't trust him. We need a medic we can depend on in this jungle."

"Alright, we'll see what a talk with the surgeon will do for his attitude."

My new medic had been assigned to the platoon while we were still guarding the bridges and had won no friends with his attitude. He would not pull guard duty, clean up his messes, or do anything except drink beer in the shade. Besides, he was dirty and had dirty habits. The guys were really upset at him.

Doc was responsible for our lives, and in a major way our psychological well-being depended upon our trust in him. Everything in a medic's manner was studied by the men as they quietly evaluated him in their minds. His habits, bearing, and attitude took on special meaning to the men who might some day have him as the only ally in a struggle with death.

Doc did nothing to reassure us as a good ally. Unfortunately, he looked like the individual he acted. He had pimples, was overweight, looked more like a slob than the rest of us, would not carry his load, was not good at making friends, and was not professional. He was constantly falling behind on the march. Medics in Nam had the option of carrying a weapon and he carried one, but it was indicative of his personality that it looked like a rod of rust.

I had bitched to Delta-Six plenty of times about getting a new medic, but they were in short supply, like everything else we needed.

The last straw had been in our first night location at the beginning of this patrol. We had formed into our perimeter defensive circle and were going about the duties of camp. Suddenly, Rueto swore.

"Goddamn you, Doc. What the hell are you doing shitting in the middle of our goddamn perimeter?"

"Fuck you," Doc replied. "I'll shit where I want. It doesn't make any difference anyway," and he proceded to continue squatting, his fat, pimply ass hanging out in the breeze.

"The hell it doesn't," Rueto hissed. "We all have to live in this circle, too. You're supposed to shit outside the perimeter."

"I ain't going out there to shit," Doc answered. "I could get killed."

"You're damn sure gonna get killed in here if you don't haul ass, motherfucker," P.G. called over.

"Alright, alright, I'll go. But someone come along to guard me."

"Shit smell like that you don't need no guard, motherfucker," P.G. answered. "Whoooeee, it smells like something crawled up inside you and died."

Everyone laughed as Doc trudged outside the perimeter to finish his shit, swearing all the while.

Maybe this talk by his boss would do some good and maybe it wouldn't.

The chopper radioed he was on the way and for us to pop smoke. The designated soldier threw a smoke grenade; it was identified by the pilot, and the soldier brought him in.

The pilot switched off his engine after settling in. The firebase was on the ridge high above us and with him he had the surgeon, who would be a while talking to the medic. Besides, we surrounded the chopper so he felt justified in relaxing. The chopper blades swished through the air as the flywheel ran down. The pilot leaned back and lit a smoke. The squads from each platoon ran out to haul off the supplies as the surgeon ran out from under the blades in a crouch to the captain standing in the grass.

I bullshitted with the other platoon leaders—Delta Two-six, Lieutenant Calhoun; Delta Three-six, Lieutenant Ordway; and Delta Four-six, Lieutenant Weeks—as the men broke open the supplies.

The older M-16 had an open-ended muzzle flash guard which was handy in twisting and cutting the stiff wire holding the C-ration cases together. Each case contained twelve meals, and in order to be fair in the distribution of the meals, the case was turned upside down so the meal labels could not be read.

Sounds of disappointment and joy about the meals depended on each man's taste. Ham and lima beans were universally hated by everyone except for the one man in each platoon who was a culinary masochist.

We all bartered back and forth with all the expertise of gem dealers, trading meals until our packs were full of the next three days' treasure.

Each platoon leader always ordered an SP pack. If we were lucky enough to get one, it was a special treat for us. The SP pack contained cartons of cigarettes, candy, soap, toothbrushes, toothpaste, chewing tobacco, shaving cream, razor blades, chewing gum, and all sorts of little nice-to-have items.

The only thing ever left behind in an SP pack were the foulest-tasting chocolate bars on the face of the earth. They tasted so bad that even the dink kids wouldn't accept them in barter. They tasted worse than chalk. We always figured some businessman had bribed the military to buy the chocolate bars he had in a warehouse left over from World War II.

One of the lieutenants was talking about his patrol while I glanced across the clearing. A group of men were being directed by a young sergeant in distributing the supplies next to the chopper, but I was interested in the two men over on the edge of the clearing. The battalion surgeon and my medic were having an animated conversation. Or at least the surgeon was. My medic's sole contribution to the conversation seemed to be a nodding of the head. Whatever the surgeon was saying, Doc was getting the picture.

The conversation over, the surgeon quickly turned and walked back to the chopper. We spread out away from the chopper as the blades slowly began turning. As the turbine wound up, the blades spun faster and faster. The surgeon jumped on board as the chopper's motor reached a level we all recognized as a sound meaning "ready." The chopper lifted up in a lazy spiral heading for the ridge behind us.

"Hey!" Delta Six yelled. "Don't you know one rocket could get all you lieutenants at once? Get back to your platoons."

We scattered quickly, chagrined and embarrassed at his words. It had been nice, though, to talk to someone else. We hurried over to our respective platoons to check our new marching orders with our sergeants and squad leaders.

Captain Sells switched his command group from platoon to platoon. He had indicated his group would be with us for the next couple of days. While his CP group was integrating itself into the middle of my platoon, I called over to Doc.

I asked him if he understood the seriousness of what it meant for me to have to call the battalion surgeon out to talk to him. Doc replied in a subdued voice that he had misunderstood what he was supposed to do as a medic for a platoon, but he promised me he would pull his load and not get smart-assed with everyone all of the time.

Doc turned to walk back to his place in the platoon. His two medic bags were crisscrossed with their straps over his fatigue jacket, the bags riding next to his hips, and his rusty rifle was gripped in his right hand. He threw on his rucksack and glanced up to stare at me for a brief moment, a sad lonely look of a young boy who was acting in the capacity of a man and hadn't had the proper training for it.

I stood in the clearing by myself as the platoon readied itself for the march. I felt bad about being hard on Doc.

A slight breeze blew for just a moment, moving the grass in waves between me and the platoon. It seemed to me that the grass moving before the breeze represented the physical force of my thoughts and actions as they emanated from me in their influence to my platoon. As the waves of grass washed around the men, so too would my decisions wash over them, leaving them another day of life or wiping out hope with death.

Delta Six's command group was composed of his two RTOs, the company medic, various attached elements, and the Fourth Platoon, which under a conventional setup was the heavy-weapons platoon. In Delta Company, Four-six was responsible for the security of the company headquarters group since we didn't have heavy weapons.

Delta Six shifted his headquarters group between his First, Second, and Third Platoons, and would travel with that platoon for a few days so he could observe that platoon leader in command. This enabled Delta Six to command his company more effectively because he got to know the men and their weaknesses and strengths.

Delta-Six and his group would travel in the middle of the platoon and he would not interfere with the platoon leader's decisions even in a firefight, except in obvious foul-ups or actual need. Delta-Six would guide and direct the company, but he left the running of the platoon to the platoon leaders for the most part. However, he was always quick to chew the platoon leaders out if he thought they needed it, and he thought that quite a bit.

He was a good man to have in command.

When we left the clearing it was my turn to have the headquarters group.

From Firebase Tempest—the battalion commander's stirring name for the firebase—the patrol had begun. The ground we had chosen was no less difficult to get over for being unimportant to the enemy.

Since leaving the meadow our patrol had moved laboriously through thick jungle growth, a dark terror-filled trail. The strain of constantly staying alert while moving through enemy territory was a drain both mentally and physically.

There was evidence of the enemy everywhere: bulletin boards standing along the trails with propaganda leaflets tacked up, punji pits, fresh spider holes, fresh bunkers, tracks. We were very jittery because it was only a matter of time until someone would die.

Brief, furious firefights would unexpectedly break out as we crossed trails with small units of NVA soldiers and Montagnard mercenaries.

Rain had been falling constantly for over seventy-two hours which delayed our resupply chopper, cutting us short on food. This only added to our misery.

9 November 1967

We were resupplied late today. Captain Sells took the company down along a river with orders for us to follow in an hour or so. He would spot a night location for us as he traveled along the river and he would go on downriver to set up a night location a klick or so away from us.

Delta Six radioed the location where we should be that night and close to evening time we reached it, a bluff. We had been following the river where the walking had been easy along the tree line border-

ing the small valley through which the river was running, but the
night location looked like a bad spot.

A thick growth of small trees were bunched on the uphill side of
the grass-covered bluff. Those damn trees would provide excellent
cover for an attacking enemy, so a full third of the platoon had to be
put along the edge of the grove. I couldn't set up in the grove itself
because it was too thick. None of us would be able to see to protect
each other and the thick growth would have seriously decreased the
effectiveness of our firepower. The grassy part of the bluff was too
small to allow me to set my platoon back from the edge of the grove.

Schaldenbrand and I walked around the position trying to decide
on the best method of placing the men. We forced our way into the
grove but quickly gave that up as being no good.

"Christ, Schaldenbrand, this position sucks. Why the fuck didn't
the captain radio me a warning about it?"

"I imagine he didn't give it much thought, lieutenant. He passed
below the bluff, from the looks of things, and he couldn't tell much
about these fucking trees from down there. It's a lick, sir."

As we were in the open, night came gently. Without the thick cover
of trees the twilight seemed to last a long time. As it darkened, I
worried about my men. We all knew the dinks had been following us
and the men had nervously talked to me as I checked their positions.

For the first time, the fear of these men was apparent. It was a fear
of the unknown, the coming night, and the sure knowledge that dinks
surrounded us. The rest of the company had pulled ahead of us and
were deep in the valley, seemingly a great distance away.

It was now, as much as during battle, that responsibility meant
something. The men looked to me for leadership. I went to each
position, reassuring each soldier of the importance of holding his
position, and to show them I was not afraid. If any of them pulled
back, our perimeter integrity would be destroyed.

I even dragged out our two starlight scopes and made sure the men
knew how to use them. The starlight scopes were a little science-
fictional, large dull-black tubes about six inches in diameter and about
eighteen inches long with a single rubber eyepiece. By squeezing a
trigger, the man looking through the eyepiece would see a greenish

shadowy outline of the terrain in front of him. The theory was that they enhanced available starlight by intensifying it, making things stand out clearer. They probably weren't worth a good goddamn in the jungle, but the men who had them immediately began sweeping the area in front.

Mann had dug a foxhole for the two of us in the middle of the perimeter. I plopped into it. I had never seen him so nervous. He started talking about his wife and the child whom he had never seen because the child was born after he left for Vietnam; they were living in New York City with her mother. For the first time since I had known him, he expressed his fear of dying before going home.

He held his latest letter in his hand along with pictures of his kid. In the dying light it was impossible to read any of the words and the baby was a blur.

I put my hand on Mann's shoulder and tried to reassure him that his wife was lonely and afraid too. I told him that he would be going home shortly. He looked up at me and said with a great weariness that, no, he didn't think he would make it home. The year had been too long.

Suddenly, there was an explosion and a hideous scream in the darkness at the edge of the perimeter. I put on my helmet and jumped out of the foxhole, crouching at the edge of it, staring into the darkness. The men all around me were instantly alert. I could feel it.

Three of my men crawled frantically to my foxhole. The one in the lead stopped in front of me, fear flowing from him.

"What the fuck was that?" I asked him. The screaming continued outside the perimeter, tearing our nerves to shreds with its piercing wail.

"I heard a sound in front of us and popped a grenade out there. That's a fucking dink I hit, and they're all over out there."

"Settle down," I told him. "You men in the perimeter hold fast," I yelled, hoping my voice sounded steadier than I felt.

"What are you guys doing out of position, for God's sake? Who the fuck is guarding that end of the perimeter with you guys out of position? Don't you know that without you there's a gap in our defenses?" I hissed. "Go on, get back over there before the dinks come through."

Nobody moved.

"I need you guys to hold that end of the perimeter. Now get back there before it's too late."

They looked at each other and stared at the black hole in the jungle from which the screaming was coming.

I gripped the arm of the man closest to me and, in as calm a voice as I could muster, explained once again how much I needed them—we all needed them—to hold the perimeter. Turning to each man, I gripped his arm to assure him of his importance.

I turned in a crouch and said, "Follow me and I'll sit over there for a while with you until we figure out what the dinks are going to do."

Hesitantly, they turned and crept back to their foxhole. I lay along the side, talking to them until they finally calmed down. The screaming had stopped, which helped settle their nerves. After a few minutes I felt I could leave them, but I explained that I had to check the other positions, and that I would be back.

All of the men were nervous, undone by the sudden terrible screaming. After speaking to all the men, I returned to my foxhole to find Mann quietly crying in the bottom, huddled up in a ball.

"Mann, Mann, what's the matter?" I whispered as I crouched on the edge of the foxhole.

"Sir, I'm scared. I'll never get to see my son, I know it."

I crawled into the hole and put one arm around his shoulders to comfort him. "Hell, Mann, you're an old-timer. You've made it this long, there's no way you won't finish out your tour." He talked about his family for a while as I sat next to him with my arm around his shoulders. I listened until he seemed to come out of it. Then, jumping up, I told him to call Delta Six while I checked on the platoon. When I got back he was his old self.

"Sir, I'm sorry I broke down on you a little while ago."

"That's alright, Mann. I needed the time myself. Besides, you owed it to yourself. It doesn't do a man any good to keep it all bottled up for so long."

"Yeah, you're probably right."

"Fuckin' A."

Morning was a welcome relief, washing our fear from us with its shower of light. We had survived the glance into our souls.

"Sir! There's a blood trail out here where that dink got hit last night."

"Good. Any sign of the dink?"

"No, sir, just a lot of blood and some flesh. That fucker died for sure."

"Alright," I answered. "Mann! Call in one for a body count. Whatever's left of that dink isn't enough to bother us anymore."

10 November 1967

This day I moved my platoon to a place shown on the map where a stream ran into the river and three trails met. When we reached the location we could see that it was a perfect spot for an ambush.

I spread the men along the path leading out of the jungle along the stream. I sent one squad of men across the stream to set up an ambush spot along the road around a bend in the river. My platoon formed a rough triangle, with the river acting as a hypotenuse and the stream intersecting its middle.

We waited there until evening and then climbed to the top of the ridge behind us to set up our night location. It was the first of many ridges stair-stepping up the mountain range. Its other side sank down into a small ravine before reaching up to the next step, a higher ridge. I imagined the whole process was repeated until the top was reached.

There were no trails along our ridge to bring the enemy to us as we straddled its jungle growth. Schaldenbrand and I decided it would make a good night location for however long the captain decided to leave us in the area.

The captain gave the new codes over the radio right after dark. The radio codes were changed on an irregular basis to confuse the enemy, who loved to listen to our broadcasts.

Before an operation, code words would be given that we would change to at a signal from Delta Six. That night he gave the signal to use "Black Night." The relatively simple code was to put numbers under the letters and use them in transmitting. For example, "Black Night" would be interpreted by substituting the number 1 for B, 2 for L, 3 for A, and so on. The area of operation was also coded so that our location on the maps was right for our code only. The map AO was also given in code. We would then outline with wax pencils the grid squares. By knowing what grid square we were operating in we could give coordinates in the clear without danger of the dinks interpreting them.

That night I copied the new codes, holding my flashlight in my mouth while balancing the map on my knee. I failed to get the exact codes the first two times and asked Delta Six to repeat them again. He got aggravated as he read them a third time. Again, I failed to get them all. With his voice dripping with sarcasm, he asked me if I had gotten them that time. Afraid to say no, I replied I had them.

"Tell the man on radio watch at midnight to wake me, Mann. I'm not going to admit to Sells I didn't get the son-of-a-bitch, so I'll call one of the other platoon leaders after the captain's gone to sleep."

Around midnight I awoke staring up at the moon. The sky had cleared. A figure was standing over me and I got the distinct impression he had just stopped.

"What time is it?" I whispered.

Silence from the figure.

I felt something was wrong. Suddenly, I realized the man standing above me was holding an AK-47. Goddamn! A dink!

I grabbed his foot and jerked hard. The man fell on his ass as I scrambled out of my hootch to grapple with him. A silent battle took place as we rolled back and forth on the ground, hitting and kneeing each other. After only a few seconds, the dink broke away to run through the edge of our perimeter. I jumped up searching for my M-16 which was next to my rucksack as he disappeared into the night. Some of the men asked me what the fuck was going on. I told them to be on guard as I turned in the direction I thought he had come. My three-man machine-gun crew was fast asleep as I came upon their position.

Dropping down on all fours, I shook them awake. Without mincing words, I told them what had happened. Still half asleep, the fear in their eyes was clear to see in the moonlight. Not fear of me but of what they had done. It turned out that Doc had been sharing their hole and was pulling guard duty. He had fallen asleep. I was still keyed up from the fight but it had seemed so unreal. There had been no sounds except our grunting. There was nothing now to prove that it ever happened.

11 November 1967

The next morning I sent Delk's squad across the stream to their ambush location.

After an hour or so we heard gunfire back up in the valley. Delta Six and the company had ambushed a dink company. We held tight to our position expecting dinks to be moving on the trails.

I called Delta Six to ask if he needed our assistance but he told us to stay put. He was calling in gunships. Soon we heard the thumping of their blades on the jungle air as they rushed to the battle.

A low ridge across the river formed a barrier between us, beyond which Delta Six was fighting. A wide field lay from the edge of the ridge across the river to form a large open area. Any dinks trying to escape would probably cross that open area to escape into the tree line farther downriver.

The gunships were working in pairs. We watched the duets circle above the ridge to sweep down into the valley where the battle was. The sounds of their machine guns was sharp against the jungle. With a tremendous swoosh the pilots fired rockets into the suspected locations at the dinks, the rockets exploding with a terrible raw sound.

We were kept informed on the progress of the battle over the radio. Most of the dinks had escaped but some of Delta Six's men thought the dinks had tossed their mortar into the river. While one platoon led the attack, Delta Six was going to have some of the other platoon's men dive for the weapons. It was important to get weapons.

Meanwhile, the gunships were having a field day blasting the jungle apart with their firepower. After all, this was what an American-fought war was all about—tremendous firepower. As the gunships would peel off from their attack one of the pilots would report he was taking fire which would cause a renewed attack with terrible ferocity.

Finally the gunships ran low on ordnance after repeated attacks. Return fire had stopped, so the pilots headed for the barn.

Later, Schaldenbrand and I were discussing reordering supplies when one of the men called our attention to some activity across the river. Three dinks had emerged from the edge of the tree line bordering the ridge where the fighting had taken place earlier. They were three or four hundred meters away and had started to run across the open area heading downstream. They had rifles in their hands and were running for all they were worth across the field.

"Fuck! They're too far away to kill," Schaldenbrand remarked.

"Yeah, but I hate to let them get away," I answered.

"There's no way to get them at this distance."

"I'll bet you a pack of Pall-Malls I can hit one," I told him. Saying this, I climbed up on the edge of a pile of dirt at the end of the line ambush.

"Shit! You're on!" Schaldenbrand and Doc stood next to me as I sighted on the black-pajama-clad figures bounding across the open area.

I laid the rifle sights on the middle man, flicked the sight to long range, and settled on his body. Allowing for windage and range, it would be a difficult shot. The M-16 at that distance just was not that accurate.

They looked like shadows in the field. I squeezed off a round. The middle shadow went down as if he had been pole-axed, his body fluttering on the ground. The man behind him reached down in midstride, picking up the weapon the man had dropped. I fired twice more but couldn't hit any of them before some small trees along the river blocked my shots.

"Good shooting. It's too bad that other fucker got that weapon, though," Schaldenbrand said as he handed me my pack of cigarettes.

12 November 1967

This morning I put one of the machine guns next to the dirt pile and spread the platoon upstream along the tree line. Delk's squad crossed the stream to its position.

Doc, Hunter, Schaldenbrand, and I were sitting close to Indian's gun. Spagg's gun was set up on the other end of the line. Both guns were to be the key in the ambush if the dinks used the trail. If they came along the trail, the guns were not to fire until the lead man had passed by the first gun and had reached the next gun. That way the largest possible number of men would be in front of my platoon hiding along the trail.

I seriously doubted that any dinks would be in the neighborhood after the ruckus the day before, but if they came, we would be ready for them.

I was standing with my side to the trail talking to Schaldenbrand, who was sitting facing the trail. His eyes suddenly grew larger. With one hand he pointed while the other patted the ground around him searching for his helmet. Our helmets had been taken off for comfort's sake.

Out of the corner of my eye I saw two small trees moving up the trail. I swung around as the first tree moved up level with my position. Four dinks had walked the trail in front of my platoon and were approaching the M-60 gun position. The two in front had bushes sticking out of their packs for camouflage, making them look like trees for a split second. All of them had small branches stuck in their helmets. They were all carrying packs on their backs and rifles in their hands.

The enemy was in front of us only fifteen feet away. They hadn't spotted us. I glanced to my gun crew, wondering why the hell they had not opened fire. Indian was hitting his gun with the heel of his hand as his two assistants stared at the dinks bearing down on them. The platoon was waiting for the signal from the M-60 and the son-of-a-bitch had misfired.

I brought my rifle up and yelled fire at the same time as I pulled the trigger. My first shot hit the second dink in the neck, practically ripping his head off. I immediately fired at the second man, hitting him in the body as a tremendous volley from the rest of the platoon cut the dinks down like a scythe.

There was nothing to see anymore but the platoon kept firing.

"Cease fire," I yelled. "Cease fire."

I walked through the grass out onto the trail, my helmet still lying on the ground behind me. The adrenalin was pumping through my body at the excitement of the brief firefight. Turning to the M-60 crew I asked Indian why his gun had misfired. He looked at me in a horror-stricken way, realizing his gun had failed him at a crucial moment.

"Indian, you'd better get that thing fixed. I was counting on you to trigger this ambush and the whole fucking thing about went down the tube."

"What happened to the lead dink?" I asked the man behind me. "All of you stay in position a second until we find the son-of-a-bitch!" Sergeant Kirkpatrick, an old mortar sergeant attached to our platoon because the company was not carrying mortars, followed me along the trail.

The jungle was deathly quiet after the firing. Only the sound of the stream and river broke the silence. Something was wrong, but I didn't know what.

"Schaldenbrand. How many dinks were there?" I asked. "There are only two dinks here and the lead dink is missing. Was there another one?"

"I think so."

I turned up the trail and found myself looking at a dink lying in a depression next to the trail. His rifle was pointing straight at my head as I stared into his face only fifteen feet from me.

My eyes registered a flash from his rifle as a thunderbolt slapped the side of my head. I screamed "I'm hit" as I spun around and blackness enveloped me. I came to lying in the grass, an intense crossfire blazing over my body. I was paralyzed from fear. The side of my head burned and a piercing ringing was blocking out much of the noise.

For a brief moment I thought I would be safer if I played dead. What was happening? The cracking sound of bullets passing over my body was terrifying. I couldn't move because I was afraid. *I have got to move!* I thought.

Everything was black; my eyes were clenched tight. I opened them to find I was staring through the grass at the dink who had shot me. He was blazing away at the platoon behind me. The blades of grass closest to me were out of focus because of my concentration on the dink.

He looked at me, saw my eyes were open, and jerked his rifle toward me.

I screamed "Cover me" and jumped up, running back to my platoon. It was a wonder I wasn't shot by my own men in that crossfire, but I made it, stumbling and falling.

I turned and fired with the rifle I had never let go of, into the depression where the dink was. Regaining my feet, I charged full of anger toward the dink, firing as I went. He had been already shot by me or by someone else, but I emptied four or five shots into him to make sure. The platoon stopped firing.

"Alright. There's one dink left. Find him and kill him," I said venomously.

Part of the platoon spread out to search the bushes in the clearing and along the trail. The men were happy we had finally seen action and killed some dinks. They were joking about it as they searched the bodies for souvenirs.

Schaldenbrand said that Hunter had been hit. I rushed up to where Doc was digging in his medical kit. Hunter's glasses were halfway down on his nose as he grinned in excitement and shock. A neat bullet hole was in the upper part of his left arm. The bullet had missed the bone and it looked like a clean wound. A little trickle of blood was running out of the hole and he stared at it in disbelief.

"Mann, call Delta Six and tell him we need a dustoff. One peanut." I talked to Captain Sells on the radio to tell him of our good luck. "It was a lick on them, Delta Six. I think one got away, but we zapped three of them, over."

"What kind of weapon was the one that got away carrying? Over."

"It could have been a light machine gun, over."

"O.K., I'll bring my unit down there. The resupply chopper is coming in this afternoon and I'll have him land there. Meanwhile, keep looking for that dink, out."

Schaldenbrand nudged me, "You shouldn't have told him that, lieutenant."

"What are you talking about?"

"That one dink carrying the machine gun. He'll have us here a week trying to find the son-of-a-bitch."

"Here, One-six, a little souvenir for you," one of my men handed me a belt with a belt buckle impressed with a five-pointed star—one of the prime souvenirs.

By this time all of the dinks' packs had been ripped apart and their pockets turned inside out.

"Hey, sir, the dustoff is coming in."

"Alright. You guys over there searching, spread out. The rest of you get ready to protect the chopper."

There were a million things going on, it seemed. The bodies were being dragged off into the brush, the searchers were spreading out, Doc was taking care of his patient, one man had a smoke grenade ready, everyone was keyed up from the action and chattering in the relief of tensions.

The dustoff called for smoke.

"Smoke popped."

"I identify purple smoke," the pilot reported in his mechanical vibrating voice.

"That's affirm."

A man ran out into the clearing to guide the chopper in.

We heard him sweeping in around the edge of the river in order to make a quick recovery and exit.

I yelled at Mann to tell the pilot to watch the upper part of the river because of the escaped dink. The pilot acknowledged and swept into the clearing. The dustoff pilots were always hot. They were experienced and good. If their blades could clear the trees, they'd make it in.

After he settled down I ran up to the pilot and shouted into his little open plexiglass window, "There's still a dink around here. Your best exit is downriver."

He gave me a thumbs up as I ran back out of the way.

The noisy fuss of a helicopter was always welcome, dustoff or not. It reassured us of the tremendous system backing us up.

The pilot lifted a few feet and did a one-eighty, heading for the river. He swung downriver, gaining altitude. He made it out; the sound faded.

All of us were calmer by now. Each man went back to his position in the ambush to await further developments. Porter, the squad leader conducting the search for the escaped dink, concluded the dink had gotten away and he led his men back into position.

I asked Doc and Schaldenbrand to look at my ear. It was burning like fury and a small stream of blood was running along its edge to drip onto my face and shoulder.

Everyone was amazed I had been so lucky. If I hadn't turned my head at that split instant, the SKS bullet would have blown off the back of my skull. If I had been wearing my helmet, the bullet fired from its low-down angle would have glanced from the inside of the helmet into my head.

When I reported to Delta Six I had been hit, my second wound, he raised hell with me for getting myself into such a predicament.

In a few hours Delta Six completed his patrol by ending at our position. We were proud of the weapons we had captured and the dinks we had killed. Delta Six sent the Third Platoon on a search for the dink that had escaped. He put his hand on my head to examine my ear.

"Hell, One-Six, that little scratch isn't worth a Purple Heart!"

There was a sudden flury of gunshots around a bush in the clearing. Three-six's men had found the dink.

"I thought you had searched this area, lieutenant!" the captain exclaimed. I was chagrined to answer; I thought we had done a good job of searching. I looked at Porter who shrugged his shoulders.

There were three or four old foxholes across the stream. Lieutenant Ordway's (Three-six) men dragged the dink across the stream to dump his body into one of them. All four of the dinks were now lying

around the clearing in depressions or foxholes, their completely lax
bodies in impossible positions at the bottom of the holes. No one
attempted to throw dirt on them because we all figured we would be
out of the area shortly.

My platoon and I had not shaved for three or four days. Delta Six
was a bear about shaving, combat patrol or not. Just because we lived
like animals didn't mean we had to look like them, was his way of
thinking.

Throwing my fatigue jacket across a bush, I grabbed my shaving
gear and told Spagg and Villasenor to accompany me. We would
guard each other as we shaved.

Spagg was one of my machine gunners, a farmer from Minnesota
and steady as they came. I had come from a farm background too,
in Indiana, and we had grown to be friends. Villasenor was about to
become one of my squad leaders whenever an opening came up. He
always seemed to see the funny side of things and the guys kidded him
that they didn't need a clown for squad leader.

We were talking about farming as I was squatting on the stream
bank shaving. Villasenor and Spagg were looking out when two dinks
in full combat gear and carrying AK-47s walked calmly out of the
jungle straight across the little stream not twenty meters away. They
must have been deaf, strolling into the area after all that had been
going on.

I dropped my razor, grabbing for my M-16 as Spagg, Villasenor,
and the dinks opened up simultaneously. I fired as Spagg's bullets tore
into one of the dinks, knocking him head over heels. The other dink
let loose another burst from his AK-47, turned, and ran back into the
jungle. We splashed across, firing as we ran. Voices from the Americans yelled to ask what we were doing. There was no time to answer.

I fired the last bullet from my magazine just as I reached the dink
lying dead on the ground. Spagg had shifted to my left and was
exchanging shots with the dink in the jungle. I threw my M-16 into
my left hand and reached down for the fallen enemy's AK-47.

It was a well-balanced weapon, easy to hold with one hand. The
thirty-round magazine was full, the safety off. I held it between my
arm and side and fired the full clip into the dink's position. The

son-of-a-bitch was still firing back at us as Spagg and I dived behind a dead tree lying along the ground.

"Spagg, do you see him?"

"No! But I know where he is. I'm going to throw a grenade in there."

Spagg heaved a hand grenade into the jungle's edge.

"Look out, the fucker's thrown it back!" Villasenor screamed.

The grenade went off by the roots of the dead tree we were hiding behind. My dog tags clinked against one of the branches from the force of the explosion. I felt a sharp stab of pain in the bicep of my left arm. I looked down in shocked surprise to see a small ragged hole from which blood was oozing.

"Goddamn! I've been hit! Are you guys O.K.?"

"We're fine. Are you hit bad?"

"No! It's only a scratch. Where's that dink?"

"I think he's gone."

We ran from our position into the jungle. There was nothing but a small blood trail to show he had been hit.

We ran back to the captain, standing next to the dirt pile, to explain what had happened. He was pleased with the weapon we had captured and complimented us both.

He was concerned over my wound though, and asked if I wanted to be sent in on the resupply chopper. There was no way I wanted to be sent in now that the action was starting. I told him I would be alright since the shrapnel was not too deep, and besides he needed me in the field. I was eager to remain in the field. He said I could stay. Grinning, he told me some men would do anything to get a Purple Heart.

Holmes, a black who was the company medic, was picking at the hole, trying to grab the shrapnel with a pair of tweezers. He cut the hole with his scapel, widening it until he could reach in far enough with the tweezers to grasp the piece of metal. A final probe and a satisfied exclamation signaled success. He handed me the little piece of grenade metal for a souvenir, and made out a med-tag to send in, thereby assuring an award of a Purple Heart. Holmes never carried a weapon, only a walking stick with a notch for every day he had been in Nam. He believed his job lay in taking care of the company and he was famous for his coolness under fire as he went from wounded to wounded.

After Holmes had finished bandaging my arm, I put on my fatigue jacket and lit a cigarette. I felt good. I had only been in-country a few months and I had my second Purple Heart (the first one had been from a wound received in October). To top it off, I had been wounded twice in one day, shot in the ear in the morning and hit with grenade shrapnel in the afternoon. Luck was with me. All three wounds had been slight.

13 November 1967

This morning we were late getting into position because Delta Six was moving his company back into the valley. We were the only platoon staying up. After they had gone, I told Delk to take his squad across to their usual ambush spot while we sat up in our position along the stream.

He got his men into marching order and moved them down off the ridge. After a few minutes we started down behind them. I came out into the clearing in time to see his squad crossing the stream. One of his men brought his weapon, a M-79 grenade launcher, up to his shoulder and fired. I heard the round explode ahead of them, followed by the scream of someone who had been hit.

Christ, I thought, *already we have action!* I told the platoon to hang loose while I took a couple of men over to Delk to see what had happened. He was calling me on the radio as I reached his squad crouching in the bushes.

Material of some sort was scattered on the trail fifty meters from his position. He explained that they had been crossing the stream when one of the men had spotted three dinks moving down the trail toward them. The front dink had had one of those long poles across his shoulder with baskets hanging from either end. The M-79 man had fired a round which had landed between the legs of the man with the baskets. They had seen him knocked down, his rifle and baskets flying in all directions. The other two dinks had disappeared while the wounded dink had run screaming into the jungle. Delk's men had fired but had evidently not hit the dink again.

Delk's squad went ahead on the trail to form a guard while we looked through the items spread around. The dink had been carrying an M-16 which was laying in the grass. The front basket had held about fifty homemade wooden Chi-com (Chinese Communist) grenade handles with holes carved down the middle. Flat sheets of tin were bundled together, precut, and hammered out to resemble what a tin can would look like if the ends had been removed and rolled. There were bits of the plastic explosive, C-4, and slabs of explosives wrapped in wax paper in the bottom of the basket.

The other basket contained pieces of metal, nails, glass, and other junk, also black powder and fuses.

What we had here was the material to make about forty or fifty Chi-com grenades. Delk's squad had ambushed a walking grenade factory!

The sheets of tin would be rolled into the shape of a tin can and stuffed with explosives and junk for shrapnel; the ends would be sealed, with a wooden handle sticking out of one end. A black-powder fuse would be run up the middle of the hollow handle which would then be capped with a wooden plug and sealed with wax. They resembled a potato masher.

When a dink wanted one to work, he twisted the plug. An abrasive surface would spark the black powder which would burn down to the blasting cap set in the explosive, setting off an explosion sending shrapnel in all directions. Crude, but effective.

Chi-com grenades were unreliable as hell, though. Sometimes a dink would twist a cap only to have the damn thing explode in his face. Other times they would throw them into our lines and the black-powder fuse would be wet, delaying the explosion or turning them into duds. Americans wouldn't touch one because they were so unpredictable.

I had the engineer sergeant take the stuff and dump it in one of the holes. We would destroy it.

As the tailend man crossed the stream, going back to the platoon,

I assisted the engineer sergeant, guarding him as he carefully buried his charge in the mound of explosives. He waved me back and lit the fuse. We yelled "Fire in the hole," ran across the stream, and turned to watch the explosion. There was no explosion. The minutes ticked by.

I asked him if his charges ever failed to go off. He replied that they hardly ever did, but this one didn't look good. The fuses he had been carrying could have gotten wet, causing them to burn out. Worse, the fuse could be only slightly damp, causing it to burn slower, in which case the damn thing could go off in his face if he went back too soon.

We waited. One of the dinks we had killed earlier was lying in a foxhole next to us. Thousands of ants were crawling over his head and hands. All over his body, I imagined, but his jungle fatigues hid the others. I moved a little farther away to make sure none of them crawled on me.

"Well, shit, it looks like the goddamn thing isn't going to go," the sergeant announced.

We waded the stream and warily approached the explosives. I was afraid the mess could still go off and asked the sergeant if we could just throw a grenade in the hole. He wasn't anxious to stick his nose in the mess and agreed that a hand grenade would probably set off the other explosives.

I unhooked a hand grenade from my web gear and pulled the pin. Tossing the grenade in the shallow pit, I whirled and ran after the sergeant, passing him at the stream. A tremendous explosion ripped the air behind us. We both turned to see an ugly cloud of dirt and smoke pushing into the air. Clods of dirt and other junk fell into the jungle and clearing, the sound of their hitting the earth drowned out in the rumbling of the explosion echoing up the river.

I reached the front of the platoon just as Delta Six called to ask what the hell the explosion was all about. I quickly explained as we started to march. The sooner we got out of the area, the better.

We marched up the ridge and after an hour I called a halt and we set up our night location.

15 November 1967

Our company had not been the only one to make enemy contact. The battalion radio net crackled with reports of fighting the other companies were going through.

This morning my platoon was working a ridge that we had followed up from our ambush location at the river. Mann had been listening in and he told me it looked like Alpha Company was going to run into something big.

Alpha Company was working the ridge right across from us when they ran into heavy fire from the enemy, who was dug in. We heard the distant pops of rifle fire and bursts of automatic fire as the sounds of the fight drifted across the valley. A little before noon I called a halt for chow, as the battle heated up. It was possible we would run into the same thing on our ridge. This might be our last opportunity to eat for a while.

The battle was shaping up to be a big one. Gunships had been called in to soften up enemy troops dug in on the mountain opposite us above Alpha, giving us a ringside seat. Shortly, the gunships arrived and we caught glimpses of them through the trees as they flew their duets of death.

It was obvious the enemy was going to make a fight of it. One of my OCS classmates was leading one of Alpha's platoons. I wondered how he was faring.

The battalion commander was up in his chopper directing the battle below. The trees kept him from seeing anything clearly, but the radios were full of traffic as he attempted to maneuver the elements of his battalion.

A bird-dog arrived which meant more air firepower was on its way. Delta Six radioed for us to continue along the ridge and to be careful. The air power was a flight of ARVN pilots in propeller-driven attack planes.

Jesus Christ! That meant as much danger to us as to the dinks. The ARVN pilots would routinely shoot at anything. The bird-dog pilot, an American, would radio instructions about the strike area back to an interpreter at the ARVN headquarters, the interpreter would then issue orders to the ARVN pilots. By the time this cycle was completed, the ARVNs could empty their whole ordnance load in the wrong spot.

I passed the word back that the ARVN air force was coming and to be ready for anything. We pushed on up the ridge, to the sound of approaching propeller-driven aircraft.

"The fucking dinks are firing at us," someone yelled.

The ARVN dinks were kicking their rudder pedals as they flew up the valley, firing their machine guns into the ridges on both sides.

We dived for safety.

This is it, I thought, but the flight zoomed by in the valley on a level with us so close we could see the pilots' faces. They must have been clearing their guns, not knowing we were on the ridge, for they soon peeled off toward the enemy mountain, firing their rockets and machine guns into the enemy positions. We breathed a sigh of relief.

Delta Six called, "One-six, you move down the side of the ridge into the valley. Set up a blocking force for any dinks trying to escape in your direction, out."

I gave the order to move out and we broke into the heavy jungle, forcing our way down through the rugged growth. The terrain was torturous, cut through with steep ridges running in all directions. Sweat poured from us as we pushed our way down for a little way, then climbed up steep embankments to stumble down the other side.

The sounds of the battle were intense—aircraft overhead, the rockets and bombs exploding, and the steady chatter of the infantry rifle fire.

After fifteen minutes or so we were approximately halfway down the ridge; the captain gave me a call.

Dragon Six had decided it would be better if I halved my platoon, marching the two elements in opposite directions in order to cover a larger area. I was dead set against this. My platoon was below strength and dividing it would be asking two reinforced rifle squads to defend hundreds of acres of jungle against a foe of unknown size.

But orders were orders, especially from Dragon Six. I passed back the word for Schaldenbrand to come up. I was pouring over my map and compass when Schaldenbrand reached me. The battle was full-blown; its sound provided background noise as I briefed Shelly on the situation and our orders.

"Shit, I don't like it, sir."

"I know, I don't like it either, but it's a lick. You got your map and compass? Good. I'll be following this heading to the east and you take this reading a hundred and eighty degrees from mine. That way we'll be going in opposite directions. Whatever you do, don't follow any of the ridges. They go in directions every which way and you'll get screwed up for sure. Just follow this heading. I'll use your radio call sign of One-five when I need to talk to you on the horn."

There should be no danger of our paths crossing. We were both worried about that. Although only a corporal, Schaldenbrand was the most experienced man I had, so he had been my acting platoon sergeant since I had taken command. There weren't any regular platoon sergeants to assign to my platoon and Schaldenbrand had been doing a great job. Now he was charged with an even greater responsibility: moving men through difficult jungle terrain during battle conditions with a vastly understrength unit.

I went over the direction he was to go again, and he acknowledged that he understood.

We split up, each little unit taking one of the M-60 machine guns. I told him to keep in constant radio contact. I had the nagging fear he would get lost or be attacked and I wouldn't be there when he needed me.

I watched him head out with his unit, paralleling the ridge heading west. I told my unit to saddle up and we headed east. The battle was to our left now, instead of our front, as we struggled over the crisscross of ridges and ravines. I wondered if Dragon Six knew how impossible this damn terrain was to move through.

The point man finally came up to a ridge so steep we couldn't climb it. At that time Mann informed me we had lost radio contact with Delta Six.

"Goddamn, what else can go wrong? Throw out the long antenna while the point tries to find a way around this fucking cliff."

The long antenna was a ten-foot foldable antenna the RTO carried with him to use when the regular antenna didn't have the range. The point man said we would have to go straight up because there was no other way. He started up, using small trees and roots for handholds as he kicked footholds out of the jungle soil.

The ten-foot antenna allowed us to hear Delta Six frantically calling us, but we couldn't call him back. Some part of the terrain between us was blocking my radio. I told Mann to go up on Dragon Six's net and have Dragon Six relay to Delta Six that One-six was O.K. and I would contact him as soon as I got out of the dead spot.

Mann was switching channels rapidly, keeping in contact with first Dragon Six and then Schaldenbrand, who reported he was still O.K.

After a laborious effort, we finally reached the relatively flat top. The flatness of this ridge ran in the direction of the battle and on the map looked to be one of the ridges at the end of the valley connecting the mountain I was on with the mountain where all of the fighting was.

At last I was able to talk to the captain, who gave me hell for losing radio contact. I wondered how the fuck I could have foreseen a radio dead spot, but instead I just reported we had reached our position.

I was in constant contact with Shelly now. He said he was still on the move but he was unsure of where he was. We discussed his compass readings back and forth, but to little avail.

Meanwhile, my unit had set up a defensive position. The M-60 was on the lower end of the perimeter facing across the flat area toward the enemy mountain. All of us were keyed up, expecting dinks at any time. Dragon Six had reported from his chopper that he had seen dinks through the trees heading in our direction.

Schaldenbrand was on the move again, obviously worried.

Another flight of aircraft had arrived to replace the first flight which had fired its ordnance and gone back. The battle was now directly across from us, no more than six or seven hundred meters as the crow flies. The sounds of the fight permeated everything around us.

"One-five, this is One-six. Have you figured out where you are yet?"

"This is One-five. Negative."

Porter scrambled on all fours from his position near the M-60 crew up to where I was kneeling on one knee with the radio.

"Lieutenant," Porter whispered as he reached my side, "we hear noises to our front. Men are moving across in front of us in the jungle."

"Hold on a second, Porter. One-five, this is One-six. The sounds of the battle should be on your right if you're going in the right direction. Where are the sounds? Over."

"This is One-five. Negative on the right. The sounds are on the left, over."

"One-five, did you say the sounds are on your left?" I was squeezing the hand set so hard my knuckles were white.

"Affirmative, affirmative."

"Jesus Christ, One-five," I hoarsely whispered intensely into the mouthpiece. "You're heading in our direction."

I could hear the sounds of men moving through the jungle below us. I whispered to Porter, "Get back down there and tell the men to hold their fire. That may not be dinks after all. Hurry."

Porter had heard my conversation with Schaldenbrand and quickly turned to carry out my order. He couldn't yell because if the sounds were coming from dink soldiers his yell would put us in jeopardy. As Porter started toward the crew, the machine gun crew opened fire.

The harshness of the gun's multiple explosions ripped across my thoughts as its sound was echoed through the handset I was holding next to my ear.

The sounds of Americans swearing and screaming rebounded from the jungle below and from my handset. "Cease fire!" I screamed. "Cease fire!"

Porter and I were running to the gun crew, both of us yelling "Cease fire! Cease fire!" the sound of their gun blanketing the screams in front of them.

Abruptly the gun quit firing.

I yelled into the jungle, "Schaldenbrand, is that you?"

"Yes! Yes! Stop firing! Don't fire!" I was answered by many voices.

I stood there an instant. The horrible realization that I had fired on my own men swept over me like a wave from an ice-cold hell.

The gun crew looked at me, their faces filled with shock.

I ran leaping and falling down to the brush line where my men were, asking the question, "Anybody hit, for Christ's sake?"

Gallagher yelled back as I burst through into a small clearing, "One man, the point man, Fonseca."

The clearing had been chopped out of the jungle sometime in the past to allow a chopper to land. Short vicious stubs of trees and bushes a foot or so high were thickly spread all over the man-made clearing. The men were strung out in a ragged line, some of them getting up from where they had dived when the firing started. Fonseca, the man in front, sat staring at his foot. Shelly and the squad leader were just reaching his position.

Doc, who had followed me, rushed to Fonseca. The toe of one of his boots was a mangled bloody mess. Doc cut the boot off while I asked Shelly how the fuck he had gotten turned completely around.

He explained he had been following a ridge running in what he thought was the right direction. He just could not understand how that ridge had turned around.

"Shelly, I told you above all else not to follow a goddamn ridge. We could've killed you guys. Why didn't you do like I told you?"

I don't know, sir. I'm just glad it was you guys and not the dinks. When that shit started flying out of the jungle, I thought it was a lick on us," he nervously smoked as he went on to explain what his men had been lucky to live through.

"How's Fonseca, Doc?" I kneeled down next to Fonseca. "Hey, fellow, you're lucky. That's a million-dollar wound. No more field for you."

His big toe was held on by just a piece of skin. The two toes next to it were mashed meat. It was impossible to tell how many toes he would lose altogether. The whole mess was covered with blood as Doc carefully wrapped the foot, gingerly pushing what was left of the big toe tightly into the bandage as he wrapped.

I stood up and waved for Mann. "Well, now comes the hard part, calling Delta Six and requesting a dustoff. He's going to ask why and when I explain that I've ambushed my own platoon, he's going to shit a conniption fit."

If there was any place in the world I wanted to be at that moment, it was not there.

Screwing up my courage, I pressed the handset button. "Uhhh, Delta Six, this is One-six, over."

"This is Delta Six, over."

"This is One-six. I need a dustoff for a peanut. We've run into a little action, over."

"This is Delta Six. What do you mean a little action? What's going on? What happened? Over."

My knees felt weak and my stomach was sour.

"This is One-six. We had a little difficulty with the terrain, and uh, uh, I ambushed One-five, over."

"What! How the fuck did you do that, One-six? You mean you ambushed your own men? What kind of an outfit are you running up there? That's the most asinine thing I've ever heard of. You get your head out of your ass, One-six, and get that platoon straightened up. You got that? Over."

"This is One-six. Affirmative, over."

"Agghhg, One-six, give me your coordinates. The dustoff's on its way. How bad is your peanuts? Over."

"This is One-six. Not too bad. He'll lose a couple of toes but everybody else is O.K., over."

"Alright, One-six, settle down. Out." He was more gentle with the last transmission because I'm sure my voice had showed the strain I was feeling. Whatever the reason, I welcomed the sound of his voice. Perhaps he understood better than I thought what had happened.

The dustoff arrived shortly and asked us to pop smoke. One of the men threw a yellow smoke grenade into the clearing. The pilot identified it and one of the men cautiously guided him into the tight clearing. Fonseca was loaded on hurriedly and the pilot pulled out immediately.

I trudged back up to my position, One-five and his men following. Mann handed me a can of coffee. I chain-smoked my cigarettes and drank coffee while the platoon expanded into a larger perimeter.

I stood facing the mountain, the battle still raging on it. One-five walked over to me, still shaken from his experience. He told me how sorry he was that he had gotten me in dutch with the captain and we discussed the operation, going over his mistake while we attempted to figure out ways to keep it from happening again if we were ever split up.

Shelly and I had been through too much together for me to blame him for what had happened. I told him so and we let it go at that. We had been lucky.

Besides, I blamed myself for what had happened. The responsibility for any unit's action ultimately rests with its commander. The leader got the glory when things worked out and he took the blame when they didn't. That went with the job. When it came right down to it, the men were my responsibility and I had failed them today.

We were to make contact with Alpha Company that day to assist them but the terrain hindered us so much that night fell before we could reach them and we were forced to logger in.

16 November 1967

We were awake early in the morning.

Alpha Six reported that the dinks had withdrawn during the night, allowing his company to secure the hill without opposition. All of Alpha's men had been warned we were on the way, but we were to move cautiously anyway.

Shortly after beginning the march we ran into evidence of the battle. Giant trees had been blasted apart or uprooted to be blasted again during the bombing and straffing attacks. In deep bomb craters smoke still drifted out of the dirt. The jungle had been torn into jagged edges, the damage more intense as we fought our way through to the top. Dink bodies lay about in various postures of death. The American dead and wounded had been flown out during the battle. Americans never left their dead bodies behind.

I spotted a friend of mine. He was Three-six for Alpha, a black lieutenant I had met when I first arrived in-country. We swapped war stories as we heated coffee.

"Hey, Downs, let me tell you something. Never travel a trail again.

I know we all do it, but not me ever again. We were traveling down this trail yesterday and walked smack into an ambush. In fact, my point man and I were through it when they opened fire. One bullet flew over my shoulder as I dived into the bush and hit my point man in front of me. The rest of the platoon was pinned down and I was so scared I would've shit in my pants but my asshole was puckered up too tight. I crawled over to my point man, grabbed him by the pants leg, and dragged him off the trail. Man, those motherfuckers never let up for a moment. We finally got into a ditch and returned fire enough to drive them off. I ain't never traveling a trail again. Those guys in headquarters want us someplace in a hurry, they can go fuck themselves."

"Sure, Anderson. But I don't see how the hell I can keep from it. There's no way in hell to travel anywhere in this country fast without using a trail."

"Well, I may be forced to again, but I'm not going to like it. That ambush yesterday was too much. You been ambushed yet?"

"No, and I'm not looking forward to it. With the proper caution, maybe I won't either."

"Bullshit! Nobody could have traveled a trail with more caution than yours truly, but I got nailed anyhow, and just when I was beginning to think I was a black Davy Crockett."

A dink was lying next to us as we talked. He had a black ace of spades stuck into his fist.

"Hey, Anderson, what's that all about?"

"That's so the dinks will know what outfit fucked them over up here. Look around. Most of the dinks got those in their hands."

Sure enough. The dinks were all holding an ace of spades.

"That's a good idea, but where did you get all of the aces?"

"One of the guys has a mom who works in a card store, so he wrote home asking her to send him a couple of packs of nothing but the ace of spades."

Why did we want to kill dinks? After all, we had been mostly law-abiding citizens back in the world and we were taught that to take another man's life was wrong. Somehow the perspective got twisted in a war. If the government told us it was alright and, in fact, a must to kill the members of another government's people, then we had the law on our side. It turned out that most of us liked to kill other men. Some of the guys would shoot at a dink much as they would at a target. Some of the men didn't like to kill a dink up close. The closer the killing, the more personal it became.

Others in the platoon liked to kill close in. A few even liked to torture the dinks if they had a prisoner or cut the dead bodies with knives in a frenzy of aggression.

A few didn't like to kill at all and wouldn't fire their weapons except to protect their buddies.

Mostly, we all saw it as a job and rationalized it in our own way. Over it all ran the streak of anger or fear that for brief moments ruled us all.

My job as platoon leader was to control the spectrum of emotions, to guide the men toward survival. I didn't believe in torturing or in allowing a dink to die a lingering death. In the jungle we never took prisoners if we could help it. Every day we spent in the jungle eroded a little more of our humanity away. Prisoners could escape to become our enemy again. Hence, no prisoners.

The philosophical arguments in favor of man's ability to resist the slide into barbarism sound noble and rational in a classroom or at a cocktail party. But when the enemy is bearing down, bent on taking your life away from you, it's not his country against your country, not his army against your army, not his philosophy against your philosophy—it's the fact that that son-of-a-bitch is trying to kill you and you'd better kill him first.

Fuck it! "O.K., you guys, let's go kill some dinks. Saddle up," I gave the order to my platoon. "So long, Anderson."

"Remember, One-six, no trails," Anderson shook my hand.

"Thanks, I'll keep it in mind."

I pointed out a trail leading in the direction we would be going to the point man. "We'll follow this for a little way at least."

About fifty meters down the trail I stumbled on a vine lying across the trail.

"Goddamn jungle!"

"The jungle had help here, sir. Look at that," Mann pointed.

The vine I had tripped over was a triggering device for a three-foot sharpened spear dipped in shit, that was held in place about waist high with three woven rings made with vines. The trigger had failed or the spear would have struck into my side.

"Oh, shit, I was lucky on that one. You can't even see the son-of-a-bitch."

Anderson had come down the trail to see what had caused my platoon to stop.

"See what I told you, One-six."

"Ahhh, fuck it. Nothing can get the kid. I lead a charmed life," I joked back.

The top of the mountain was one of a chain of mountaintops climbing across the top of the jungle. We moved into a saddle leading to the next highest mountain. The trail we were following seemed to bear off to the right, leading out onto a high ridge running down into a different valley.

Two or three hundred meters of traveling along the ridge brought us to an area of tall trees with a small amount of brush covering the left side of the ridge as it dropped steeply down into the jungle below. I studied the map to see if there was a junction farther down in the mountain's lap where streams running from the many ridges converged.

There was a spot about midway down the mountain marked in blue. That meant something bigger than a stream. If I were an enemy commander, that would be a perfect spot for a camp. High mountains on three sides, a good water supply, thick jungle growth, and escape paths in any direction.

If he had decided on that location, the enemy commander would be counting on an attack from the valley up toward his location. He would have his back guarded but not very heavily, or so I reasoned.

"O.K., Porter, take your point down the side of this ridge. Maintain silence, and we'll move toward this stream somewhere below."

He studied the map with me and agreed the dinks would like a hole like that.

I passed the word back to the men to watch themselves and to be quiet. We always moved with a minimum of noise, but this time it would be tricky.

Slowly we pushed down the side of the steep mountain. With the high canopy of trees, the undergrowth was not as thick and we were able to move through a forest-like environment instead of the usual thick jungle we were used to.

Two of the point men started tumbling and flailing around with their arms and legs. Not a sound issued from their lips except grunts and low growls. Porter and I checked our movement, bewildered at their actions.

Zap! Zap! "Hornets," I whispered loudly to the men behind me, flinching from two stings as they buzzed my head and shoulders. Porter jerked as they hit him. We ran sideways, slapping at the hornets as they stung us again and again. I clenched my teeth to keep from yelling. Better a sting than a bullet. Porter and I ran downhill, stumbling on the steep terrain, maintaining our footing by grabbing at branches and small trees with our free hands, gripping our guns with the other.

Finally, we panted to a halt with the two point men. The bumps swelling and burning like fire, the pain brought tears to our eyes.

"Uhhh, those motherfuckers hurt," one of the point men groaned.

"Yeah," Porter agreed. "Those fuckers are definitely dink hornets."

I moved the men a little farther down the hill and called a break for lunch.

Soon after we had eaten, we were on the move again. Shortly, Porter held up his hand signaling a stop. We discussed the leveled-off area we had come upon and decided to follow it. During a heavy rain, water would flow down it to the stream.

A little ridge ran along our left and the steep ridge we had just deserted was on our right. As we neared the possible location of the area we thought might have dinks, the ground gently sloped downward until the level area we were on turned into a small ridge itself.

The point stopped and waved me forward. I got out the map, studied it, held my finger to my lips, and pointed ahead. Nodding, the point crept forward, guns ready.

The point stopped abruptly and waved me up. Watching where I put my feet, I crept forward cautiously. To our left a small ravine had formed, a meter below our position, with a small stream running down its middle. Across the stream a small ridge ten or fifteen meters high rose up to drop off into another ravine on the other side with a stream. The two ravines ran together forming a "Y" a few meters to our right. I could see around the corner of the ridge a little way up into the other ravine.

Suddenly, Porter grabbed my arm hard with one hand and pointed with his rifle across the stream. Not ten meters from us a man was emerging from a large bush set a little above the stream on the other side. No! Not a bush but a hootch. Like an ink blot that changed totally in design, the whole scene became recognizable.

My God! There were dink hootches set up and down both ravines. Camouflage underwear and clothes hung on lines, men were moving around at camp duties not more than a few meters away. They were totally unaware of our presence in the middle of them. Surely they would notice us soon.

The word was passed up the line by men touching their comrades and pointing. No one made a sound.

I moved a little further down the ridge toward its end and stopped above a bunker built into the bank below my feet. The men crept after me, all eyes on the enemy camp.

Finally, the men were spread out along the ridge, every weapon pointing at the enemy. It was incredible! They still hadn't noticed the platoon.

The camp was at least company size, meaning we were outnumbered three or four to one. This had to be done right or we'd all be dead. I pointed to a couple of men to face the other side of the ridge we were on to guard our backs.

I looked along the line of my pitifully small number of twenty-six men, their weapons pointed into the enemy camp. Fear and anticipation filled their faces. They kept glancing at me for a signal. My stomach was full of butterflies, my knees felt weak. The adrenalin pumped through my body. I was struck with the realization that there was no way out. We were trapped, just as they were, and would have to fight.

For just a split second I thought of the consequences of my next order and was afraid. "Open fire!" I bellowed and at the same time I pulled the trigger, dropping a dink ten meters away.

A tremendous cacophony of sound exploded into the jungle as hundreds of bullets tore into the camp. Hand grenades and M-79 rounds exploded amid the smooth sound of M-60 machine-gun fire and the rapid firing of semiautomatic and automatic M-16 rifle fire.

One dink was ripped apart as he attempted to dive into a bunker. Others died where they stood, and many were wounded. The wounded ran away if they could, following their comrades who had escaped the initial burst of gunfire. They must have thought a whole battalion had dropped right into the middle of their camp.

Our surprise had been complete. Mann and I ran in a crouch down the ravine, across the stream, to huddle next to a bunker. I popped a grenade into one of the entrances. The grenade must have set off other explosives because one wall of the log and dirt bunker blew out on top of us.

Our blood was up. Some of the men ran into the camp, clearing bunkers as Mann and I had done. Others stayed on the ridge to provide covering fire.

Mann was so excited he forgot how short in-country he had left and dropped into a bunker. He poked his head out grinning and held up an enemy rifle he had liberated.

There was no more firing. We couldn't believe it. We had pulled it off and not one of us was hit. Goddamn, this was the way to kill dinks!

Men were running through the camp now. Exploring hootches and discovering all types of things.

Schaldenbrand was up on the ridge calling the captain when one of the men let out a shout. The bunker I had been standing next to at the outset contained two Russian 82-mm mortars, complete with base plates and sights. I yelled to Schaldenbrand to tell him to report this find to Delta Six. Goddamn! No one in the battalion had yet captured anything like this and we had two! I was tickled pink.

The camp was complete. It had officer hootches, a barbershop, mess hall, bunkers, and hootches for the enlisted men. Everything was made out of the materials in the jungle. Each officer hootch had a small part of the stream diverted into a little pool in front of the hootch so the officer could wash his hands and shave. We were amazed at its completeness.

I examined the mortars' lethal tubes of steel and called the serial numbers of the weapons to Schaldenbrand who repeated them over the radio to Delta Six. By this time, Dragon Six had been informed and he was as excited as any commander could be at the success of the operation.

Yoder, Iding, and Torrey from the Second Squad had started to climb the other side of the far ridge. Shots rang out followed by the tumbling of the men back down the hill. They had not been hit but the dinks were starting to form up in the jungle above us. Occasionally they sent blind shots down into the camp. We returned their fire with a ferocity intended to belie our small numbers.

It was time to get out while we still had our asses.

"Let's get the fuck out of here, Schaldenbrand, before everything goes to hell."

"It's a lick, lieutenant. Dragon Six is sending Alpha Three-six down to assist us and we're supposed to wait for him."

"Shit! We don't need any assistance. We need to get our young asses out of here before dark."

"I know it, but Dragon Six said to wait."

There was nothing to do but wait, so I started looking through the pack of intelligence material we had captured. The dinks never failed to amaze me. Included in the papers we had put together in the pack was an American publication entitled *The Hippie Handbook of Love*.

"Son-of-a-bitch, now where do you think the dinks got that and why would they have it out here?"

"One of their agents probably stole it out of a trashcan. The dinks out here probably use it to show the troops how decadent Americans are," Schaldenbrand mused.

"Yeah, I suppose so. Hey! Look at this!"

Big as life, the three bridges my platoon had been guarding before the operation were traced out on tablet paper. All of my gun positions and bunkers were clearly marked as to location and type of weapons.

"Look, sir, they've even got your name down as the lieutenant."

"Yeah, that would be easy to figure out, but this is what I don't get. They've even got that machine gun marked in the right position. I took pains to keep it covered up during the day so they couldn't guess its location."

Everyone was more interested in *The Hippie Handbook of Love*, and passed it around while I chain-smoked cigarettes and wondered where the hell Alpha Three-six was.

In an hour or so Delta Six called me on the radio and told me that Alpha Three-six was in the area but couldn't find us. Would we pop a cap?

That was all we needed. The dinks were moving in the jungle around us and Alpha Three-six wanted us to pop a cap.

I told one of the guys to fire his rifle in the air. Alpha Three-six had switched to Delta's frequency so I called him to ask if he had heard the shot. He had reported he would be arriving in a few minutes. I got my platoon into order of march with our booty and kept chain-smoking.

Finally, one of the men yelled that Alpha Three-six was spotted. Anderson's tall lanky black frame materialized out of the jungle, his face all smiles as he came over to me.

"Hey, Downs, good show. We heard you had captured a couple of Russian mortars. The whole battalion is talking about it."

"Yeah, I know. Delta Six told me the firebase was mortared last night so the battalion commander is really pleased. We got the whole shebang, mortars and mortar shells." I was inordinately pleased. "Let's get this fucking show on the road. Its getting late and I want to get out of here before the dinks figure out they've got us outnumbered. My platoon will take point. We're going down this creek until we reach the river. Delta Six will be waiting for us there."

"Roger, my platoon will pull rear guard. Let's get going."

I rushed to the front of my platoon and gave the order to move out.

I hadn't gone fifty meters when an explosion went off behind me in the camp.

"Mortars," I yelled as I dove into the brush. *Fuck! we haven't made it out,* I thought.

There was just the one explosion. I ran back up the trail to see what had happened, Mann following with his floppy antenna.

"What happened?"

My men were crouched in various positions of defense, well-trained men reacting to a dangerous situation. They were glancing about them trying to spot the enemy. The smell of powder hung in the air as I ran back into the enemy camp toward a small cloud of smoke around which some of Three-six's men were milling.

One of my men yelled to me as I ran by that it was Three-six's platoon. He thought it was a mine.

At the fork of the "Y" was the bunker Mann and I had blown up. Three-six's men had walked down the middle ridge around the bunker and hootches when they first arrived. Since they were in single file, most of the platoon had still been spread up the ridge while Three-six and I were discussing our moves. They had waited until my platoon had filed out of the camp. Three-six had then fallen in behind my platoon, waving for his men to follow him. His platoon had slowly filed out of the jungle following in their platoon leader's footsteps.

Three-six's point squad had been with him when he had first stepped into the camp and had been filling the platoon's canteens at the stream when Three-six waved the rest of his platoon on. The point squad was tossing the canteens up to the men as they filed by with the intention of falling in behind the end squad as it passed.

One of the men in the file had stepped over to the edge of the ridge to catch his canteen as one of the men standing in the stream had tossed it up to him. The spot he stepped into was level with the head of the man below him in the stream, but that spot contained a land mine. Quicker than thought, a mine had exploded, blowing one of his legs off about three inches above the top of his boot and throwing his body up in an arc over the stream to land on the other side.

The man who had been standing in the stream tossing the canteens had taken a load of shrapnel in the head. Two other men were knocked down by the force of shrapnel flying into their bodies.

A scene from hell greeted me. The men around the explosion were still in shock, just beginning to move. The man who had had his leg blown off was sitting on the bank rocking back and forth, clutching his stump with both hands, trying to stop the bleeding and holding the bloody end out of the dirt. His face grimaced in pain, the muscles in his face outlined as he gritted his teeth to keep from screaming out. His boot with the bloody, mangled stump sticking out the top was standing up a few meters from him. A white bone glistened brightly in the flesh. No, two bones! My eyes traveled to the stump the man was holding to match the separate pieces.

The man who had taken the shrapnel in the head was sitting in the stream, slumped forward with his head under water between his legs, his pack thrown up over his shoulders, the weight holding the head down. The other two men were lying on the ridge writhing in pain.

Three-six and the men closest to the wounded men were slightly disorganized from shock but were quickly regaining their senses.

My medic pushed by me, running to the man in the water. Needlessly, I yelled to get his head out of the water before he drowned. Doc yanked the man backward and dragged him to the side where he started working on him. Three-six's medic simultaneously rushed to the man holding his stump and started his lifesaving procedures.

Three-six and I were both yelling orders to the men around us to take care of the wounded, set up a defensive perimeter, and for our sergeants to report.

Three-six was still on Delta's frequency. I told him I'd handle the dustoff while he got the men squared away.

Schaldenbrand ran up to me while I was calling Delta Six. Delta Six was on the horn immediately. I explained what had happened to Three-six's men and requested a dustoff, fast. There were four peanuts but Doc thought the man with the head wound was in bad shape. His breathing was irregular and he hadn't regained consciousness. This man would be a Kool-Aid pretty soon if we didn't get him out fast.

I told Schaldenbrand to get me some men with machetes to chop out a hole in the canopy so the dustoff could lower a sling to lift the wounded out.

One of my machine gunners, Spagg, overheard and volunteered. We only had a couple of machetes so the men worked in twos. The trees were close together and when one was cut, it would tilt only a little before it caught on another tree. Chopping through the thick

trunks was hard work with a machete, but the men worked frantically, racing against time.

I wondered at my platoon's luck that we had not stepped on the
damn mine. I had walked that very area many times that day, as had
my men. Who would expect a live land mine in the middle of a camp?
Leave it up to the dinks to think up something like that. Christ!
Sometimes you just couldn't figure out the goddamn dinks. They did
the weirdest things.

The dustoff pilot radioed he was coming and to pop smoke.

I told him we would pop it, but it probably would not get up
through the trees.

"This is One-six. Try to find this fucking hole."

I grabbed a machete from one of the men. With quick frantic chops,
I worked on one side of a tree while Spagg chopped on the other side.
When it started to fall, three or four of the men pushed against it to
force it as far over as they could.

The hole still was not big enough. The sound of the chopper blades
brought on a frenzied renewal of chopping on the tree that seemed to
be holding the others up. I threw the machete to another man while
I ran to the radio.

"This is One-six. Do you see anything yet?"

"Yeah, I think so. Stand by while I hover over. If it's the right hole,
I'll drop a life vest through."

The immense bug shape of the chopper slid into view, silhouetted
against the sky in the small hole above us. A couple of the men started
waving.

"This is One-six. You got the right place. Lower the sling, we're
running out of time. One of the peanuts is fading fast."

A man leaned out of the chopper's door fifty feet above us and
threw down a couple of vests.

"Three-six! Get those men up here!" I yelled.

The two walking wounded were helped over to the space. Other
men helped them put on the nylon vests while the crewman swung
out the arm of the sling and lowered the cable.

My men had stopped chopping as the tree fell over a little more,
widening the hole.

One of the men grabbed the cable as it came within reach and hooked it to the ring in the vest of the first man.

I gave a swirling signal with my hand to the crewman above. The wounded man was pulled off the ground as the cable was winched up.

The dustoff pilot was good. The sweat must have been pouring off him as he manipulated the controls of his craft, keeping the man centered in the hole as the winch drew him up.

When the man reached the top the crewman swung the arm in to bring him into the chopper. After unhooking, he swung the arm out and lowered the cable again, throwing the vest back down. The procedure was repeated for the other walking wounded.

The third man to go up was the guy with his lower leg blown off. We fastened the harness on him as the medic hovered around him like a mother hen.

A tourniquet had been tied around his stump and was held in place with a two-foot stick. The medic told him to hold this stick for all it was worth. One of the men lit a cigarette and stuck it into the wounded man's lips.

The signal was given and the cable pulled him off the ground. About half way up he waved to all of us, grinning like a cheshire cat. Blood dripped on us.

It was a picture I shall always hold in my mind. A man dangling from a cable, holding a stick fastened to a tourniquet on the stump of his leg, waving at his comrades with his other hand, the cigarette dangling from his lips.

"One-six, this is getting hairy up here. We're starting to take rounds," the pilot reported.

"Hold on, there's just one more."

Spagg and I lifted the unconscious man up while we slid the vest onto him. Someone handed me the cable which I hooked into the ring.

The unconscious man was winched upward, dangling like a limp doll at the end of the cable. Spagg and I stood underneath, watching this final exodus. As the crewman reached out to grab the man, something went wrong. The man had become unhooked somehow and fell through fifty feet of sky toward us. We jumped back as the man fell in a heap at our feet.

The medic and I pulled the man over.

"Fuck, he's stopped breathing."

The man's skin was bloodless but maybe we could make him live.

"Hold his head, lieutenant, I'm going to give him a trache. Quick, someone give me a knife."

Spagg handed the medic his large sheath knife.

The medic ran his fingers along the bones of the man's throat while I held the head. Satisfied he had found the right place, he stuck the top of Spagg's knife into the flesh. He cut smoothly through the flesh of the throat, between the bones and into his esophagus. The naked darkness of the man's throat was exposed to light. Pink shone wetly through the bloodless cut.

"That's all I can do. He's breathing again, but I think he's already dead. Haul him up," the medic said to me.

Jumping up, I arched my head toward the chopper as a man hooked the rig. I gave the signal and once again the man was pulled into the air. As he was safely pulled inside, the pilot put his chopper into motion and sailed up and away.

"Three-six, it's almost dark. We've got to get out of here and the only way is up the side of this ridge my platoon was on this morning. We'll go as far as we can, but if we don't reach the top we'll just have to stay strung out in a long line until morning."

I gave the point orders. We started up the steep side, the men of One-six dragging the heavy mortars and other captured goods with them. We spent the night clinging to the side of the mountain and fought our way to Captain Sells the following morning.

We continued to patrol the ridges and jungle trails for days, searching for and fighting the enemy.

Sometimes one of their soldiers would wait next to a tree lining a trail. When our point man was almost upon him, the NVA soldier would whirl around the tree, spraying a full thirty-round clip from his AK-47 into the point element. Sometimes they would fire at us from hidden bunkers and spider holes.

The attrition rate on both sides was like a steady trickle of blood from the body. We were able to fill in the spaces and keep going, although weaker than before.

The attrition on our side was terrible on our morale. Although we killed and wounded many of the NVA we never knew how much it hurt them. It seemed there was an unlimited number to take their places. But on our side, when we lost a man we all knew it and it wore heavily on our minds.

The constant marching and fighting demanded two things of us—strength and absolute reliability.

This was never more evident than on the twenty-second of November 1967.

22 November 1967

Early that morning Captain Sells marched us up the trail a couple of hundred meters to one of our former night locations. He was going to stay there with the Fourth Platoon while the other three platoons moved down the trail to cut left on a heading down the ridge toward the stream at the bottom. We were in need of water but were tired of fighting, so we were not to look too hard for dinks. Just travel to the stream, top off our canteens, and head back to Delta Six.

We would leave our packs (thank God!) with Four-six. Lieutenant Weeks, Four-six, promised us that no one would raid the packs while we were gone. Everything would still be there when we got back. Well, maybe not everything. Four-six kicked my pack and asked if I still had any fruit. He laughed as we kidded each other. Lieutenant Cohoon (Two-six), Lieutenant Ordway (Three-six), and I joked with Four-six about the easy job he had just sitting while we did the work. We were not kidding each other, though. Even with our joking we knew the danger he would be in by staying behind. His platoon was smaller than any of ours. If he were attacked, he would be hard put to hold off an attack of any size.

Four-six was up to the task. He informed us that he had to protect Delta Six or there wouldn't be anyone to chew our asses on a regular basis.

Three-six left first since he had the farthest to go. Next was Two-six. They were going to hike down the trail, then cut down the ridge about a hundred to a hundred fifty meters apart, thereby sweeping a large section of the ridge. My platoon was going to go down the ridge from Four-six's position. Each platoon would be far enough apart to cover a large section of the jungle and yet close enough to lend a hand if one of the other platoons ran into trouble.

My point element that day was Delk, Jesse, Yoder, and Bell. Mann and I would be traveling between Delk and Bell in the point. Altogether I had about twenty-four men, counting Four-six's Sergeant Kirkpatrick.

We moved off the ridge. Delta Six and Four-six told us to be careful. There were dinks everywhere.

Yoder was the point man. He was experienced and full of good humor due to his promotion to door gunner. A good man to have on point any day, he was aggressive and unafraid. Even though he was going in soon, there was no question of putting someone else in his place on point. It was his turn and he would not have it any other way.

It had been overcast and slightly rainy the past few days but the sun broke through the clouds as we moved cautiously down the ridge. I called a halt for chow about 1100 hours, figuring we were approximately halfway. After eating, I rested on one arm while talking to Yoder. We had gotten to know each other pretty well over the months I had been in-country and I had come to depend on him as a man to get the job done. He reminded me of a hillbilly, with his coarse language, mannerisms, and humor. I was always asking him when he was going to get that front tooth replaced. That missing tooth made him look more like a hillbilly than anything else. He always laughed and said, "Fuck, sir, I ain't about to let them fucking army dentists work on me. Shiiit no, that would be a lick on me."

"Alright, you big dumb fucker," I would reply. "Let all your teeth get crooked and then say you should have listened to your old wise lieutenant." He always got a kick out of that.

Today I razzed him about his tooth again and told him I wouldn't be able to worry about his dental health since he was leaving me. I again congratulated him on his promotion and new job.

"That's right, sir, I'll be flying above all you poor humpers, shooting up the dinks in style while y'all are sweating like a goddamn preacher in a whorehouse."

I took one last drag on my cigarette, offered him one, and lit them up for both of us. We sat in silence for a few minutes lost in our thoughts.

I was watching a couple of brightly colored birds perched on a limb a few feet away and wondered if everything in the jungle had been discovered and classified by the scientists. Probably not, I reflected. No scientist had ever been this far back in this jungle.

Oh, well, back to work.

"Saddle up," I told the point. The word was passed back up the file of men. We all grunted as we stood up and adjusted our web gear with all our ammo and other equipment.

Yoder had moved only twenty or twenty-five meters when he stopped and waved me up. He pointed to a narrow muddy trail twisting down the ridge in the general direction we were going. Yoder whispered, "Fresh dink trail."

I nodded and reached for the handset. I reported to Delta Six that we had run across a fresh dink trail and that we were going to follow it.

"This is Delta Six. You follow that trail, but be careful. We've been in this area long enough that every dink in the jungle knows we're here someplace. Watch for an ambush, out."

"O.K., Yoder, follow this trail, but move slow and cautious. This trail can't be more than a couple of hours old," I whispered.

He nodded affirmative and moved out in a low crouch. We moved very slowly down the side of the ridge, aware of the tremendous danger.

Soon we reached a flat area with a little gully running next to it on our left. The undergrowth was very thin along the flat area we were on. Yoder waved me forward and whispered that he thought he had heard movement in front of us. I whispered back to take it easy. Word was passed back that dinks were ahead. I put my hand on Yoder's shoulder to signal him to move ahead. There was noplace else to go and we were there to find the enemy.

Yoder crept forward in a crouch, looked back at me, and grinned. I grinned back and nodded my head. Yoder stepped over a tree root holding up part of the small gully bank.

At that moment, all hell broke loose as a Chi-com machine gun strafed the point element. Yoder was hit in the body and fell forward into the gully. The machine gun acted as a key which triggered a complete ambush. We had walked into a classical "U-shaped ambush," with the machine gun being at the base of the "U."

As the terrifying sounds of the bullets ripped by our bodies, we dove for cover. Delk stepped behind the tree with the root. Yoder yelled that he had been hit. Jesse fell flat on the ground at Delk's feet. Bell and I dropped where we were, clutching the ground desperately with our fingers digging into the gravel and dirt.

The cacophonic sounds of explosions, machine guns, and rifle bullets ripped through the air and ricocheted off the ground and trees around us. The noise was overwhelming. Men were screaming and yelling, trying desperately to get to cover—or screaming when they were hit or thought they were hit, which was almost as terrifying.

My face was pressed into the ground, my eyes clutched shut for a few moments, my fingers curled into the earth; I prayed none of the bullets would slam into my body. Rocks were thrown against my body from the force of the bullets hitting the ground around me. I shuddered each time a rock hit me, thinking it was a bullet.

I looked up to see the RTO, Mann, huddled behind a low rock. Green and red tracers were crisscrossing the complete perimeter of my little platoon. The end of the "U" had closed completely, encircling us in its death grip.

We still had not seen any of the enemy in the thick growth around us. Most of us in the point played dead. I lay trying to get my thinking organized as to what to do.

Yoder was moaning to himself that he had been hit. Delk kept trying to turn around the tree so he could fire at the as yet unseen machine gunner. Jesse was lying where he had fallen, not moving a muscle. Bell was lying next to me, near my feet.

I could hear Yoder crying on the other side of the root where he had fallen. He cried out for me to come and get him.

"Lieutenant, I've been hit, I've been hit bad. I'm dying. Please come and get me, please come and get me, oohh."

I turned my head in his direction. Twigs and bark from the trees were falling like snow all around us, as the terrible shrapnel and firepower ripped through the jungle around us. I was terrified.

Yoder's cries cut me like a knife.

"O.K., Yoder, I'm coming!" I yelled.

I jumped up into a crouch and ran toward Yoder. Bell jumped up at the same time on my right and was running with me. We were going to pull Yoder back up from the edge of the gully into what we hoped would be a more secure area.

In two or three steps, we were at the edge of the gully. The mountain was old lava rock and the rock was showing through along the top edge of the gully. The machine-gun bullets struck the rock at our feet, throwing rock shrapnel into our faces and bodies. We teetered on the edge of the gully for a split second, shocked at the sight of the rocks exploding at our feet and at the pain of the rock shrapnel. Another burst of machine-gun fire raked Bell and me from right to left. As the machine-gun bullets swept across Bell, one of them hit the M-79 grenade launcher he was carrying at port arms across his chest. It exploded and the force of the explosion knocked us down.

I lay stunned, sprawled along the edge of the gully, facing in the direction of the machine gun. Bell was lying in the bottom of a small depression to my right, his face a bloody mess. He was curled into a ball as he tried to make sense of what had happened to him.

The machine gun raked us a few more times. As the bullets hit the rock in front of me, the rock shrapnel dug into my face. My lips and cheeks were burning fiercely and I thought I had been wounded more gravely than I was. I lay absolutely still, pretending to be dead.

My eyes were looking right at Yoder lying a few feet below me. His hands were fumbling with the first-aid pack on his web gear as he was trying to staunch the flow of blood from his body.

I looked up in a daze, forgetting I was supposed to be dead. I saw the machine gunner pull back the bolt in his machine gun. He was dug into the opposite bank only fifteen or twenty feet away. *He must be reloading,* I groggily thought. Then he lowered the barrel of his machine gun a few inches and fired a burst into Yoder's moving body. Yoder's body shook from the shock of the bullets.

I pushed myself to my knees, knowing I was next. He fired at me as I fell backward and I felt a powerful blow on my hip. *Oh, fuck, I've really had it this time,* I thought. I hugged the ground as flat as I could.

I yelled up to the main body of the platoon to ask how they were. The platoon was sort of shaped like a figure eight with the point element forming the bottom circle. We were separated from the platoon and were in the killing zone of the ambush. I couldn't believe we were still alive.

Mann yelled at me that Delta Six wanted to know what in the hell was going on. I yelled back to tell him to tell the captain that we had been ambushed and I had one Kool-Aid and three peanuts. After a few seconds Mann yelled back, "Damn it, Delta Six wants to know who the Kool-Aid is."

I told him it was Yoder. There was a brief lull in the firing as Mann relayed this information to the captain. This would go hard on Captain Sells. Not only did it bother him to lose men, but Yoder and he had come over on the boat together.

Mann yelled down that Delta Six wanted to know my exact position. As I reached for my map in the pocket of my trouser leg, my body rose up off the ground and the machine gunner once again fired at me.

I immediately dropped, lying completely still, afraid he would fire into my body as I had seen him fire into Yoder's body. I yelled back to Mann that I couldn't get to my map. Mann relayed this to the captain.

The captain knew I was in serious trouble and the only way out was for me to take direct action. His deep concern for our well-being coupled with his strong personality came over the horn.

Mann yelled that Delta Six was depending on me and that I had to let him know where I was so he could send help.

I could not let down the captain, nor my men. I inched my hand along the side of my body until I reached my map case. I unbuttoned the leg pocket and slowly inched the map up until it was next to my face. With the map between my nose and the ground, I read off the coordinates which Mann relayed to Delta Six.

Mann yelled back that Three-six and Two-six were on their way. Four-six had taken some rounds but so far they were still O.K. Mann

yelled down that Schaldenbrand had taken a round through the arm-
pit of his rain jacket but was O.K. Everyone else was in good shape
up there.

I didn't know why we hadn't taken more casualties, but that fucker
with the machine gun had been shooting at me the whole time and
I wasn't hit bad yet. If we couldn't see them very well, maybe they
couldn't see us.

I looked up at Delk and asked him if he had seen that fucking gun
yet. He said he had not seen him but he had a good idea where he
was. Delk flipped around the tree and fired a burst into the opposite
bank. The machine gun answered by spraying Delk's tree with two
or three bursts of bullets.

The tree exploded into splinters as bark and pieces of wood flew in
all directions. Delk clutched his elbows in tight, gritted his teeth, and
clenched his eyes shut as death hungrily slobbered around his narrow
protection.

"Well, he ain't going anyplace," Delk dryly remarked. "We ain't
either until that son-of-a-bitch decides to call it quits."

"Fat chance," Jesse spoke up.

"Hey, lieutenant, Delta Six just called. Two-six ran into an ambush
and their point man was killed. Two-six is heading back up the ridge.
He says he can't get to us," Mann yelled. "Three-six is still coming,
though."

"One-six, Delta Six wants to talk to you."

"You tell him I'm trapped and can't get to the radio. What the fuck
does he think I'm doing down here anyway?" I yelled back.

"He still wants to talk to you. He said to get your ass on the horn."

"Fucking captains. Alright, tell him I'm coming. You guys give me
covering fire. I'm going to slide along this hill and then run up." I was
pissed.

I immediately stuck my hand into a pile of dink shit. "Agghhh,
there's shit all over this place. This is a fucking dink latrine," I
exclaimed. What a hell of a note—to be ambushed in a dink latrine.

The machine gunner started firing at me again. I ran on all fours
and finally stumbled next to Mann and his low rock. There really
wasn't room for both of us but it would have to do.

"Delta Six, this is One-six, over."

"This is Delta Six, About time you got on the horn. What's going on? Over."

I explained my predicament through bursts of gunfire. We were still surrounded. Occasionally I caught glimpses of the enemy moving in the jungle around us. Sergeant Fitzpatrick and I fired on three dinks and they dropped out of sight. It was impossible to tell if we had hit any of them. The firing was too intense so Mann and I crawled up to a larger rock.

Delta Six called to tell me that Three-six, Lieutenant Ordway, had run into an ambush and was stopped. They hadn't sustained any casualties but they would be a while fighting their way through. Delta Six said our best bet was to pull back.

I said I couldn't. I still had people on the point element trapped in the area below us and I couldn't leave them behind. He started to say something and I handed the phone back to Mann.

I lay bare-headed behind a rock just tall enough to conceal me as long as I was laying flat. My helmet had fallen off and had rolled down the hill during the initial contact. A hand had reached out to grab it for a souvenir. Some souvenir, I thought. Some day that fucking dink will be a grandpa with my helmet setting on his mantel. My helmet covering was camouflaged jungle green with my name and rank inked in. There were a few other items written on it that would embarrass his womenfolk if they ever had it translated. Examples: "Fuck Nam," "FTA," written on by one of my men (which meant "Fuck the Army"), and other assorted goodies. I hoped the son-of-a-bitch tried to drink the bug juice that was fastened to the helmet with the large rubberband holding the helmet cover. It would serve him right.

I yelled down to the point element and asked them if they could make it back up to us if we provided covering fire. Delk and Jesse said they could.

Bell yelled back, "No, sir, help me. I'm blind."

I let out my breath. "Bell, can you make it back if I can get you?"

"Yes, sir, I think so."

Fuck, I'm going to die, I thought.

I yelled back that I would come get him.

"Delk! Jesse! When I give the word everyone will start firing to give you cover. Bell, I'm going to run down and guide you back."

I laid my rifle down. There would be nothing I could do with it. I would need both my hands to drag Bell up the clear space. I actually thought I was going to die. There was no way I could get down across that open area to Bell and back safely, but I felt I had an obligation to him and to my men to get him out of the situation I had gotten us into. Besides, there was no way I could live with myself if I left him down there. I might as well be dead.

Porter looked over at me. "I'll go after him, sir," he laid down his rifle and started forward.

"No, Porter, you stay here. I want all you men to give me covering fire. Throw grenades, smoke grenades, fire your rifles, machine guns, scream and yell. Do everything you can to keep their attention away from me and try to keep their heads down."

Porter and the men looked at me. Without sounding melodramatic, I could see in their eyes and expressions that they thought I was going to my death, that I was going to get killed for doing this.

I lay flat behind the rock and took a deep breath. I looked at the open area I had to cross and the butterflies knotted my stomach up. Damn, what was I doing?

I said, "Alright, now when I yell fire, give it everything you've got, yell and scream as loud as you can." I was trembling and I was scared, yet at the same time I was calm because I was thinking that there was nothing else I could do.

I yelled to Bell that I was ready to come and get him, and I told Delk and Jesse that when the firing started they were to take off as fast as they could.

I bolted upright yelling "Fire."

Everyone started firing, yelling and screaming, and throwing smoke grenades.

I took off running. The machine gunner started on me as soon as I leapt out from behind the rock. As I ran in a crouch, zigzagging toward Bell, tracer bullets from the machine gun and other guns zipped all around me. As they zinged by me, I know there were four or five that I couldn't see.

After an eternity, I reached Bell. I grabbed him by the back of his
fatigue jacket and literally jerked him out of the small depression he
was in. As I was pulling him up, one of the machine gun bullets grazed
across the back of my left hand, ripping off the skin. It didn't really
hurt, but it burned like hell and surprised me. It was almost like I was
in another world. The blood rushed from the back of my hand. I threw
Bell's arm around me and put my body between him and the machine
gun. I started back up the hill with bullets flying by us and ricocheting
off everything around us.

Bell was able to help me but he couldn't see anything. He limped
and crawled, I pushed and swore, as we continuously fell in our flight
back up the hill. I said, "Come on, boy, we'll make it!" In the middle
of all that I immediately regretted the use of the word "boy." I had
not meant anything by it, but Bell was a black from Atlanta, Georgia,
and probably couldn't stand the word "boy." To my dying day I will
regret that word. Although it was said in innocence, Bell might have
taken it wrong.

As I pulled him up the hill, one of my feet was shot out from under
me. I had been shot in the heel, one of the bullets knocking off a piece
of my boot heel, and the force had knocked me down. I got up again
and again felt a tremendous blow to my hip, knocking me down. *Hit
again,* I thought.

Finally I got Bell up behind a rock. Doc was there and started
working on him. I lay on my back looking up at the sky through the
jungle canopy, not believing that I had actually made it down there
and back.

Yoder was still down there and although I had witnessed the bullets
hitting him, I didn't want to leave. I had to be absolutely sure he was
dead. I would never forgive myself if I pulled back and he was still
alive.

Meanwhile, Three-six was moving closer. They had hit another
ambush but had fought their way through and weren't too far away.

We were getting low on ammo. About one magazine of M-16 and
a hundred rounds of M-60s. We could see some of the dinks as they
moved around us. Oddly enough, some of them were wearing uniforms that looked white. We kept firing but only at sure targets.

I was ready to call artillery in on our position if we were overrun.

After an undetermined amount of time, the firing began to taper off. We returned fire conservatively. Finally, Three-six said he was entering a dink camp which had been vacated. His unit was now below us on the ridge. There had been no firing from the dinks for the last few minutes and we thought they must have pulled out.

Three-six confirmed this by entering the empty enemy camp. They were moving up the gully toward us. We heard voices as they neared our position and we began to believe the fight was over.

We saw their point man come into sight, moving cautiously up the gully. Two or three men came into view and waved at us. We were safe. That American unit was a very welcome sight after the ordeal we had just been through.

We all stood up. A couple of my men and I ran down to where Three-six's point was standing over Yoder. I leaped over the edge of the gully and stopped at Yoder's body. Kneeling down, I turned his body over. He had died with his head lying downhill. His face was a dark blue from the blood which gravity had pulled into the downhill portion of his body.

There wasn't much blood on his body but numerous bullet holes were cut into his fatigues covering his stomach and chest. His eyes were closed. I looked at him for a moment, my thoughts running back to our many conversations in the past. Once we had discussed whether we would go to the aid of one of our fellow soldiers if he was in trouble. I had told him I would always respond to one of my men if he needed help. He had replied it would be a lick on me.

I wondered if he had known that I tried to get to him. He was the first man under my command to die.

I went through his pockets, recovering his watch, ring, and other personal items. I checked to see if his dog tags were around his neck. Graves registration would need them for identification. I put the handful of his personal belongings in my pocket for the captain, who would have to write the letter to his folks.

I looked up to see some of my platoon and Three-six's platoon standing over a dink body lying in the gully. Three-six had an Indian in his platoon and I had an Indian in my platoon. They drew their knives and slashed the enemy's body in frustration. This was the only dead dink the men could find. One lousy dink for all that pain and suffering. At least we could take our hate out on that son-of-a-bitch.

Three-six had taken one dink prisoner in the enemy camp. Delta Six radioed to blindfold him so he couldn't see that his comrades had killed one of us.

I told Schaldenbrand to have some of the men get Yoder's body ready for traveling. Sticks were put through Yoder's fatigue sleeves to carry the upper part of his body. His legs could be carried by grabbing his fatigue trousers.

He was a big man, over six feet tall, and he weighed at least two hundred pounds. Carrying all that dead weight proved to be an ordeal in itself.

We would go straight up the ridge to Delta Six. I put two men with machetes behind the point man to chop out a path for the men carrying Yoder's body.

As I directed my platoon into marching order, I turned to find the blindfolded prisoner standing next to me with his hands tied behind his back. I had forgotten about him and I was surprised. The NVA soldier was dressed in neat green jungle fatigues. He was young, about five feet tall, and of small build.

"You lucky son-of-a-bitch," I said to him. "If Delta Six hadn't ordered us to bring you back, I'd kill you where you stand."

"Let's go." I headed to the point.

Dragging and carrying Yoder's heavy body up the side of the mountain kept us cussing and sweating. The machete team was moving slowly, but they managed to keep ahead of us as Yoder's body kept slipping from our grasp to fall on the jungle floor. Goddamn, he was heavy. Three-six's men helped.

My men were beaten physically and emotionally from the strain of the ambush. We were tired and all we wanted to do was reach the top. Both flanks were traveling parallel to us and they would switch positions with the carrying detail to help out.

Finally Four-six yelled down that we were almost there. We struggled up the last few meters to the excited conversation of Four-six's men and the relative security of the ridge top. The carrying detail laid

Yoder's body next to the dead man from Two-six's platoon.

Our rucksacks were lying where we had left them in a neat group. The platoon was still coming in, the men drifting over to retrieve their packs and set up around the perimeter. I was watching them when Captain Sells put his hand on my arm.

"Fred, are you hurt bad? Where are you wounded?"

I started examining myself. My hand was bleeding slightly but it didn't seem bad. My trembling hands explored my body. Five bullet holes and their exit holes were spread through my fatigue shirt, evidence of the nearness of death. One ammo pack on each hip was mangled where a bullet had plowed into them. Each ammo pack contained three magazines of M-16 ammo. The steel sides of the magazines were torn and the pack's canvas covering was ripped from the striking bullets. I pulled the magazines out of the pack, marveling at my good luck. The two blows to the hips had been from the force of the bullets hitting my magazines.

"I, I think I'm O.K., sir. My luck held," I said as I examined the twisted, torn magazines. My hips ached dully, my face still stung, my lips were swollen from the rock shrapnel, and my hand burned. I was shaking all over from relief at still being alive.

Captain Sells went over to the dead men. I stood where I was, the men milling around me and occasionally asking how I was. I always replied "O.K.," but I was not O.K. I was scared. Goddamn, that had been close. I had almost bought it that time.

I held a match up to a cigarette but my hand was shaking so bad I just held it in front of the cigarette, watching the flame vibrate. A couple of the men gathered around me telling me what a brave thing I had done to run down there to pull Bell out. One of them lit my cigarette. I nodded my head, afraid to speak. Reaction was setting in.

"How's Bell?" I finally asked. I was looking over at a unit of men who were helping Doc wash Bell's face of the blood and dirt.

"He's O.K., his sight is O.K., he was just blinded by the blood and other crap."

"Thank God," I murmered. Doc was wrapping a bandage around Bell's head. Bell was sitting on the ground smoking as Doc worked on him.

This is it, I thought. I'd been wounded four times in battle. I had done my job. Captain Sells had asked after my third wound if I wanted to be sent back. Anyone with three wounds was due that. All it took was two wounds to get you out of the field. Surely four would let me live with myself. What was I trying to prove? But I answered my own question: The men depend on me. It's my job to keep them alive by giving them good leadership and looking after them. They need me.

Yeah, but shit, what did I owe myself? I had a wife and two little girls who needed me; the ten thousand dollars in insurance money wouldn't do them much good. Where did my duty lie?

I was still shaking. I couldn't go through this again.

Reluctantly, almost against my will, I started walking toward the captain.

"Captain."

"Yes, Fred."

"You asked once if I wanted out of the field after I had been wounded for the third time?"

He turned and looked into my face. "Yes."

"Well, I, I think, I mean would you think I was letting you and my men down if I did?" I stammered.

"No, I wouldn't. You've done your job. I could get you a good job with S-2."

"I, I think I want out. I don't know if I can do this again. Maybe I can't cut it."

"That's nonsense! You're a hell of a fine officer and the men will understand, but you think about it."

"O.K., I will, let me think." A little bit of confidence returned at his words. I handed Yoder's things to him. I wandered back to the packs, thinking I should find Yoder's pack.

Bell had stood up and was coming toward me when he saw the blindfolded dink. In one motion he swung his fist into the dink's face. He hit him again and again, knocking the surprised dink down in a burst of fury. Bell started kicking him. It was obvious Bell was going to kill him.

The other men and I stood smoking and watching. We were going to let Bell kill the dink. Bell had the right.

Captain Sells yelled and ran over to us, pushing me out of the way and pulling Bell off the dink. "Here! What's this? What's going on? We're not going to have this in my company. This man's a prisoner. Lieutenant Downs, what are you doing just standing there?"

I looked at him in surprise. "Bell was killing this motherfucker. What's wrong with that?" I retorted.

"You know goddamn well what's the matter with that, lieutenant. This man is defenseless and our prisoner. Now let's get this prisoner back to the LZ."

I wanted the dink dead but the captain was right. "Saddle up," I called to the men around me.

Two-six was the point platoon. He was ready to go, and at a signal from the captain he moved his men on. Some of his men picked up the body of their comrade and started down the trail behind the main body of the platoon.

We were next. The men from Yoder's squad picked up his body and we moved down the slippery, muddy trail. Both carrying teams were having trouble with the bodies as their feet kept slipping in the mud and the strain of carrying the awkward weight caused them to slide and fall, dropping the bodies in the mud.

Finally we reached the landing zone and the two bodies were laid on the grass at the edge. The dustoff was on its way.

I walked over to the bodies. Yoder's eyes were partially shut and I leaned down to push them closed. Not that it did any good, but for some reason I thought it was better that way.

I stood there with one hand on my aching hip, smoking and thinking. Yoder's face was all muddy from the numerous times he had been dropped in the mud and there was a trickle of blood at the base of his throat.

This is the way it will always end, I thought. Men being killed in the jungle, other men dragging their bodies out, putting them on choppers, and the rest of us going back to the fighting. When they left on the chopper, it was as they had never been. Man's beginning and man's end would always be attended by only a few. Those that bore him at birth and those that bore him at death. The only important thing was what he did in between. Good or bad or indifferent, he would touch those around him in some way and then be gone.

I wondered if a salute would be in order. Not necessarily in the military sense, but a salute from one who had known him and would never forget him. I decided it was and I raised my hand to my forehead in a farewell.

I turned around as the beat of chopper blades sounded through the jungle air. "Get that prisoner ready," I yelled. "Some of you men come over here and put the bodies on board the chopper when it lands."

Smoke was popped and the large chopper swung in toward us for his landing. The doors were pushed back and I saw the door gunner on the side facing me look around, anxiously searching for the omnipresent enemy. *Good man,* I thought, *not trusting a goddamn thing even with an American infantry company surrounding the LZ.*

The men who were going to load the bodies picked up the two dead men and hurried toward the chopper, bending over as they ran under the swiftly turning blades. The pilot was not staying on the ground any longer than he had to. After the bodies were loaded, the dink was hurried over to the chopper by two men who roughly threw him on the chopper where one of the crew members grabbed him and sat him on the floor.

The men who had thrown him on board wiped their hands on their trouser legs as if to rid their hands of any contamination with the enemy.

Captain Sells decided that enough was enough for one day. He told the platoon leaders to set up a company defense perimeter.

That night I lay on the ground talking with Schaldenbrand. The long day had made us both reflective. I relayed my fears of being a capable leader and of the shock of losing Yoder.

He told me in an embarrassed manner that the men and he had thought that what I had done for Bell that day was a hell of a thing. They had gone to Captain Sells and told him they wanted to put me in for the Distinguished Service Cross, but Captain Sells had suggested instead the Silver Star. Schaldenbrand and the guys had written it up before dark.

I tried to say something appreciative but too many thoughts were crisscrossing in my mind. Above everything else ran the thought that I could not abandon my men. I felt ashamed that I had asked Captain Sells to pull me out of the field earlier when I was still shaken. What would the men think if they found out I was doing such a thing? Worse, what I think of myself?

The next day was Thanksgiving.

On Thanksgiving Day the company gathered for a hot meal flown in by a chopper to the same LZ where the dead men had been picked up the day before.

Delta Six let us have a couple of hours for dinner, then we started to march back up the ridge. A dink sprayed the front of the column with an AK-47, wounding the point man. The chow chopper which had just picked up the empty food containers was called back to pick up the wounded man.

It was a day like all the others.

My only consolation was that my RTO, Mann, had come to the end of his year and I put him on the chopper to go home. I really missed him but I was glad he had made it. He was going back to the "world." He had beat the infantryman odds.

Skelly, a blond, quiet man from Florida who was Schaldenbrand's RTO, became my RTO for the remainder of the operation.

Our success at finding the enemy caused the battalion commander, Dragon Six, to keep extending our time in the field each time we had a firefight. We were tired and the constant series of extensions made us wonder if our luck would run out. Each day the patrol was extended was another day of fear, anguish, and physical exhaustion.

Finally, Delta Six informed us that we would finally be lifted out to the firebase for sure. One of the other companies could then go out on patrol.

All of the platoons of Delta Company rendezvoused at a clearing on a high mountain ridge and waited in the endless rain for the Chinook helicopter.

2 December 1967

We all stood around in the rain praying the clouds would lift. Finally we heard the welcome news that choppers were on the way.

The men were divided into lifts. The choppers had hardly settled until all the men were on board to be lifted out. A short hop put us into LZ Tempest, the firebase we had blasted out of the jungle four weeks ago. It had gone through a remarkable metamorphosis. The soldiers had sandbagged each foxhole and had scrounged around for odds and ends to make them more comfortable.

The grass within the perimeter had been beaten down until the whole area on top of the ridge was practically bald. All of the hootches had been reinforced with extra sandbags. The wooden ammo containers had been broken down so the individual boards could be used as flooring and as part of the roofs. Concertina wire was strung around the whole perimeter.

Dragon Six assigned sections of the perimeter to the companies, which in turn assigned sections to the platoons. One-six was assigned to the southwest edge of the perimeter. We immediately began to make ourselves at home.

"Lieutenant."

"Yeah, Skelly."

"Captain Sells called and said for you to report."

"We just got here, I wonder what he wants."

"I don't know, he just said for you to report."

I left my pack with Skelly with instructions to get our hootch ready for the night. As usual, I left my web gear and bandoliers of ammo on. I hurried across the firebase to the CP where Captain Sells was busy talking to the battalion XO.

"Downs, your platoon has to provide men for two of the listening posts tonight," Captain Sells said as he turned his attention to me. "Have them report to me on the double. I'll have someone show them where the LPs are. They'll have to eat their chow and get out there before dark."

LPs were dangerous as hell and no one wanted to go out on them.

An LP, or listening post, was a two- or three-man position set up at night outside the perimeter away from the main body of troops. The men in the position were to act as an early warning system if the dinks were getting ready to attack. The dinks were unsure of exactly where the edge of perimeter was in the darkness and so would send scouts ahead to probe the line. The men in the listening posts would hear the movement in front of them and throw grenades toward the sound. It was almost certain death if they gave away their position, so they rarely fired their rifles. Their job was to report movement, throw grenades, and pray the dinks didn't find them. The LP didn't dare try to go back into the perimeter for fear of being shot by their own men. If a fight broke out, the LP was generally caught in a crossfire. Any way you looked at it, an LP was not the place to be.

When I got back I called Delk, Porter, Jose, and Gallagher to give them the bad news. Two of the squad leaders were to pick three men and send them to me. The men all groaned at our misfortune. We all figured we had a rest coming.

The men who had been picked gathered around my hootch for instructions. The LP's radio codes would be Voodoo One and Voodoo Two. To maintain noise security with their radios, they were told that the RTO would conduct a radio check every hour by clicking his handset once. They would reply by squeezing the handset twice. When we heard the two clicks we would know they were alright. After supplying them with extra hand grenades, they reported to Captain Sells.

I had always read about night coming swiftly in the jungle, but up on the ridge away from the trees the evening was as gentle as a cloud-covered sky. After a last cigarette I checked One-six's section of the perimeter, making sure the ends of our platoon tied in with the ends of the adjoining platoons. Satisfied that everything was strack, I returned to my hootch and called the LPs for a radio check.

"Voodoo One, this is One-six. Radio check, over."

"Click-click."

"Affirmative, Voodoo One, out."

"Voodoo Two, this is One-six. Radio check, over."

"Click-click."

"Affirmative, Voodoo Two, out."

"That's it, Skelly. Make sure your relief knows to check with them every hour on the hour."

"O.K., sir."

Skelly was not that well known to me so we got to talking about where we lived back in the world, our families and the other conversations soldiers talk about when cooped up together. Skelly was a good troop but he didn't make coffee like Mann. I missed that.

We all carried paperbacks to read when we weren't doing anything else, and he and I swapped for new reading material. I lounged back in my hootch for a good night's rest surrounded by the security on three sides of three layers of sandbags and the dryness of a poncho for a roof and sides. Even one end, the end facing the inside of the firebase, had a poncho across it. Heaven.

I was awakened by Skelly shaking my shoulder. "Sir, something's wrong with Voodoo One. They aren't answering the radio check."

"Let me have the radio. Voodoo One, this is Delta One-six. If you hear me, hit the handset twice, over."

Both of us listened intently to the static, waiting for the two clicks of recognition. Nothing. I called Voodoo Two and received an answering two clicks. At least they were O.K.

I tried a couple of more times before calling Captain Sells to tell him something was wrong with one of the LPs. He told me to keep trying and to keep him informed. He would alert the perimeter.

I felt helpless as I continued to call Voodoo One. I couldn't go out there nor could anyone else. All I could do was anxiously stare into the blackness as I willed the LP to answer the call.

If they had fallen asleep I would be perturbed but relieved that nothing had happened to them. Not knowing was torture. My mind conjured up everything that could happen to an LP, the worst being capture by the enemy. The frightful stories we heard about captured Americans were full of enough truths to keep us all leary. It was a fact that American ground troops were executed out of hand. Anytime an army fights a war as long as we had without the enemy having more prisoners than they did was proof enough.

"Click-click." The sound startled me.

"This is One-six. Is there movement in front of you? Answer by squeezing the handset twice, over."

"Click-click."

"This is One-six. Do you think there's dinks out there? Over."

"Click-click."

"This is One-six. Wait one . . . Delta Six, this is One-six. Voodoo One says there are dinks out there, over."

"Tell them to throw a grenade, over."

"Affirmative, out."

"Voodoo One, this is One-six. Throw a grenade, over."

"Click-click."

An explosion broke the blackness. Pure silence followed.

The whole perimeter was on alert now. Every commander had called his men. Infantry, artillery, and mortars were all prepared for an attack. Every man was trying to pierce the darkness with his sight, searching for the enemy.

"One-six, this is Voodoo One, over," a barely heard whisper came over the radio.

I whispered back, "This is One-six. What's going on out there? Over."

"This is Voodoo One. It sounds like the whole dink army is out here. There are all kinds of sounds. We'd better come in, over."

"This is One-six. You can't come in. Just stay put until daylight. If the sounds don't come any closer, don't throw any more grenades. You might give away your position. When it gets daylight, check out the area to your front. Radio check will be every half hour from now on, out."

Nothing else happened for the rest of the night but the perimeter stayed on alert wishing for daylight.

After a while, I dropped back to sleep with orders to be awakened before daylight.

"Sir, it's time," Skelly shook me awake again.

Everyone in the firebase was awake. The best time for the dinks to attack was at dawn and we meant to be ready for them.

Light gray gave way to regular gray as the sun came up over the cloud cover. Captain Sells radioed to send Voodoo One out to see if their grenades had gotten anything the night before. The whole perimeter was waiting.

"Voodoo One, this is One-six. Check the area out to see if you got anyone with that grenade and report, out."

Again the waiting. Everyone waited.

"Delta One-six, this is Voodoo One, over."

"This is One-six, over."

"Uh, One-six, this is Voodoo One. I think we found something, over."

"This is One-six. Well, what is it? Over."

"Uh, One-six, there's a big dump out here that the firebase has been dumping their junk in and we've found out what made the noise last night, over."

"Well, don't keep me in suspense. What was it? Over."

"Uh, One-six, it's hogs, over."

"*Hogs!* Are you shitting me? Over."

"No, One-six, it's hogs. In fact, there's an old sow and a bunch of half-grown pigs. We killed one last night, over."

"Wait one . . . Delta Six, this is One-six. Did you get that transmission? Over."

"I got it, One-six," Captain Sells's voice dripped sarcastically. "You mean to tell me *your* LP kept this perimeter on alert all night for a bunch of hogs? Over."

"This is One-six. I guess so, over."

"Well, tell them to get their butts in here before the hogs attack them, out."

3 December 1967

The chaplain flew out to hold a memorial service for the men who had been killed on the operation. He set up some C-ration cases to spread his purple cloth across and put his cross and cup on top of the cloth. The sky was cloudy and drizzly as the chaplain prayed for the souls of the men who had been killed and for understanding of the fight we were in.

Some of the men drank in his words like the desert sand drinks in moisture. To some of us the moisture fell on bare rock to be carried away by the empty winds. To others the water was held in a pool of unknowing.

The chaplain tried hard but the men had been lost fighting for survival and not for God.

The service finished, the chaplain climbed back on the chopper to return to the security of the base camp.

5 December 1967

The word was passed down that the battalion was going to abandon LZ Tempest and return to Base Camp Thunder or Montezuma at Duc Pho. Delta Company was assigned the job of policing the area after the battalion pulled out and patrolling for a few days in order to watch for dinks who might nose around the abandoned base. The evacuation was conducted in reverse order of the first day. First, the big Chinooks hovered above the artillery guns to lift them out one by one. The four-deuce mortars were broken down and loaded aboard other Chinooks. Then equipment, and last the men. Soon we were left by ourselves with the sound of the last chopper fading to the east toward the base camp at Duc Pho.

I had never put any thought into what had to be done when a firebase was evacuated. I just assumed that the men and equipment were lifted out and that was the end of that. As I wandered around the deserted base, I was appalled at the mess the battalion had left behind. None of us could believe the numerous hand grenades, smoke grenades, artillery shells, mortar shells, and other odds and ends of explosives and weapons laying around on the ground. It was no wonder a company had to stay behind to police up. We dumped everything into one pile and then blew it up. As we moved off the ridge I looked back and thought how much it looked like a deserted carnival ground with the earth all churned to mud with trash lying everywhere.

8 December 1967

From a neighboring ridge we watched the abandoned base for two days. Dinks occasionally appeared and prowled over the base. We would call in artillery on them and wipe the ridge clean.

But today we were going to be lifted out. The operation was finally going to end. If only the rain clouds would lift enough so that the Chinooks could land. We had been delayed one day by the rain already.

Schaldenbrand and I played checkers. A breeze was blowing, carrying the clouds over our ridge. Occasionally there would be a break in the clouds and we could see the lowlands. The bottoms of the clouds were below us. If they just lifted a couple of hundred meters they would clear the top of the ridge we were on. The breaks in the clouds were becoming longer now. The clouds had lifted enough so we could see the ocean off in the distance during the breaks. Just a little more.

Delta Six told us to get into position. The choppers were on the way. We stood nervously in the mist, hoping that we were going to get out this time. We were ready to hump to the ocean rather than spend another night in the jungle.

We heard the choppers circling above us, out of sight above the clouds. We were packed and ready to go, the checkerboard was tied to Schaldenbrand's pack—we were ready.

"They're coming. Pop smoke!"

The big Chinooks appeared during a break in the clouds and settled in. We ran aboard on each side of the chopper.

The machine carried us away. I looked over my men sprawled along the sides of the chopper. They had removed the magazines from their weapons before boarding and now were holding them close to their bodies. The men were dirty and unshaven, their clothes in various stages of disrepair, jungle boots worn and torn with clods of mud between the cleats. There were dark rings under their eyes and their faces were drawn and tired. Some of those faces were new men, sent out to replace the faces that had started the operation and were erased. We had experienced the worst of life and the most challenging. We had survived.

The platoon I took back was not the platoon I had brought out.

SECTION 3

Back
to the
Bridges

10 December 1967

After two days of standdown at Base Camp Montezuma at Duc Pho, the company was assigned an area of operations on Highway 1 just south of where we had been in October. This time my platoon had responsibility for only one bridge.

We loaded into deuce-and-a-halfs and headed to the new location. We were dropped off at Bridge 100, three kilometers south of the bridges we had guarded in October. The lieutenant in charge took me on a tour to point out the bunkers, possible lines of attack, and problems associated with this stretch of road.

A large freshwater lake lay next to the road and spread east three kilometers where it was separated from the South China Sea by a narrow strip of sand. The mountains bordered the road on the west; six bunkers were spread along the road south from the bridge. A couple of rolls of concertina wire circled the complete perimeter enclosing the bridge and bunkers.

After he had shown me around, I assigned the men to the different positions. The lieutenant and his men were going to be lifted out by choppers later that day to go into the jungle.

Rueto, who had hurt his leg earlier in the operation, had rejoined the platoon while we had been in base camp. I had made him RTO and had sent Skelly to be Schaldenbrand's RTO. Rueto, Schaldenbrand, Doc, and I would be together in the CP bunker.

While the men were settling in, I wandered around to familiarize myself with the new area. The other platoon was packed and ready to go, clustered along the road waiting for the helicopters.

Their rucksacks lay on the ground bulging with belongings, each man's weapon leaned across his pack.

I watched these strangers as they prepared to be lifted into the jungle. They were nervously puffing on cigarettes and writing one more letter home. Their lieutenant was moving from one group to another, checking equipment and seeing to last-minute details.

I stood alone on the side of the road, smoking a cigarette and thinking, perhaps for the first time, that we could lose this war. Standing alone under the cloudy sky, I felt alien in this land. We had just finished an operation back in the jungle and these men now were going out to a different part of the jungle to play the same deadly game of hide and seek with the enemy, probably with the same inconclusive result.

Why were the Americans doing the fighting? It seemed that ARVNs should be doing their own fighting in the jungle, not us. Our tactics also seemed wrong. We had spent over a month humping and fighting in a certain section of the jungle. Just when we had become familiar with the land, the mountains, and the streams, and knew where we would find the enemy and how to use familiar terrain to our advantage, we were pulled out. Sure, we wanted to pull out, and we needed the rest, but the unit now going in had never been in the jungle. They would have to learn everything from scratch.

To be successful in the jungle, the commanders should send us back into that area after our rest. We would then be able to strike right at the enemy. After our patrol, the unit now going in could turn about and go in when we came back. Instead, we never went back to the same place. We were always dropped into a completely new area to continue our tactics of search and destroy.

Of course, the Americans never owned anything except the ground they stood on. We were supposed to be winning the war, but we didn't dare move outside our perimeters at night.

The people all around us in this part of Vietnam were known Vietcong sympathizers. We didn't speak their language, they didn't speak ours. We were supposed to win their hearts and minds—but how could we compete with countrymen who could speak to them, live with them, were related to them? If they didn't have a common philosophy, all Vietnamese had a common desire—to see us go home.

I threw my cigarette down and mashed it with my foot. *Oh, well, I'll change things when I'm in power,* I promised myself. I enlisted because I wanted to see what a war was like. I guess I was romantic about war, but reality was fouling up my ideas. I was a soldier. My country thought it was doing the right thing and I did, too. It was just that it could be done a lot better than it was. My skepticism quickly faded. I knew we would never be beaten.

Someone yelled "Pop smoke."

I stepped to the side of the road and scanned the sky for the choppers. Little dots to the north expanded into the bulbous shape of Hueys. The smoke from the grenade drifted in a low stream across the road, marking the LZ for the flight. They landed in groups of three on the road. The traffic had been stopped to allow them to land. The road was just wide enough for the choppers to land perpendicular. The men were waiting in queues of the proper number for each chopper. As one chopper was loaded, it would take off to make room for the one coming in behind.

I walked along the ground until I was standing in front of the nearest chopper, looking up at the pilot and co-pilot. Their helmet-covered heads were moving back and forth, their sunglassed eyes alternating between their instruments and the men loading. At a signal from the crew chief, the pilots increased the speed of the blades, their eyes looking over the path of probable flight. The co-pilot stared at me for a moment. We briefly studied each other. I was squatting on one knee, smoking a cigarette and balancing my M-16 against my body. I envied him his job, sitting day after day in a graceful machine that magnified his body movements into the proportions of flight. We depended on him for food, ammo, protection, for lifting out our wounded and our dead. Yes, his danger was great. He presented a prime target. But he and his machine were one. If I should be married to any machine, let it be a flying machine.

Did he envy me? I doubted it. Who would walk when they could fly?

He nodded a greeting which I returned with a wave.

The pilot's mechanical body roared free of the earth, moving up and forward over me. I squinted to keep out the dirt from the powerful blade wash. The sound dwindled as the chopper moved out over the lake to climb into a holding pattern. God, how I wished I could fly!

19 December 1967

We were sitting in the sun, basking, shooting the bull, writing letters and whatnot, just enjoying the beauty of the day, when I received a call from Captain Sells. He asked if a lot of fishing boats were out on the lake. I replied in the affirmative. The villagers were evidently taking advantage of the weather to get in some fishing. He said that that was good because an MI team was going to fly out later to conduct an operational sweep of all the dinks on the lake. We should be ready.

The single chopper came from the direction of Thunder Mountain where the CP was located. Rueto hollered to pop smoke. A couple of the men stopped traffic while the pilot brought it in.

My old friend from the mission into the village next to the lake conducted on the last day of our earlier bridge-guarding duty, the mysterious field agent, jumped out followed by his equally mysterious helper, the Chou-Hoi, Fouel. The chopper took off and headed back home while the agent and I shook hands. Our last time together we had had good results.

The agent said that his Chou-Hoi, Fouel, in snooping around the villages in the area, had learned that a lot of the fishermen on the lake were in fact Vietcong guerrillas. The guerrillas were in the process of resupplying the different VC units in the area with the fish caught and the rice the villagers had stored.

I called my sergeant and squad leaders together to give them the layout of the plan the agent and I had devised. The agent had two gunships laid on to arrive in about thirty minutes. Their job would be to drive all of the boats toward us into the little cove formed by the bend in the road. The platoon would fan out along the road to corral all of the dinks as they reached shore. In order not to arouse the suspicions of the fishermen, everyone was to stay at his regular location until the gunships arrived. The traffic would be allowed to move until the dinks were driven ashore.

Everyone was tense. They checked their ammo, hooked grenades to their web gear, looked for their steel pots, and gave a last-minute check to their weapons. This would be a perfect operation. All we had to do was stand along our own perimeter and collect the guerrillas as they landed on shore.

As the agent and I were discussing the operation, someone let out a loud roar. Fouel had wandered down to the south bunker where he was not recognized. When the men sitting around the bunker noticed a dink in black pajamas and carrying an M-1 rifle nosing around their bunker, they almost shot him.

Rueto hollered down the road that the gunships had called and would be there in a few minutes. The agent ran up the road to get on the horn. He explained to the chopper crews what their job was as I told my men to get ready.

Two small air force-type observation helicopters zoomed low around the bend to sweep out over the lake. They were not the big gunships we were used to seeing, but they carried some kind of machine gun arrangement. They started at the far end of the lake, spraying the water with bullets as the choppers buzzed like gigantic mosquitoes back and forth across the lake, forcing the boats in our direction.

The boats were dugouts holding three or four people each. Most of the dinks got the message quickly and started paddling toward where our platoon was lined up on the bend in the road. Three boats tried to go the other way, the men paddling like crazy for the opposite shore. The gunships riddled one of the boats, sinking it. One made the far shore, and one turned back in our direction.

The gunships were very thorough. Their machine guns swept like a sickle across the water as the choppers darted past each other driving the boats. Occasionally, a stream of bullets would come dangerously close to any boat that lagged behind.

The little cove was soon covered with thirty or thirty-five boats bobbing gently on the small waves of the lake. The people in them stared at us, lined up along the road and beach with our weapons trained on them. The fishermen were dressed in traditional native garb of black pajamas, some of them bare to the waist. Some clung tightly to the sides of their boats, staring at us, the hate in their faces almost a force. Others showed no emotion at all.

Fouel was eager to start. He waded into the water to grab at one boat to pull it into the rocky shore. With his rifle he poked the first boatload out onto the rocks and proceeded to interrogate them. His method was to slap one of them around a bit, questioning him in rapid Vietnamese. Satisfied as to his identity, Fouel would shove him into the group of innocents or into the group he considered Vietcong. Then he would wave his rifle at another boatload and repeat the process.

We were surprised at the large number of guerrillas he was finding. Fouel had once been a guerrilla in this area and seemed to recognize many of the Cong. Whenever he spotted one he knew, he would yell out, become very agitated, and strike the person with his rifle butt. The dink who was hit always threw himself on the ground, crying out a long lament while he held his hands around his head for protection. Fouel never smiled. As each guerrilla was pushed into the group, one of my men pulled the shirt down from around his shoulders to check for callouses.

As each boat was unloaded, the men would search through it to see if they could find anything incriminating. There was nothing in any of the boats except for the usual fisherman's equipment—line, hooks, nets, and bait. Sometimes there might be a small tin box with tobacco or betel nuts, but that was all. The guerrillas would long since have thrown all weapons overboard anyway.

The choppers radioed us good luck as they sped back to their base after one more low pass over us.

It took two hours to empty the boats. The guerrilla group was squatting down with their hands across their knees, staring morosely at us and at Fouel as he relentlessly went through the other group again, checking and rechecking to make sure no guerrillas had slipped by. All of the villagers were silent except for an occasional word spoken in answer to a question from Fouel.

Fouel was finally satisfied. To those in the group who were supposed to be regular villagers, Fouel gave a speech. We couldn't tell what it was about exactly, but the drift was clear—if they were again caught harboring the enemy, they would be severely punished. As an example, he went over and stomped a hole in the bottom of one of the boats, threw a couple of heavy rocks into it, and sank it. The owner of the boat screamed in dismay, but stopped when Fouel went over to him.

When Fouel screamed and motioned them into their boats, the people silently passed by him until all of the boats were occupied, then paddled quickly to their village on the other side of the lake.

We looked over our group of guerrillas; there were eighteen. Soon a jeep and a duece-and-a-half drove down the road from the north, stopping next to the prisoners. A dozen Vietnamese soldiers jumped down, laughing with anticipation, arrogant as hell, kicking the Cong up into the back end of the truck and pushing them around just for the hell of it. I didn't like them, the lazy bastards. Why weren't they out on patrol instead of us.

The ARVN officer in the jeep congratulated us on the capture of the guerrillas. He said they were well known in the area as part of a larger force that specialized in land mines and early-morning ambushes.

I told him sarcastically, I hoped, how pleased we were to be of such service to his country, and that anytime he needed help, just give us a call.

As Fouel and the agent boarded the jeep and the little procession hurried back before dark, I looked at the sunken boat. That boat had taken a lot of hours to make. It was a shame to sink it.

20 December 1967

Captain Sells called on the horn. He said a chopper would be landing in a few minutes to take me back to base camp. It turned out the battalion commander had given me a three-day pass as a reward for capturing the Russian mortars. Unfortunately, a day and a half was already gone, but if I could catch a ride on an airplane back at the base camp, I could get one night in the main base camp at Pleiku.

Elated at the news, I ran around collecting my pack and rifle and hurriedly told my men of my good fortune. I gave Schaldenbrand command of the platoon just as the chow chopper landed. I jumped on board and the pilot immediately took off. He landed back at the base camp where I reported to the first sergeant, who had a jeep laid on to drive me around to the airstrip.

I hitched a ride on a C-123 to Pleiku. At Pleiku I hitched a ride in a deuce-and-a-half that was going across town to the main camp, where I would stay the night. I studied the town as the driver crept through the traffic.

Pleiku belonged in the Dark Ages. I had been patrolling through the farming and fishing villages. Those people were alive in their quaint hootches with dirt floors and woven grass sides and roofs. The people in this town looked depraved by comparison. I saw them as in a stop-frame of life: a toothless, black-gummed woman, a naked baby crawling in the gutter, prostitutes of all descriptions, filthy stands selling black market goods. Beggars everywhere. Babies barely old enough to walk were smoking cigarettes. God! How could people live like this?

Out of the downtown area on the road from Pleiku to the main base camp some of the people were different. These were the lucky Vietnamese who had well-paying jobs in the camp. They were better dressed and better fed than those who had been on the road between the airport and in Pleiku.

Off to the side of the road was a gigantic dump. Hundreds of Vietnamese crawled over it. The driver explained that the dump was the one the Americans had built, and the dinks, or gooks as he called them, rooted through it every day for items they thought were important. Plastic, cans, magazines, you name it. Many Vietnamese were carrying suitcases that looked as if they had been covered with stickers from American products. It turned out the Vietnamese took all the beer cans, oil cans, and other cans to their homes and shops. They would then cut them open, hammer them flat, solder them into large sheets of tin, and then fold them into the shape of trunks, suitcases, or boxes.

When we arrived inside the camp I checked in with brigade headquarters and went immediately to the PX. After a turn around the PX and mailing home two Christmas gifts, I walked back to brigade headquarters to find a place to eat. Rounding a corner of one hootch I came upon a sight hard to believe. A gigantic American house trailer was set majestically in an open space, complete with grass and ground rock walks. Electricity ran to it.

Through the windows, I could see an electric stove, a dishwasher, a living room, and a bedroom. I would have looked in the bathroom had I been tall enough. A nameplate stated that a general lived there.

A sergeant at headquarters told me that if I hurried, I could catch the movies that were shown nightly at the Officers' Club. After the general's house trailer, I expected something grand. It wasn't. It was just the Officer's Club that was used by the infantry. It was a wood and tent affair that had been built by fitting two regular barracks hootches together.

The bartender said he didn't have any beer or mixer. After ordering whiskey, I looked around to see if there was anyone I recognized. The club was pretty vacant and looking the group over didn't take long. There was only one officer my age, but he was sitting with an older man who was gesturing as he told some sort of story. The other men sat by themselves or in small groups. The solitary men just seemed to be sitting there in order to drink and smoke, lost in their own thoughts. They didn't want company but I wanted companionship, so I tried to strike up a conversation with a couple of them. I received noncommittal grunts from them, discouraging any further attempts at friendship on my part. This club was not a place of entertainment for them but a place of refuge. They were old career men and it was almost Christmas and they were facing the prospect of spending their holiday with their mute surrogate family—the mother, father, wife, and child of their lives, the army.

I had made a mistake in coming to this Officers' Club. I should have searched further for one of the clubs where the men were alive, the music loud, and the behavior rowdy. This was a select club belonging to those few men who had nothing but the military life to sustain them; I was an intruder.

I thought about leaving, then decided to hell with it. The bartender was setting up the film for the night's picture so I bought three drinks and found a chair close to the screen. The club didn't have a movie to show but they had three hour-long T.V. shows that had been canned without the advertisements and sold to the army. I watched "Combat," "Gunsmoke," and "Bonanza." What better fare for a group of soldiers?

Around midnight I was feeling no pain. The shows ended and the bartender was anxious to get rid of us. I stood outside under a starry sky for a while getting my bearings and wondering if I could find another club still open. There were no lights but the stars provided enough light to see by.

One of the men drove his jeep into a deep ditch when he missed the drive out onto the road. He cursed as he drunkenly tried to change gears fast enough to rock it out, but to no avail. The jeep was stuck proper.

I decided to see if he needed help. I walked over to stand on the culvert so I could see better while I smoked a cigarette. He finally noticed me.

His voice was sad and slightly drunk.

"Hey! Ain't you that lieutenant that was in the club tonight?"

"Yes, sir."

"Saw you were alone. I wondered what you were doing here. You just get out of the field?"

"This is my only night of a three-day pass from the field. I was kind of hoping for more, but it was O.K. I guess. At least I enjoyed the films, but I would have liked beer better."

He put his foot up on the dash to support himself better against the downward leaning jeep.

"I've been in the army over thirty years. This is my third war. In World War II I was an enlisted man, but now I'm a major. The army is my life. This is your first war, but don't let this fucking country ruin your perspective. The people aren't all that bad, they just don't care."

He was fairly drunk and felt like talking so I lit us up a couple of cigarettes and listened. "The army life is a good one. Why, hell, I've got friends all over the world. Once you make a friend in the army, you're bound to run across him again if you stay in long enough. The only trouble is that people don't appreciate you after the fighting is over. I know, I've been through it before. When the war gets over the people don't give a shit for you anymore. Just be there to die for them when the next one starts, that's all they care about. In between, a soldier is just an embarrassment to them. Like a fucking pregnant daughter in the family with no husband. Someone to hide and make excuses for until the bastard kid grows up to prove himself. Yeah, that's the army. Something that's fun to fuck but nothing you'd want to marry. That's me, an old bastard that's been fucked over so many times, the only one who still loves me is my family, the army, and they won't love me if I don't get this jeep out of this ditch. I borrowed it from the chaplain."

"You mean that's the chaplain's jeep?"

"Yep, probably even has a cross in here somewhere," he rambled around in the back seat.

"I hear some troops coming, sir. From the sound of them they may be drunk, but I'll get them to help."

"Young punks, they don't give a shit either. The army isn't what it used to be, lieutenant, no respect."

"Well, I'll see if I can talk them into it anyway. . . . Hey, you guys! Can you help us get this jeep out of this ditch?"

There were about eight of them, singing and walking drunkenly down the road. They stopped at the sound of my voice.

"Hey, who's there?" one of them yelled.

"No, you fucker, it's 'Who goes there?' " one of his friends said.

"It's the chaplain," I replied. "Can't you see the cross on the plate in front?"

"Oh, yeah, I see it now." One of the guys stumbled forward to stare at the bumper. "Hey, you guys, it's a chaplain and his assistant."

I cringed at that, but I decided to be a smartass. "Yes, the chaplain and I were coming back from a late service when some drunk officers came out of the club and forced us into the ditch."

"Fucking officers. No offense, chaplain, but that's just like a fucking officer." They all chimed in, "Yeah, bet you they came out of that lifer's club."

"Fucking lifers."

"I bet my captain was one of them."

I couldn't see them but I imagined the major's knuckles were turning white from where he was gripping the steering wheel at hearing this blasphemy.

The major outdid himself by jumping up and practically falling. "That's enough, sinners! The Lord has a place in Heaven for lifers, too."

"Yeah," someone snickered. "He calls it the army."

They all laughed like crazy at that one.

"Come on, you guys, help us out of here," I implored.

They all rushed behind the jeep and to its side, yelling encouragements to each other. The major got the jeep started and let out the clutch with a vengence. With all of us pushing, the jeep shot up out of the ditch to run madly across the road, with the major's drunken foot on the accelerator, into the equally deep ditch on the other side. The motor ground to a halt.

The major turned to me with a bloody nose as I ran across the road. He was pissed.

"Now, chaplain, you just hold on and we'll have you out of here in nothing flat." I didn't want him to explode yet. He was still stuck.

The fire from his eyes looked anything but angelic as he stared ahead with both hands tightly gripping the wheel.

The men stumbled over to our new location and started to push as the major started the engine again.

This time he was ready. He slammed on the brakes before hurtling into the other ditch again. When I saw he had the jeep under control, I thanked the men and told them they would be in my prayers that night. They staggered on down the road.

"Well, sir, there you are."

"Did you hear those snots? They called me a lifer. I've got half a notion to get their names for insubordination."

"That's no way for a chaplain to act, sir. Besides, they were doing the Lord's work. You aren't in the ditch anymore."

"No, I'm not, am I? Jesus! My nose hurts, though. You think they did that on purpose?"

"Now, all they did was push. You ran it in the ditch."

"Yeah, I guess you're right. The hell with it. You want a ride?"

"No, I'm going to walk back. It's a pretty night."

"Well, O.K., but remember—the army isn't bad. It's only Christmas and I always get lonely on Christmas, you understand?"

"Yeah, I understand. You want a cigarette to get back to your hootch on?"

"No thanks, its not far."

It was a beautiful night and I enjoyed the walk back. Out of curiosity I walked by the general's house trailer. It was lit up and I could hear soft music. Damn, he had it nice!

It was cold in the Central Highlands at night. The cot felt good. I laid my hand on my rifle to check if it was still by my bedside as I drifted off to sleep.

The next morning my head hurt and my tongue felt furry but I was in good enough shape to catch a deuce-and-a-half heading for the airport.

22 December 1967

Captain Sells called early to say that he wanted me to take a patrol south on Highway 1 for about five kilometers. I checked the map to find that we would travel out of my AO into Charlie Company's area. It seemed odd to leave our area, but I didn't question it.

I called Sergeant Marley and the squad leaders together to brief them on the patrol that day. I wanted as many men as possible to go. Only a few men would be needed to hold the bridge area while we were gone. We rarely got a chance to travel down roads on patrol, so we reviewed the procedures we would follow. Each man would be responsible for maintaining a proper interval from the man in front of him. We would travel in two lines, one line on each side of the road. Packs would be left behind, of course, and only web gear would be worn.

This would be Marley's first patrol as sergeant. Schaldenbrand had left me the day before. Schaldenbrand had survived his year in Vietnam. Twenty-two years old and he had finally gotten his sergeant's stripes after acting as platoon sergeant for so long. Before he left he bought a plastic sack of marihuana cigarettes from one of the dinks that peddled the stuff along the road. At that time a guy could buy three hundred joints for about five dollars or 500 P. Schaldenbrand thought he could sell them for a dollar apiece back in Philly. He opened a whole carton of cigarettes and emptied the American cigarettes. He then refilled the whole carton with his special cigarettes. He had packages of cigarettes in every pocket and had visions of making close to five hundred dollars back in the States. I asked him if he was worried about getting caught, but Shelly wasn't concerned. After a year of combat, sneaking five hundred joints back into the States didn't have him worried.

Delk had also completed his tour and was going home.

As usual, I had mixed feelings about losing my old-timers. I was glad they had made it and were going home, but I hated to lose their experience.

Now Shelly was gone. His advice had helped me over many rough spots. I was going to miss him.

Marley was my new platoon sergeant. He had been a team leader when I had taken over the platoon. From Utah, he was a good man and Schaldenbrand thought Marley would make a good sergeant for me. Marley was only a corporal, and had been in the Army only a little over a year, but I felt confident in his abilities. I reshuffled my men, making Villasenor and McCovey squad leaders.

This patrol would be a good chance to see these men in their new positions. I told them to get the men lined up and ready to move out. They checked the men's equipment and reported everything was O.K.

I yelled "move out," and led the point south around the bend in the road. About one klick ahead of us on the east side of the road on a little hill was a camp of about six hundred dink soldiers being trained by an American Special Forces group. We never had any contact with these men. The camp was off-limits to us, and the Special Forces thought they were a cut above us amateurs so they never came down for a visit. We occasionally saw them moving up there against the sky, but this patrol would be the closest we had ever been to them. We would go right by the bottom of the hill where their camp sat.

The road curved under a railroad bridge before climbing steadily uphill past the camp to a short pass acting as a portal to a small plateau. As we approached the camp I looked up to see a group of dinks looking down at us. They were laughing and pointing at us as they waved to their buddies to come for a look-see.

The top of the flat hill was only about fifty feet above us where the road cut through the growth. We could see their faces clearly and they were making fun of us. We couldn't understand why they would do that. We were determined to show them how a real infantry platoon moved on a road patrol. The smart-ass bastards!

I looked back down the road to check my men. They were all aware of the watching camp by now. My platoon looked perfect in their order of march: five meters between men and staggered opposite the men on the other side of the road.

This camp represented what we were always bitching about. These dinks had been in that camp many months supplied with American arms, clothes, and food, but they never went out on any patrols. They never fought. We patrolled all the time, set ambushes, got into firefights. All the while those bastards sat on their smug asses up on that hill. We didn't understand it.

The point element and I had just passed the intersection with the road that led up to the main gate of the camp when automatic rifle fire cracked over our heads. We dived into the ditches, sprawling in the mud while twisting around to prepare for defense. After the initial burst of gunfire, there was silence. We frantically searched in all directions with our eyes trying to find the enemy. Laughter sounded from the camp above us. I crawled out on the road to get a better look up at the camp.

A number of dinks were standing by the edge of the camp, laughing and pointing at us. One of them saw us looking up at them. He pantomimed pointing his rifle above our heads and firing. They were making fun of us!

We cautiously stood up, perplexed at their motives. We cussed back at them. Some of my men wanted to fire back. I told them no, it wouldn't prove anything. We would go on with our patrol and ignore them.

I turned my back on the camp above us and started marching, seething with hatred. Those fucking dink sons-of-bitches. Those fucking shots had been right above our heads. I had been shot at enough to know! Why, why, why? They were our allies and yet they had mocked us. We had never done anything to them. Why, hell, they never even left their camp, and where were the Special Forces assholes? Surely they would have questioned the meaning of the gunshots, but they had never appeared on the scene. I looked back at the camp as I topped the pass. The dinks were still standing there, watching the rest of the platoon pass on the road below them.

Maybe the people in Nam are worth saving, but their army isn't worth shit, I thought.

The road wound leisurely over the plateau passing by clusters of hootches next to the road. Some of the hootches had open storefronts with their wares showing to entice any prospective customers. One hootch I particularly remember had orange bottles of pop setting on a table out front. A toothless old woman in black pajamas sat on her haunches mixing up a batch of betel nuts in an old 20-mm shell casing. She smiled up at us with her betel-stained gums. Leaning in the doorway was an ARVN soldier dressed in the typical ARVN uniform of tightly pegged camouflage fatigues. His M-16 was leaning against the hootch wall. He smiled at us as we passed. His buddy, dressed in the same type of outfit, was lying in a hammock spread between two poles holding up the porch roof. His camouflage hat was pulled down over his forehead. A cigarette hung out of the corner of his mouth. His smile was insolent. He said something to his buddy in a harsh tone. His buddy stopped smiling at us, grabbed his rifle, and went into the hootch. The man in the hammock looked back at us with his insolent smile and put his hands behind his head as if to flaunt the fact he was resting while we were marching.

The son-of-a-bitch!

We reached the edge of the plateau. The road dropped gently down to the tidal flats that lay between the edge of the bend where the road ran and a low peninsula from the plateau running parallel to the road about a klick to the east. The tidal flat was about two klicks long. South, there was a small gap where the southern tip of the peninsula was separated from the land by a hundred meters, through which the ocean poured at high tide.

We could see the first bridge that Charlie Company was guarding on the road next to a small low island about five hundred meters from where we were. The men guarding the bridge watched us as we marched down the road toward them. The sight of another American sister unit was always a welcome relief from boredom.

When we reached the bridge I called Delta Six to tell him we had arrived at the farthest end of our patrol. I told him we would head back after a short rest.

I sat on the bridge railing watching the Vietnamese in the tidal flats. The tide had gone out, trapping a number of sea animals which made up the stable diet of the people along the coast. Women, kids, and old men gathered up the bounty, carrying baskets in the ankle-deep mud. A young man was sitting on the shore looking out over the villagers working in the mud. I wondered why he wasn't with them. I found out when he jumped up, balancing himself on a pair of crutches. His right leg was missing below the knee.

I remarked on it to one of the men guarding the bridge. He explained that the man had stepped on an old mine, blowing off his leg. No one was sure who had planted the mine, according to the villagers, but it had happened about five months ago.

He hobbled toward the road, planting the crutches and swinging his good leg in a pendulum motion as he moved awkwardly over the uneven ground. I felt sorry for him. I couldn't stand the thought of losing a limb, but losing a limb in a country like this would be the end of life itself, with no hospital and no artificial limbs and no livelihood. Well, it was a lick on him. Everybody around here supported the Vietcong.

I couldn't forget the look on his face as he passed by me. For the first time in my life I saw the look of total dispair. In a conflict of emotions, I got up from the bridge railing. My thoughts were whirling around in my brain. I couldn't sit as this one-legged man with his soul mirrored on his face passed by me. I had to stand to protect my own dignity. This man was trapped forever in a world I could not imagine and I could not belittle him in mine.

His image decreased in size as his black-clad body moved south toward the village.

23 December 1967

This evening we were sitting with the APC crew, singing songs. After a couple of hours Rueto decided to climb up the roadbed to cross over the road to the abandoned bunker to take a piss. He was about halfway across when bullets cracked around him, throwing sparks where they hit the road around his feet. I had been standing behind him and I heard the whines, close. We both dropped.

I looked up over the road to where Rueto was lying. His eyes were wide with excitement and fear. He pointed toward the flooded paddies to the northeast.

"Over there," his voice quivered.

He crawled rapidly toward me as more shots cracked over our heads and ricocheted off the road.

The shots had the same effect as kicking an anthill. All up and down the road men had rushed out of their bunkers and hootches to take up guard positions.

I instructed everyone to hold in position while I checked out the location of the gunshots, then radioed Delta Six.

The track crew was manning their powerful fifty-caliber machine gun. I told them to fire toward the area of the shots. The man in the cupola did this with gusto, raking the paddy and the area behind it. The ugly red tracers flew gracefully through the air to bury themselves in the ground or ricochet at strange angles into the sky.

The village was in a line behind the paddy. The fifty-caliber raked the earth farther and farther out, methodically sweeping the area until the bullets were flying into the village hootches three or four hundred meters away. I didn't give a thought to the village except to wonder if the dinks had come from there.

I told the gunner to stop firing, that I wanted to have a look-see. Rueto, another man, and I ran in a crouch across the road and tumbled down the other side, then stepped carefully through the concertina wire to the edge of the paddy.

The lake was to our right. The beach was only ten meters away. An empty hootch was to the right. I could see the top of the APC sticking above the road and my men at the side of the bridge.

In front of me was the flooded paddy containing some type of slender-stalked plant taller than our heads. I told the men on the bridge not to fire because we would be in that stuff and I didn't want them hitting us by mistake.

We crept forward in the boot-top water as we slowly penetrated the growth. We could hear movement to our front. We crouched forward, continuing our progress until we came to a small earthen dike. I stepped over the dike and continued forward. After seven or eight meters there was a thrashing in the water to my left, right next to me. I thought it was Rueto, but unknown to me Rueto and the other man had stopped at the dike and had lain across it. As it turned out, the dike was the home of an ant colony. Trapped on the dike by the rising water from the lake, the ants swarmed over them.

"What the hell is going on back there, Rueto?" Silence except for the splashing behind me. "Rueto?" I harshly whispered, "Rueto?"

"What, sir?" Rueto's voice sounded from the direction of the dam.

"What are you guys doing?"

They had settled down by now. "We got into a nest of ants on the dike."

"We? Are you both back there?"

"Yes, sir."

I immediately swung around in a low crouch because whoever was next to me was a dink, not an American. I couldn't fire, though. He was between me and the men on the bridge, too close.

The men on the bridge shouted over to ask if everything was alright. I was scared but I thought the dink wouldn't dare open fire. He had heard my voice on one side, and the voices of Rueto and the other man behind him, and the men on the bridge. I took a chance.

"Spagg and you guys on the bridge. The dink's in here with me. Can you see Rueto O.K.?"

"Yes, sir."

"I think we have this dink trapped. Don't fire at the reeds moving around because it might be me. I'm going to try to maneuver to a position where I can fire without hitting you."

I crept over to a small piece of ground to my left. I slowly stood up, straining my eyes into the growth looking for reed movement.

I thought I saw movement and fired as I dropped to the ground. Nothing fired back.

I crept back into the water toward the spot I had fired into. I reached the location but could find nothing. The reeds around me were like thin rod walls cutting me off from all contact. I stood silently, waiting for a sound to give him away. My heart was going a mile a minute from the closeness of death.

From a distance of three or four meters, a deafening sound of an automatic rifle opened up on me. The tracers zinged by, missing me by inches. I dropped flat into the water. Luckily he had only guessed where I was.

Then he splashed through the water and reeds to the north. I ran after him and the men on the bridge were firing, firing uncomfortably close to me. I exited the other side of the reeds to face a dry paddy with a taller dam running across the end. He was gone.

Early the next morning I took a couple of men over to explore the paddies. We found only a spider hole dug into the larger dry dam. It had paper wrappers in the bottom and shell casings were lying around the outside. It was evident he had made his home there. He had waited until dark, a target had presented itself on the road, and then he had opened up.

We went back to the road for a breakfast of C rations and to wait for the mine-clearing crew that would be along in a couple of hours.

True to routine, the mine-sweeping crew arrived on schedule at a walk—three men swinging their equipment back and forth in front of them as they walked quickly toward us. A small caravan had built up behind them hoping to gain extra minutes on the road to their destination.

They had just passed by the village when a group of distraught villagers ran out of the village. In their midst was a teenage girl with blood all over the upper part of her body.

The mine-sweeping crew stopped at this unexpected interruption. The villagers were strung out in a ragged line from the village with the headman and his group on the road. They were gesturing wildly, pointing down the road at us and offering up the girl as evidence of something we had done.

We had gathered on the bridge, wondering what the hell was going on. I decided to take a few of my men up the road to find out.

The mine crew watched us approach as though we were lepers. The crew, part of the convoy, and the villagers were all milling around the girl who, it turned out, had been hit with one of the fifty-caliber bullets the night before.

We stood apart.

One of the mine sweepers asked what the fuck we were doing firing into a dink village. I hotly replied that it was just tough shit the girl got hit. They should have been in their bunkers, and besides, they were friendly to the guerrillas who had fired on us last night.

One of the mine crew yelled to me to call in a dustoff and I replied that they could call in their own dustoff, which they did.

Their good deed done, the mine-sweeping crew swept by us. Both sides exchanged stony looks, each glad to be rid of the other.

It makes a lot of difference where you sleep. The mine crew could see only the girl—she wasn't badly wounded—but we remembered the night before.

SECTION 4

North
to Tam Ky

North
to Tam Ky

30 December 1967

The Eleventh Brigade arrived from Hawaii to replace us in the area. The Eleventh was new-in-country, so when the bridge replacement platoon began to set up I tried to explain how things were to the new lieutenant. But there would never be enough time to explain.

Our battalion flew north to Chu Lai further up the coast, a tough area made tougher by the oncoming Tet offensive, although we didn't know that at the time.

Chu Lai was a free-fire zone. I was instructed to shoot at everything not American, ROK, or ARVN. The brutal war of the highlands had come to the flat farm ground of the South China Sea coast.

We made a combat assault into a hot LZ. The area was deserted of villagers and the terrain was the most wartorn I had seen. A steady drizzle fell from low clouds, heightening the scene of destruction and desolation.

It was as if a stage had been set for war and all acts played except the last.

Captain Sells led us across a low, wide hill with scattered thin pines. At the bottom of the hill we saw a number of lakes on the east side of a long earthen dike which protected a very large series of rice paddies on the west. The lakes were interconnected by canals. It looked like it once was an orderly arrangement of some type of plantation, but it had long since fallen into disrepair. The whole area was flooded and abandoned.

On our side of the dike the villages were all vacant. We saw no sign of human existence other than the inanimate objects left behind. There was a large village to our left, but there was no one there. A trail ran down to the dike to intersect a trail running along the edge of the lakes and rice paddies. Another trail led from the village. We stood at the intersection, obviously a major point on anyone's travels through the area. The dike was the only connecting link between the two land masses for klicks in either direction.

To the west of the intersection the trail ran along the edge of the rice paddies, passing a large red brick schoolhouse. By some quirk of fate it had remained standing even though a bomb had passed through the roof and ceiling to explode at ground level. All of the windows were blown out. The doors were gone, parts of the walls were blown away. Some of the two-by-fours holding the ceiling were still in place and sections of the tiles on the roof were intact.

The building had been built by the French. Like all of the French buildings, this one had been well built, functional in a pretty sort of way with its red brick and orange tile. I called it a school because it reminded me of a one-room schoolhouse that had been on a corner of our farm in Indiana.

Captain Sells decided we would set up a perimeter around the school for the night. My CP group and I entered the building through a hole in one wall. We looked up to determine which section of the roof was large enough to give us protection from the rain. We decided to settle down against the far wall, only two-thirds of which was still standing. It didn't offer much protection from the rain, but for some reason it felt good to be in a building again.

Four-six was a little farther down the trail from us, set up in bushes on the edge of the rice paddy. One of the little dikes ran right up to his position and a dink squad was following that right toward his position.

Captain Sells told Four-six to wait until the dinks got closer and then to order them to surrender.

It was not to be. The dink acting as point man spotted something he didn't like and fired into Four-six's position with a Thompson. Four-six's men opened up on the squad, killing the dink with the Thompson submachine gun and wounding a few others; the survivors ran back across the paddy. Four-six's men ran out to the dink they had killed to retrieve his weapon. They didn't find any more bodies, but they did report a couple of heavy blood trails.

My platoon turned its attention to setting up a defensive perimeter around the schoolhouse.

Spagg had set his gun up to cover the large dike. He and one of his men had crawled out on the dike to set up a ground flare with a trip wire. If any dink used that dike in the night and stumbled across that trip wire, he would be cut to ribbons by the bullets from Spagg's M-60. In a situation set up like that, the men on duty would start firing at the instant the flare went off. Since the gun was already set on that position, the gunner only had to pull the trigger to get a kill.

I ate a miserable cold meal of C rations and then smoked until dark. I thought about the area we had been lifted into. It had once been a very prosperous area, I surmised, with its large fields of rice and many French buildings. A lot of work had been done to the land at one time. Now only the Vietnamese used it, and not very effectively.

Of course, this far north the people were always in conflict. The protection offered the people was not very good down south in the delta, but it was better than in the north. The government agents didn't last at all out in the field. The local Vietcong cadre were strong in the north. They executed out of hand any troublesome government village chiefs, policemen, and soldiers they caught. It was a sorry business in a sorry land.

I leaned back against the wall trying to figure out why I felt depressed. Everything that had happened that day would not have done it—that was part of the job. *It must be the strange area coupled with the dreary rain,* I thought. How about my new replacements? These young men I was responsible for. Would they leave the field alive or dead or wounded? I thought of the other men who had been with me.

I drifted off to a fitful sleep. The wind was noisily blowing through the trees, driving the rain into every corner of dryness. Sometime later a bright light shattered the dark pool of night. In the course of a split second the rugged explosive sound of Spagg's M-60 focused my eyes on the brightness of red tracers spreading in a narrow beam from the gun's position in front of me to the brilliant flare burning furiously on the dike.

The white light was outlining a macabre scene of restless shadows of trees and bushes moved by the wind and the figure of a man who was outlined for an instant in a grotesque ending of life at the end of our beam of power. The rain added a surrealist tint to the vision of reality.

"How many, Spagg?" I called.

"That was it, sir."

"Good job. Keep an eye out for any more dinks crossing tonight. Tomorrow morning, go check out the body."

I slept without interruption for the rest of the night.

3 January 1968

Captain Sells split the company into platoons and assigned each one of us an area in which to set up ambushes for the first part of the day. My platoon received the easy duty of guarding the intersection next to our camp.

When the rest of the company moved out after breakfast, I placed my men, putting one squad down the trail twenty or thirty meters from the schoolhouse. They were to hide in the growth on one side of the trail. The rest of the platoon would remain at the intersection with me in a small grass and mud hut with three walls, in a relatively thick clump of bushes and small trees. The area all around the inter-section was free from thick growth. We would be able to spot anyone coming toward us.

It had stopped raining, but the day was still overcast.

Spagg and I sat talking about farming and our future. He guessed he would be going back to the farm. I had received notice that my application for Army Flight School had been approved. I was pleased about that! Assured now that I would be a pilot, I also felt I had a future with the army. As soon as my tour in Nam was over, I would report to Flight School.

As we talked and smoked, we kept an eye on the terrain around us.

Spagg touched my shoulder and pointed. We fell silent and all of us shifted into firing positions. I was standing, peering through the veil of brush in front of me at a group of seven dinks coming toward us.

Two boys, twelve to fifteen years old, were in front of two old men and three middle-aged women.

Goddamn! Thoughts rushed through my mind as I tried to decide what to do.

Women, old men, and kids. Obviously noncombats.

But this is a free-fire zone. There are not supposed to be civilians in this area.

Yeah, but dinks occasionally ignore those warnings about free-fire areas.

Maybe they are the point element for Vietcong or NVA traveling behind them. Maybe they're supposed to give the warning if stopped. It's happened before.

In that case, some of my men could come under fire and be killed or wounded.

Four-six killed that one dink last evening and he had a Thompson. There was a whole squad of Cong in that group.

There was some incoming fire when we made the LZ.

A dink tried to cross the dike last night.

These people look innocent enough.

They may be carrying supplies for the Cong in the area, food and/or ammo.

It's a free-fire zone. Everyone is to be considered the enemy.

I'm responsible for my men. They'll get killed if I make the wrong decision.

These dinks coming toward us mean nothing to me; my men mean everything. What if the dinks aren't innocent? My men depend on me to keep them alive.

I spoke softly to the men around me. "It's a lick on them. When I give the order, open fire." I brought the M-16 up to sight in on the dinks.

Spagg was standing to my right, his M-60 machine gun supported on his hip by a sling around his neck and shoulder. He reached over and touched my arm. His whispered voice reflected the agony of doubt in his face. "No! Sir, you can't! Kids, women," he motioned toward the file of people coming toward us.

I felt ashamed. Spagg was right.

"Wait one," I whispered to the men around me. "I'll call for them to surrender."

I felt relieved. Capturing them was the best solution. If they were the point for a VC group, I would just make sure none of us was exposed to fire when we captured this point.

The dinks were almost to the intersection.

I stepped through the brush with some of my men. *"Dung lui, dung lui,"* I warned. They were only ten to twenty meters from us.

They all glanced at us standing with our weapons trained on them. We had them dead to rights. They had no cover and no place to run to. A perfect capture situation.

Almost in midstride they all moved with astonishing speed. The two boys in the point split up. The front one ran past us, heading down the trail past the schoolhouse. The other boy, the women, and the old men started running back toward the bridge.

"Stop! Stop! *Dung lui, dung lui,"* I yelled to no avail.

I could not order the men to run after them. It could be a trap. Neither could I let them get away. Why were they running?

In the split second those thoughts ran across my consciousness, I gave the order to open fire.

An irrevocable wave of death swept in front of us.

After the initial burst of gunfire, I yelled, "Cease fire."

Two women survived long enough to cross the bridge and enter one of the hootches. Three of my men crossed over the bridge and threw grenades in the hootches.

We hurriedly looked over the bodies on the trail since they were lying in the open and we had no desire to be caught exposed. The men reported that some of the dead had been carrying hand grenades and ammo in their packs. I felt somewhat relieved. Those supplies could not have been for anyone but the Cong.

I received a report from the squad down the trail. The firing had alerted them barely fast enough to fire at the teenager running toward them down the trail. Someone hit him in the shoulder and knocked him down. Surprisingly, the boy had jumped up and run past the squad to safety somewhere in the brush.

I had no pleasure in reporting to Delta Six that we had killed six dinks and wounded one. I knew he would ask how many weapons we had captured. I stared at the grey horizon a long time before answering that the dinks were not carrying weapons, only supplies and grenades.

I felt low. This putrid war! I thought of so many ways I could have done it differently. So easy to think afterward. After all, now I knew there was no dink squad behind on the trail. This episode would be the darkest of my career.

I called my men together for a march up the slight hill to Delta Six's position, forcing the dinks out of my mind.

4 January 1968

Delta Six put the company on line to traverse a large area criss-crossed by hedgerows, jungle, hootches, villages, trails, streams, and other obstacles. The day was overcast but the high clouds seemed to indicate a dry day.

It was difficult to maintain control moving through terrain like this. The maze caused us to become separated and some fell far behind. I urged the men to keep in sight.

The squad leaders were doing their best to keep marching order, but the growth was too lush and the trails through and around the villages and hootches funneled groups of men through small areas while other groups fought their way through thick growth.

There were tunnels everywhere. The purpose of the sweep was to flush dinks out ahead of us, but it was obvious to all that the dinks were hiding in those damn tunnels. Every time we passed the entrance to a tunnel, someone would throw a hand grenade into it. Cries of "Fire in the Hole" rang out all around the area.

What with all of the starting and stopping, the platoon was barely maintaining its integrity.

My RTO and I split up to cover both sides of a cluster of hootches. Doc went with Rueto while I inspected a narrow trail leading off in the direction I wanted to go. When I got to the other side of the cluster of hootches, a thick hedge separated me from Rueto and Doc.

I called over to Rueto and Doc to continue walking. We would connect up at the end of the hedgerow which I figured only ran for twenty or thirty meters. The farther I traveled down the trail, the

more concerned I became. The hedgerow had developed other hedgerows. Rueto and Doc were moving at an angle away from me. I didn't
want to get separated from my radio, but every step forward was
taking me farther from it. I glanced back; no chance. Surely the next
bend in the trail would connect me up with my men.

I was now moving through enemy territory alone. Rueto and Doc
were ahead and to my left quite a way. The rest of the platoon had
moved far ahead of us. The growth had blocked everyone from view.
I hurried to catch up. I glanced at my watch. Only three or four
minutes had passed since Rueto, Doc, and I had headed around that
hootch in opposite directions.

The trail rounded a bend where an open area off the trail on the
right side contained a hootch, an old bunker, and more hedgerows.
I kept on the trail for a second, then decided to hell with it. That
bunker looked too enticing to pass up. I was already behind so a few
more seconds to throw a grenade in the bunker wouldn't hurt.

As I stepped off the trail toward the bunker and started to unhook
a hand grenade, out of the corner of my eye I noticed movement.
Reflexes took over. I dived to the other side of the shoulder-high dirt
hill covering the bunker. The cracking sound of bullets ripped the air
next to me as an automatic weapon fired in a descending arc until the
bullets tore into the dirt bunker. I crawled quickly around to the other
side of the bunker while bringing my M-16 up into firing position.

There was no time to plan anything. I knew I couldn't stay in one
spot, so I was still crawling with the idea of fighting back fast and
hard. I jumped to my feet in a crouch, facing in the direction I thought
the dink would be. I squeezed the trigger on full automatic but missed
him as he dived behind a well next to a ridge of dirt beside a trench.

I had gotten a quick glimpse of him, enough to answer my question
about the sound of the gun. He was dressed in green fatigues, had on
web gear, and was carrying a Thompson submachine gun.

He was stocky too, unlike most of the soldiers we had run across.

As these thoughts were rushing through my mind I was back-
peddling toward the hootch with the idea of running around the other
side to take the dink under fire.

The few seconds I was in the open allowed the son-of-a-bitch the
opportunity to open fire on me again. I threw myself sideways through

the door of the hootch, landing heavily on my right side. I was frightened. One of the rounds in the last burst he had fired had been a tracer. It had seemed to come so slowly, yet it was traveling a couple of thousand feet per second.

I was not in control of this fight. I had been on the defensive since stepping into the clearing—and I still was.

After falling to the floor of the hootch I quickly pushed myself back up to lunge out the door. The hootch was a death trap and I wanted out. My M-16 fired about three rounds and jammed before I had taken two steps. The dink had run from his hiding place by the well and trench to the bunker as I exited the hootch. He fired at me as I hustled back into the hootch, cursing the M-16.

Mere words cannot describe my will to live at that moment, my fear of dying, or my frustration. I was about to be shot down in a stinking dink hootch because my M-16 had jammed. How stupid to have gotten myself into this mess!

Without stopping my momentum, I continued on across the hootch in desperation to crash through the opposite wall. The wall was very weak where I hit it, exploding outward and causing me to sprawl on the ground outside.

I shrugged out of the rucksack I had unconsciously been carrying throughout the fight and groped for a triangle bayonet I had taken from the rifle of a dink I had killed some time before. An explosion in the hootch warned me the dink had thrown in a grenade to finish me off.

Sweat covered my body and I was gut-scared. My heart was pounding, on a rampage. I left the rucksack and the useless M-16 on the ground as I ran toward the corner of the hootch and around it, thinking I could surprise the dink before he had time to react. I had no other hope.

He was in front of the hootch with his back to me as he approached the door of the hootch.

I ran toward him and he heard me, starting to turn just as I ran into him. We both stayed on our feet and stumbled forward a few steps.

I grabbed his fatigue shirt near the back of his neck with my left hand and jerked back on it as hard as I could while at the same time

I swung my right hand with the bayonet in a short vicious downstroke into the side of his neck. The bayonet was a long narrow one with a sharp point. It slid down into the base of his throat as I continued to pull him back and down.

He had thrown his Thompson away, using both hands to reach back frantically at me. He reached over his shoulder to grab the front of my fatigue jacket with one hand while the other hit me weakly on my side. A moment of pity for him was quickly replaced by a cold mental block. He was to be killed, period.

The bayonet was not sharp and would not cut sideways. I withdrew the blade and drove the point into his throat again. He was on the ground by now so it was easier. The bayonet had gone deep both times but the soldier was still alive. I wanted him dead but I didn't want him to suffer. Once more I drove the bayonet into his throat. He died.

I got up. I wanted out of there. I had never killed a man in that manner before. Where were my men? All of this goddamn firing and not one man had heard it. I retrieved my pack and rifle, shaking, tired, and disgusted with the war. I went through the dink's pockets.

In his billfold, protected by a plastic cover, was a picture of a woman with two children. His uniform indicated he was NVA. I wondered if his family in North Vietnam would ever know that he had been killed. Did the dinks report things like that to the families of dead soldiers?

For a brief moment I wondered what kind of person this soldier had been.

I threw his billfold and his Thompson down the well and staggered in a daze onto the trail. I had won.

5 January 1968

The company was lifted out to make a combat assault into what would probably be a hot LZ, near a village by the sea a little further north, in Tam Ky Province near Chu Lai. The Vietcong controlled the area. Our job, as usual, would be to search them out and kill them.

I sat in the door of the chopper observing the terrain below, swinging my feet back and forth above the skids.

The South China Sea was mostly to the east of us, although the crooked coastline waved back and forth, sometimes placing us over land, sometimes over sea.

My concern was not with the flight but with the LZ. I leaned out to look ahead, hoping to catch a glimpse of the area.

The pilot started dropping rapidly. The door gunner hollered that we were coming in and started firing his M-60 at probable enemy positions. We leaned our weight forward with our feet on the skids. We heard incoming rounds.

The pilots of the choppers were going to land in a field next to a hedgerow lining the southeast side of the village. As the chopper settled, I could see that the village lay next to a large cove and was built up over a long, low sandy ridge that ran through the middle of the village.

Both door gunners were firing as we jumped off the skids and ran toward the hedgerow. Men were crouched along its edge looking for places to push through to a trail on the other side.

My platoon sergeant, Marley, the squad leaders, and I found places in the hedgerow where we pushed through to regroup on the other side. The dinks kept firing at us and the choppers.

Choppers were landing in a steady stream behind us, forcing us to go forward to make room. The lower end of the village was to our left. We moved across it until we formed a line.

Captain Sells joined us and gave the order to sweep forward up the sandy ridge to the village. The other platoons were scattered to the right of the line. Mine had the left side. We moved forward cautiously. The village was abandoned. Hootches were set haphazardly with footpaths running between all of them. There was no growth to speak of so it was easy to move steadily forward on line, rather like moving up a beach dotted with small shacks and tunnels everywhere.

A couple of the new men dropped down to explore a few of them, but hurriedly backed out after crawling into the pitch darkness. Men new-in-country were much more willing to crawl into tunnels. I never ordered anyone into one of those stinking holes, nor would I go in myself. Of course, I occasionally asked for volunteers but I never had any from the old-timers.

We were content on this sweep simply to drop explosives down. We probably never got anybody, but you never knew. Cries of "Fire in the Hole" sounded across the village, followed by muffled explosions.

We were sprayed with automatic rifle fire from many locations on our sweep, but each time the dinks would escape us. After an hour of fighting we reached the other end of the village.

Captain Sells called a break at the beach. The area was the most beautiful spot I had ever seen in Vietnam. The village was behind us and of course did not look too nice, but the land ran out on a wide grassy point into the sea to the east of us. The beach to our left was a beautiful sandy strip running in a wide curve in an almost perfect half-circle to the north. We could barely see the other side of the opposite point.

Big rows of sand dunes paralleled the beach, rising in height to seventy or eighty or a hundred feet before dropping back down to the level of the fields two or three hundred meters back from the shore. Tall skinny pine trees covered the dunes all around the cove.

Next to where I rested smoking a cigarette was a small enclosure fenced with short ornamental black iron stakes. In the middle of the fenced area was a stone structure a little taller than a man. On the side facing the sea was an enclosure with a religious figure inside looking toward the South China Sea. The gate in the iron fence was locked. Although the fence was only a couple of feet high, no one jumped it for a closer look at the figure.

If anyone had thought about it, Captain Sells reminded us that he would have any man's ass that he caught inside that fenced-in area.

All of us were sitting or standing on the slope above the beach when someone yelled to call our attention to two helicopters flying toward us over the land at a high rate of speed.

Five dinks suddenly broke loose from cover a hundred meters down the beach from us and frantically ran north along the beach away from us. Somehow the choppers had flushed the dinks. Why the dinks ran into the open none of us could guess, but it was to be their last mistake.

The lead chopper bore down on the running dinks. The machine guns opened up. We saw the bullets spraying the sand around the dinks at the same time the sound of the guns reached us. The roar of the lead chopper changed in pitch as the pilot completed his run to climb in a circling turn preparatory to strafing them again. The wing man opened up as the lead chopper climbed.

In a beautiful ballet, the two choppers moved with precision in a series of aerial maneuvers that ended in the death of every dink that had broken cover.

We thought it was quite a treat to have such excellent seats to this drama. The choppers had flown so low they had at times been level with us and as close as fifty meters away.

The black clothes of the men on the beach were like silhouettes in the sand, outlining their bodies in various positions of death.

We waved at the choppers as they made low passes over us on their way back to base.

6 January 1968

The area was strange, too quiet. The village and outlying single hootches were all vacant. Many of them were booby-trapped. As we marched, we found ammo hidden in tunnels, and in the hootches we found explosives but few of the enemy. They were evading us, not even sniping. We could smell a fight coming. It was just a matter of when.

We followed a sandy road running in a straight line between abandoned hootches in another village by the beach. The platoon was spread in a double column moving steadily.

Still no resistance.

The morning had been gloomy but around noon the sun broke through the clouds, bringing the terrain around us alive. We were away from the scrubby beach area now, into open cornfields divided by hedgerows. These small fields with their straight rows of corn reminded me of Indiana in the fall after the frost. I moved between the corn stalks, trying not to stomp them down, and for a moment I lost all touch with the war. The slight breeze, the hot sun, the corn ready to cut into sheaves reminded me of Indian summer back in Indiana. Reluctantly, I reached the edge of the field. I looked back to watch my platoon coming through the corn. The farmers and poets stepped around the different stalks, while the others crushed the stalks down.

Bell, who had returned from the hospital after his wounds had healed, and Hunter were point men that day. They found paths through the hedgerows into the adjoining fields as we moved toward a rendezvous with Captain Sells where the map indicated a small cluster of farm hootches.

Rueto called to me, "One-six, Delta Six says he has us spotted and for us not to shoot him."

"O.K. Bell, you hear that?"

"No sweat!"

We wandered into the edge of the rendezvous area on a grassy trail. Captain Sells and Four-six were there to greet us with the news that we would not be moving much farther before settling in a night location. This was good news. It was still early afternoon, time enough to write letters or rest. The whole company would logger together, making us a formidable force to reckon with.

The men were searching through the hootches when a commotion broke out. Captain Sells and I went over to check it out.

One of the new tunnel rats, Glover, had crawled inside a bunker and flushed two dinks. One was an old man, but the other was a rare find indeed—a young man in his late twenties or early thirties.

"Man! Would you look at this. A dink this age in this area and not in the army. He has to be VC," one of the men exclaimed.

"No shit, and look at this!" Another man ripped the dink's shirt off to expose several freshly healed flesh wounds on his chest, side, and arm.

"This is a dink for sure." The flat statement cooled the excitement of before. The two dinks fearfully looked around at the circle of Americans. There were the captain and his CP group, me and my CP group, and the point squad. The rest of the platoons were spread out through the area in a defensive position. The dink started pointing to the sky and then clutched himself.

"Downs, I think he's just a farmer who got caught in the open by one of our gunships," Sells said.

I glanced back at the dink. "I don't think so, sir. S-2 says that the only people in this area are the enemy, especially this AO. It's controlled by the Vietcong. This guy is the right age for the army and he isn't in it. Let the old man go, but not the young one."

"No, Downs, let both of them go." It was a firm order.

A couple of my men gave the two dinks cigarettes. They squatted on their haunches and smoked while we took a break.

"O.K., saddle up!" I called out. Bell, Hunter, and I consulted the map and compass to decide on the direction we wanted to go. We were to head back toward the cove. There was a long field in that direction. The grain had been harvested and the field was surrounded by hedgerows.

Bell headed straight out across the field with Hunter, Rueto, and me right behind. The point cut back and forth through some low bushes at the beginning of the field until he broke out to travel the right side of the field.

Bell, Hunter, and I, as usual, discussed the options as we moved. The platoon with attached elements was spread out in a zigzag file behind us. At the hedgerow at the far end of the field, Hunter and I bunched up while Bell searched back and forth along the hedgerow for a way through. He found a likely opening and pushed his stocky body into the shoulder-high hedgerow. Hunter and I stepped forward to follow him through, Hunter slightly ahead of me.

The air was rent by a thunderous explosion. Dirt, sticks, powder, and shrapnel shredded the calm, sunny afternoon air around those of us in the point.

Hunter was thrown violently against me. I felt things whiz by. My ears were ringing with painful intensity. I staggered backward a couple of steps from the force of Hunter's body and the explosion. Everything spun crazily as I fell helplessly down. I tried to stand up but I couldn't raise myself any higher than my hands and knees. Someone was yelling.

I pushed my buttocks back on my heels as I tried to balance on my knees, gazing up at Hunter who was still on his feet, standing a few feet away, facing me with his arms held out in front of him like a Frankenstein monster.

By going first, Hunter had taken a full load of shrapnel from head to toe. The front of his body was in tatters. Blood ran from tiny wounds over all his exposed surfaces and his clothes were cut in dozens of places. He leaned forward, smiling in a dazed way as blood dripped from his face and arms onto my outstretched hands. I wiped my hands on my fatigue shirt.

We were both laughing in grunts from the shock. A piece of shrapnel had pierced his pack and shaving cream was spurting out the top of the pack in a long stream up above his head, raining white goo down on us.

I dropped back on all fours because everything kept spinning. Then I began coming out of it a little bit. The shaving cream stopped. Hunter stood, still holding his arms out in front because of the pain. I saw the other men in the platoon crouched in different positions of defense, those closest to us moving forward to give aid. Captain Sells came running through the field toward us.

I looked toward the hedgerow. There was a small crater where a section of the hedgerow used to be.

I crawled toward it yelling, "Bell! Bell! What happened? Where are you? Bell! Bell!" I was distraught. Had the explosion blown him apart? He was nowhere in sight. There was the crater, a trail, and another hedgerow on the other side of the trail. The hedgerow was low but I couldn't see over it.

I pushed my hands into the dirt in the crater trying to find something.

"Lieutenant, be careful. There may be another booby trap."

I looked over my shoulder at Captain Sells.

"It's Bell, sir! He's disappeared," I screamed. "I'm going to jump over this to the other side of the hedgerow." I pushed myself to my feet. Captain Sells was here to take command. I was frantic. Bell was my man and I was responsible.

I lunged up and out as far as I could and there was Bell, sprawled out in the field on the other side of the low hedge. I crawled over to him, feeling tremendous relief.

"Bell! Bell! You O.K.?"

His head was turned toward me and his eyes were open. "I stepped on something, heard it go click, and leaped forward just as it went off. Son-of-a-bitch. I didn't have time to warn you."

"Doc! Hey, Doc. Come on down," I yelled. "Bell is O.K., but he's in a little shock and he has some shrapnel wounds in his feet."

I was beginning to regain control of myself as the shock wore off. I had a terrible ringing in my ears but that seemed to be the extent of my damage. That and some small shrapnel holes in the corner of my fatigue shirt was about it. Then I remembered.

"The dink! That goddamn dink back in the hootch. He could have warned us." I turned to Villasenor. "Get back to that hootch and bring in that dink."

"It's too late, lieutenant. We already had the guys at the end of the column check and those dinks are long gone."

"I had a feeling we should have killed the miserable fuckers."

7 January 1968

Captain Sells sent my platoon to patrol the area to the east. The sun beat down with more intensity than the day before.

In midmorning the point and I decided to travel along a wide grassy path running in a straight line past separate hootches spread haphazardly along its edge.

Ahead of us on the left side were two or three hootches sitting in the sun. A small grove of trees was spread out in the neglected fields behind the hootches.

Two dinks stepped out on the trail, dressed in combat gear and carrying weapons, unaware of our presence. They noticed us at the same time we were maneuvering to take them under fire. We fired as they frantically ran back into the hootch. We ran forward in a fire-and-maneuver procedure designed to offer us protection while advancing.

We rushed the hootches but the dinks had disappeared in the growth behind them. I split the platoon into squads to fan out in a search pattern. The hot, humid air was causing us to sweat with an intensity that we had come to accept as normal.

I was on line with my squad when I heard gunfire from the squad on my left. I ran over to see what was going on.

An old woman was standing at the edge of some bushes with some of my men standing next to her. I ran up to inquire what happened.

The men in the squad had seen a black-pajama-clad figure in the bush. They had opened fire, then ran forward to see what they had hit. When they ran the dink out of the bushes, they discovered it had been an old lady. We looked her over.

She had been hit in the jaw. Her eyes were registering shock. The flesh along her lower jaw was ripped to the bone and blood was dripping in a steady flow down the front of her chest.

"Jesus Christ, an old woman," I said to no one in particular. "What the fuck is she doing here? What happened to those two soldiers?" *This is crazy,* I thought. *The enemy is all over the place, everything is booby-trapped, there aren't supposed to be any civilians around here, and here is an old woman with a gunshot wound in the jaw.*

I looked around at my men. The sun shone on all of us in this peaceful field. I didn't feel bad about the old woman. I wouldn't let myself. She wasn't supposed to be there; since she was, she had to accept the risks.

"Goddamn, I wish the fuck we were back in the jungle. Everything is so much simpler back there."

By saying that I had switched my mind to something I had often argued with Schaldenbrand about. He liked the jungle fighting but I detested the closed-in feeling. I had always preferred the open areas, but damn! the open areas were always occupied by civilians. I was ready to go back to the jungle. I didn't mind fighting but I hated to have these goddamn civilians mixed in the middle.

"Let her go and let's get on with the patrol." The old lady hobbled into the brush and disappeared. I wondered what would happen to her.

Later in the afternoon we were spread out when Spagg and his assistant gunner called for me to come look at what they had found. Trees and bushes were spread through the area with small paths that cut back and forth leading from one hootch to another.

I followed them past a well they had discovered. They led me to a hootch to proudly show me their find. Inside on a table were two Buddhas. They were cast metal about sixteen to eighteen inches high.

Before I could stop him, Spagg picked one of them up.

"Goddamn, Spagg, you know better than that. These are perfect for booby traps. You could have been killed!"

Spagg guiltily stood there with the Buddha in his hands. He realized I was correct. He had made a grave error but he had survived.

"Well, sir, I know you're always talking about getting one of these for a souvenir and so is the captain. Here are two of them. I guess I wasn't thinking."

"Those are beauties and I thank you, Spagg, but damn! don't take a chance like that again. Let me see them."

He handed them over. Perfect. We took both of them back to the well. The rest of the platoon was resting there after filling their canteens.

"Hey, look at that! The lieutenant's got two Buddhas."

Some of the men wouldn't touch them. All of the old-timers had a superstitious fear of them. Everytime someone had taken one for a souvenir, something had happened to him. The men swore the Buddhas were jinxed. I had always laughed that off.

The first sergeant was flying in later. I would give the Buddhas to him to store back in the company area so I wouldn't have to lug them around. I called Captain Sells to tell him we had a Buddha for him. He was pleased.

10 January 1968

The last night of my Vietnam War, we climbed a small sand dune with a flat top. It was just the right size for the small perimeter my platoon would form. Other small sand dunes were spread around us, but with our deep foxholes we would be in a good position to repel any attack.

It was a beautiful evening. The moonlight gave the area around us a soft tint. The sound of waves breaking on the beach drifted across to us like the steady pulse of eternal life.

I was in excellent spirits. Everything was right with me in the world. I had been in the war barely five months and had already won the Silver Star, the Bronze Star with V Device for Valor, and the Vietnam Gold Cross of Gallantry. I had been wounded four times, winning three Purple Hearts. My men thought I was invulnerable; I did too. I had the respect of my men and full confidence in myself as a combat leader. I had orders for Flight School.

For the first time in my life I could look forward to a new life, free from the false starts, heartbreaks, and indecisiveness of my past. I knew I had the resolve to complete my last year of college. There were no clouds on my horizon. I had finally become victorious in the battle with myself that each man fights in order to grow.

I lay on the sand late that night, staring at the stars and thinking the pleasant thoughts of any young man who stood on the threshold of a new life.

11 January 1968

The morning's early light added to my feelings of well-being. The crispness of the fading night combined with my view of the light haze over the ocean reminded me of a verse I had read or heard somewhere. It went something like this: "The dawn comes up like thunder out of China across the bay."

I called my sergeant and squad leaders together to review the orders for the day. We would take the short march across the sand dunes to the edge of the village and set our ambush in the same location as the day before. Today we would catch those dinks with the heavy weapons.

"Saddle up," I called.

The squad leaders sorted out their men. At the last moment I made a decision. "The same point squad as yesterday will take point today."

The men looked at me in surprise. This was a deviation from my iron-clad policy of alternating point squads every day. I saw their looks and hastened to explain.

"We ain't going very far and the point knows the way." I walked forward. "Let's go."

We could see the village from our night location. The point weaved back and forth through the sand dunes toward the edge of the village. At the edge was a trail leading up to the small hill of our ambush location the day before.

I was the third man in line. We had just turned up the gentle climbing trail when we spotted a dink skittering among the hootches right next to us on the left side. The platoon stopped as the point element searched among the tunnel holes and hootches for the dink who had disappeared.

The point stepped back on the trail. "No sign of the dink, sir! He got into one of them holes. This whole area is like an anthill with the Cong hiding under the ground."

"Yeah, I know. Luckily, we aren't traveling much farther. The dinks have booby-trapped and mined this whole area, I imagine. Watch your step."

We moved forward to the gate at the top of the small hill. I instructed the two point men in front of me to check the gate and the trail beyond carefully for booby traps, and they slowly searched the sandy trail for mines and the edges for booby traps. I stood resting my weight on one hip, smoking my cigarette and watching the two men conduct their slow search forward.

About five meters past the gate the two men turned to me and waved me forward. "All clear, sir."

"Let's go, Rueto."

I passed through the gate. My right hand grasped my M-16, my left held my cigarette. I was humming "The Blue Tail Fly" as I mentally ticked off the positions around the saddle where I would set my men. I noticed the time—0745 hours.

My foot slipped backward a fraction of an inch, hitting the trigger mechanism of a mine.

I never heard the explosion. Black powder and dirt flew by me. My eardrums were ripped. My body was flying through the air. I threw my arms in front of me in a reflex motion to balance myself. My eyes registered the horror of a brilliantly white jagged bone sticking out of the stump of arm above where my left elbow had been. Ragged, bloody flesh surrounded the splintered bone. My mind cursed as utter helplessness and despair overwhelmed me.

Another part of my body coolly calculated what had caused the explosion—it had been a land mine. But what kind would blow off my arm instead of my legs? Of course! It had to be a "Bouncing Betty," a mine that flies up out of the ground after being tripped and explodes waist high. That would do it!

My M-16 had been in my right hand. The rifle was shattered; my hand was mangled. I stared in horror at what remained of my right arm. The flesh had been ripped away, exposing the two bones in my forearm from the wrist to the elbow. The bones looked like two white glistening narrow rods buried in the raw bloody meat. Thinking *My God! My God! My God!* I felt the total defeat of my life as I landed on my feet five yards from where the mine had exploded.

After landing, I staggered forward two or three steps and then collapsed. My legs wouldn't work. The mine had gone off about six inches from my left hip. From the waist down my body was mutilated and torn where large chunks of flesh, muscles, blood vessels, and nerves had been ripped away by the hot exploding shrapnel. My buttocks were blown away. The backs of my legs were ripped to the bone down to my heels.

I rolled over on my back, being careful to keep my stump and right arm out of the dirt and sand. My body was sending so many pain signals to my brain that it was overloaded like an electrical circuit. It caused me to feel a racing, humming numbness.

I lifted my head to view a scene from hell.

My pack had absorbed the majority of shrapnel that would have entered my back and spinal cord. It had been blasted to splintereens. My belongings were scattered in a wide area around me. Ammo, C rations, poncho and poncho liner, my precious horde of almost three hundred heating tabs, extra canteens of water, my green cat songbook, my grandmother's gift book of *Readers' Digest Condensed Stories,* and various odds and ends were lying among the pieces of flesh and fragments of my uniform spread around the ground.

Rueto, my RTO, who was close behind me, was sitting on the ground, astonishment on his face, screaming in a terror-filled voice that he had been hit. From the waist down he had been shredded; blood covered him like a sheet. The man behind him, Robbins, had caught shrapnel in the guts and was screaming. Two men behind him and one of the point men had also been hit with shrapnel. They were quiet. Altogether, six of us were hit.

The infantryman's soul-tearing cry of "Medic! Medic!" sounded through the air. My ears were working again.

There was initial confusion but long hours of training took over as the men moved to perform the functions they had been taught since entering the army.

I saw Doc rushing forward from his position in the middle of the platoon. *"Ah, good,"* I thought. Putting my medic in the middle of the platoon offered him the best protection from harm and it was paying off.

The squad leaders were directing some of the men into a defensive perimeter around us as other men rushed to the aid of their comrades. My friend Spagg reached me first. I looked at the shock in his eyes as he knelt over me to cut off my web gear.

I yelled at Rueto, "Shut up, Rueto, I'm hurt worse than you and I'm not yelling."

"Sir, I've been hit bad. My legs, my legs, it hurts like hell," he wailed.

"I know it," I bellowed. For some reason it took a great effort to answer him, "but shut up!"

I watched a couple of men run by me to the wounded point man. They would only glance at me sideways as I lay there holding my bloody stump in the air. They seemed nervous.

Some of my men ran toward me, then turned suddenly away at the sight of my torn body. They stood near me but hesitated to come too close, as if their movement through the air would make it worse.

Spagg asked me to turn sideways a little bit so he could pull my gear free. There were tears in his eyes as he worked over me.

With a grunt, he pulled the belt out from under me.

"Is there anything I can do for you, sir?" Spagg asked.

"Yes, run over there and pick up my arm and bring it back to me. I don't want to leave it in this stinking village!"

He ran over, picked up my arm with the wristwatch and colorful bracelets attached, brought it back, and laid it across my stomach. He then picked up my right arm that I no longer could control and also laid it across my stomach. He gently bent the bracelets off the bloody wrist and threw them away. Then he ran over to the bushes where I think he got sick.

Marley, my platoon sergeant, rushed to my side. I asked him if he had radioed Delta Six for a dustoff. He replied that he had and asked if I was alright. He said that Delta Six was on his way.

I said, "He'd better hurry if he wants to see me!"

Doc pushed Marley out of the way. I told him there wasn't much he could do. He ignored me as he hurriedly gave me a shot of morphine and tied a tourniquet around my stump.

My medic had the bad habit of always telling a man how bad he was hit. I had chewed him out a number of times about this as I had about many things. I decided this would be a good time to see if all those ass-chewings had made any impression.

"Doc, it looks bad, doesn't it? I probably won't make it, will I?"

Doc agreed, "Yep, it's really bad, sir."

"Doc," I grimaced, "if I've told you once, I've told you a hundred times you don't tell a man he's bad off when he is."

He looked at me kind of funny.

"I'm thirsty, Doc. Let me have some water."

"I can't, sir, you may have internal injuries."

"I don't have any internal injuries, Doc. I would know that. Let me have just one sip."

"No, sir, you know better. I can't."

"I suppose you're right, Doc." I was cold and it was a very hazy day. *That's funny*, I thought. *I thought the sun was coming up like thunder across the bay.*

I told Marley to get my squad leaders.

"Go take care of the other men, Doc. They need you."

I looked up. Marley and my squad leaders were standing in a rough line along my right side. I asked who was hurt. I was feeling weaker and weaker. It was so goddamn cold. As my body fought for life, my thoughts ran to my men and my platoon. I felt I was cheating them by leaving when they needed me most. When I had joined the platoon as their leader, they had taught me the ways to survive in combat. A second lieutenant who was new-in-country" and they who were "old-timers"—eighteen, nineteen, twenty, but old to the ways of combat and death. As I gained experience and confidence as a leader, I became an "old-timer," having to make decisions that had put me in the position I was now in—wounded and maimed, facing death.

My men were still there looking at me, despair on their faces. Their invulnerable leader had been brought down.

"Marley."

"Yes, sir."

"I want your men to get the dink who planted that mine. I want him dead! Get him!"

"We will, One-six, don't you worry about that."

They looked at each other, then back at me.

The grey haze of the day was strong. I pushed it back to look beyond my men.

It was colder now and harder to see. I was thinking of my Grandma Downs and her farm, of the woods and fields of Indiana I loved so much. If only I could walk them one more time. *I'm only twenty-three years old and I'm dying. What a waste! There are so many things I had meant to say and do, but I hadn't. Now I will never get the chance.*

A familiar sound broke through the haze. A chopper. It swept across my line of vision. It had a big red cross painted on its side. I saw the dust swirl up as it settled to rest.

If I could only stay awake, I might make it to the field hospital.

There was a fury of activity as the wounded were loaded aboard. A path was cleared through my men as a stretcher was brought to me. It was flipped open and thrown beside me in haste. I was lifted by my men onto the stretcher and rushed to the chopper. The man carrying the head end of the stretcher got sick and dropped me. Spagg grabbed the handles and lifted.

I looked at my platoon as I was carried through them to the chopper. God, I hated to leave them! Their faces reflected the forlorn hope that I would make it. I kept trying to smile to show them that I would.

My stretcher was locked in the bottom tier and I felt the chopper lift off. The medic who accompanied every regular dustoff lit a cigarette and stuck it between my lips. It tasted great. He leaned down and yelled in my ear, "Can I do anything for you, sir?"

"Take my left boot off, my foot is killing me!" I croaked back. The medic took out his scissors and cut my boot off. Wonderful relief. My foot was hurt the least, but its pain signals were somehow registering in my brain.

My eyes traveled around the chopper and its passengers. Sitting in the jump seat was one of the point men, not badly wounded, a Jewish

boy who had only recently joined my platoon. He looked back at me
with great compassion on his face. I glanced at the chopper medic who
had given me the cigarette. He was a black man about my size. Over
the medic's shoulder I saw the pilot study me a second, then speak
into his lip mike. The medic nodded, turned to me, and yelled above
the noise of the chopper, "Ten minutes to Chu Lai."

I tried to yell back, "I'll make it!"

It didn't seem to take ten minutes. The chopper bumped hard
against the landing pad as the pilot brought it in hot. We were quickly
unloaded into a square army ambulance with red crosses on the doors.
Just like a war movie, I thought.

After a very short ride the back doors were thrown open and we
were hustled into the Second Surgical Field Hospital.

There were six teams of medical people in a large open room with
bright lights. The chopper had radioed ahead. The nurses on both sides
started cutting my bloody combat uniform from me. One cut off the
other boot. Two doctors, one on each side of my shoulders, started
working. Needles were stuck into me. I watched as one doctor handed
my left arm, still in reasonably good shape, to a nurse. Another doctor
held my stump and cut the tourniquet off. "Who the hell tied this
tourniquet?" he remarked to no one in particular. He put a scapel next
to my stump and cut down into the flesh to a blood vessel which he cut
and tied off.

Goddamn! It didn't even hurt. I must be really zapped, I thought.

A lady stood at the foot of my stretcher, dressed in grey. She kept
asking me my name, rank, and serial number. I kept telling her.

"I'm Second Lieutenant Frederick Downs, Jr., 05337689, First
Platoon, Delta Company, Third Brigade, Fourth Division."

She asked me again.

I felt very tired.

Western Union Telegram

Mr. & Mrs. Frederick Downs Sr, Don't Phone
The Secretary of the Army has asked me to express his deep regret that your son, Lieutenant Frederick Downs Jr, was placed on the seriously ill list in Vietnam on 11 Jan 68 as the result of multiple metal fragment wounds to the body, with traumatic amputation of the left arm above the elbow and neuro vascular damage to his right arm. He was on a combat operation when hit by fragments from a hostile booby trap. In the judgement of the attending physician his condition is of such severity that there is cause for concern, but no imminent danger to life. Please be assured that the best medical facilities and doctors have been made available and every measure is being taken to aid him. You will be kept informed of any significant changes in his condition. He is hospitalized in Vietnam at the 2D surgical hospital, APO San Francisco 96394. Address mail to him at that address.
Kenneth G Wickham Major General USA The Adjutant General (46).

After five days I was transferred from the 2nd Surgical Hospital at Chu Lai to the 85th Evac. Hospital at Qui Nhon, Vietnam, and ten days later to the 249th General Hospital in Japan, where I spent two weeks before flying stateside to Fitzsimmons Army Hospital in Denver, Colorado, for a year of treatment and rehabilitation. By the fall of 1968 I was more or less on my own, able to reenter college as an outpatient and to work myself toward my present job and my present life.

AFTERWORD

My Wounds

The Killing Zone ends when my heart stops on the operating table at the Second Surgical Field Hospital in Chu Lai. When I regained consciousness hours later in postsurgery, through the fogginess I stared in disbelief at the stump of my left arm, gone above the elbow. I was further distressed to learn that I might lose my right arm and had suffered critical wounds to my hip, buttocks, legs, and feet. According to the doctors my chances of regaining a normal gait were slim. Searing pain enveloped me. I didn't know one could experience so much pain and still endure life. Dr. David Pilcher, the trauma surgeon who had saved my life when I came in from the battleground, had already written a letter to my family telling them that while I had lost my left arm, "there was cause for concern but no immediate danger to life."

After four or five days in Chu Lai, the medical staff judged me stable enough to transfer to the 85th Evacuation Hospital in Qui Nhon, where I spent a week and a half before being medevaced to Clark Air Force Base in the Philippines and on to the 249th General Hospital at Camp Drake outside Tokyo, Japan, where I stayed for two weeks before being loaded onto a medevac back to the States. On February 11, one month to the day after I stepped on the Bouncing Betty, a planeload of the wounded, me among them, landed at Buckley Airfield. Air force and army military staff and volunteers met the plane, loaded us into litter buses, and drove us to Fitzsimmons Army Hospital in the town of Aurora, east of Denver, Colorado.

For the next five months I rode a roller coaster of pain, multiple surgeries, and emotions. At times I felt sure I had gone crazy, at other times I didn't see how I could survive another day. But I was getting better.

The army medical teams managed to save my right arm, save my legs, repair the damage to the rest of my body, and restore function in my limbs. The hospital experiences figure in my second book, *Aftermath: A Soldier's Return from Vietnam.* The two books had different aims. In *The Killing Zone* I tried to set the record straight about our soldiers who fought in Vietnam. *Aftermath* was truly a catharsis—an attempt to purge my soul of the emotional and mental anguish piled up during the war and my painful recovery and rehabilitation.

A third book, published twenty years later titled *No Longer Enemies, Not Yet Friends*, chronicles my return to Vietnam, where I am finally able to complete my rehabilitation.

The Men

Meanwhile, back in the war, what happened to Platoon Delta One-six after we six soldiers were taken from the battlefield? We had endured fierce fighting on the Bataganian Peninsula while working out of the battalion firebase, LZ Uptight, but unknown to us the enemy was preparing for their major military attack of the Vietnam War, which would become known as the 1968 Tet Offensive. The six wounded by the Bouncing Betty I stepped on were a portent of the ordeal Delta Company and the other companies of the First Battalion, Fourteenth Infantry (Golden Dragons) would go through in the days to come.

Originally the platoon had been assigned forty-three men and an officer plus another five men attached to the platoon. In reality, there were never that many men in the field at the same time. Although our platoon looked to be full strength on paper, in actuality we operated at half to three-quarters strength during combat operations. At any one time, a number of men from the platoon would be in the hospital recovering from wounds or sickness. Others were at the dentist, on a three-day leave, taking rest and recreation (R and R), or in transit. A few were even dead but still on the roster because of slow paperwork. Sometimes a new man would join the platoon and be wounded or killed within days or weeks of his arrival. By the time I received a new roster from company headquarters, the man could have come and gone.

The company roster dated 3 January 1968 listed the following men in my platoon. I have noted "KIA" (killed in action) or "WIA" (wounded in action) for those for whom I could find that information. At the end of the Delta One-six platoon list, I have included men from the other platoons who were KIA. There was a constant inflow of men to replace the wounded and dead, so I have also included the names of the men killed and wounded in Delta One-six during the Tet Offensive who joined the platoon after January 3.

Unfortunately, the list is incomplete. I have gathered information from letters, after-action reports, and the memories of men I interviewed. Men who were killed or wounded were often not mentioned by name in the after-action reports.

Delta One-six roster, 3 January 1968:

Downs, Frederick, Jr.	2LT	WIA
Marley, Bradford D.	SGT	
Villasenor, Joel C.	SGT	
Bell, John W., Jr.	SP4	WIA
Collins, Ronnie R.	SP4	
Foster, Eddie G.	SP4	
George, Paul, Jr.	SP4	WIA
Hunter, James W., Jr.	SP4	WIA
Johnson, Clarence	SP4	
McCovey, Leonard L.	SP4	
Muto, Homer M.	SP4	
Payton, Ronald E.	SP4	
Porter, Arthur L.	SP4	WIA
Ruto,* Robert	SP4	WIA
Skelly, William E.	SP4	
Spaag,* Steven C.	SP4	WIA

*Spaag's and Ruto's names are misspelled in the original text, where they are referred to as "Spagg" and "Rueto."

Torrey, Clifford P., Jr.	SP4	WIA
Vesquez, Jesse	SP4	
Austin, Clarence	PFC	WIA
Benford, Walter H.	PFC	
Board, Billy G.	PFC	
Cripps, Donald R.	PFC	WIA
De Cos-Hernandez, Pedro L.	PFC	WIA
Fanelli, Garry F.	PFC	
Glover, Donald Lawrence	PFC	KIA
Hahn, James F.	PFC	WIA
Irish, Rodger H.	PFC	
Johnson, Larry Eugene	PFC	
Kissinger, Norman Charles	PFC	KIA
McCormick, Patrick D.	PFC	WIA
Nault, Eugene	PFC	
Peterson, Basil R.	PFC	WIA
Richards, James E.	PFC	
Robbins, Gerald A.	PFC	WIA
Seaton, Robert Wayne	PFC	KIA
Sexton, Denver	PFC	
Shaffer, Eugene L.	PFC	
Somers, Kenneth J.	PFC	
Sparks, Leonard E.	PFC	WIA
Subbiondo, Charles J.	PFC	
Thomas, Roy L.	PFC	WIA
Thomas, Vincent J.	PFC	
Thompson, Jerome D.	PVT	WIA
Woods, Millidge, Jr.	PVT	WIA

Delta One-six men who were not on the 3 January 1968 roster:

Mann, Frank	SP4	
Delk, Collete	SP4	WIA
Iding, Gregory Thomas	SP4	KIA
Gallagher, R.	SP4	

Schaldenbrand, Michael	SGT	
Fonseca, Juan B.	PFC	WIA
Serrao, Frank N.	PFC	
Carney, Louis E.	PFC	
Fanelli, Larry F.	PFC	
Hoffman, Charles Edwin "Doc"	SP4	KIA
Miller, James Garrett	PFC	KIA
Yoder, James Strong	SP4	KIA
Weeks, Steve	2LT	WIA
Williams, R.	PFC	WIA
Harff, William Henry, Jr.	PFC	KIA
Brown, James	SP4	WIA
Edenfield, Jessie	PFC	WIA

Second Platoon:

Anderson, Steven Richard	SP4	KIA
Nelson, Lewis Charles	SP4	KIA

Third Platoon:

Ordway, William Dwight	2LT	KIA
Miller, Paul James	PFC	KIA

Unidentified platoons:

Cortez, Jose G.	SP4	KIA
Torliatt, Charles Peter, Jr.	PFC	KIA
Martin, John C.	2LT	KIA

After the Bouncing Betty Exploded

Brad Marley, the platoon sergeant, call sign Delta One-five, had been in the middle of the platoon with the RTO and Charlie "Doc" Hoffman, our medic, as I led the long file of soldiers through the village of Phu Nhieu 2 on the Bataganian Peninsula. We were about ten kilometers north of My Lai and twenty-five kilometers northeast of Quang Ngai.

South of us was the battalion firebase, LZ Uptight. When I triggered the Bouncing Betty, those not wounded immediately dropped to the ground in defensive positions. They thought we had walked into an ambush. Several cried for the medic to come forward. Telling the men to hold their positions, Marley, his RTO, Bill Skelly, and the medic, Doc Hoffman, ran to the front of the line.

When Marley saw so many of us wounded, he was shocked at the carnage. Six men were down and blood had sprayed everywhere—on the sandy path, the grass, on trees and bushes, on men in front, and in back of those who were hit. My RTO, Ruto, was screaming as blood poured from his groin and legs. Pete Peterson ran forward to apply tourniquets to Ruto. After Pete had applied the tourniquets, Ruto ripped them off to see how badly he had been damaged. I lay in a mangled pile; my arm had blown onto the sand about twenty feet away. Another man clutched his stomach and moaned, sitting where he had been blown backward by the force of the blast. Three other men were bleeding from wounds. The contents of my rucksack and the equipment of the other wounded men littered the ground.

All of the men still operational were asking Marley what to do. He said he nearly panicked when he realized he was in command—the commotion and sudden violence had shocked and unnerved everyone. Gradually, Marley recovered his composure. He saw that Steve Spaag, one of the M-60 machine gunners, and other men were attending to the wounded. Doc had pulled open his medical kit and begun to work on me

Jim Hahn, the point man that day who had followed my instructions to proceed through the gate, turned to look back after the explosion and saw no one standing. The two men who had been with him on point were on the ground bleeding, and the men behind them in the gate area were either on the ground wounded or crouched in defensive positions. He saw "Indian's Gun," Clarence Johnson, an American Indian who was the platoon's other M-60 machine gunner, running forward to set up security. Hahn saw me lying in a bloody mess on the ground and was startled when I yelled to ask him if he was ok. Thinking the explosion was the signal for an enemy ambush, Hahn ignored the screams of the wounded as he scanned the area for the enemy. Seeing none, he climbed onto a nearby berm to provide security, thinking this was the prelude to a full attack.

Each soldier carried one first aid bandage, but with carnage so massive, Doc had to improvise. He asked Spaag to cut bamboo to use in tourniquets for Ruto's legs and my legs. When Spaag returned with the bamboo sticks, Doc asked Spaag for his Sears Roebuck hunting knife to use in cutting off strips of our uniforms to use as tourniquets. Later in the day, after the platoon had left the area, Spaag asked Doc to return his knife. Doc told him he had left the knife sticking in the sand next to where he had been working on the lieutenant.

Marley told me later that his year of combat experience in Vietnam had helped to prepare him to gain control of himself and the men that day. He got on the PRC-25 radio to call the company commander, Captain Harold Sells, Delta Six, to report what happened. Then he pulled out his map to give Delta Six the platoon's coordinates. Captain Sells acted rapidly after learning the platoon's whereabouts and extent of its casualties. Sells, who regularly moved his five-man headquarters command group from platoon to platoon, was one and a half kilometers away with Lieutenant Steve Weeks, Delta One-four, and the Heavy Weapons Fourth Platoon. After the call from Marley, he force marched his five-man HQ group and the fifteen men of the Fourth Platoon across the heavily mined area toward our platoon's location.

After he called Captain Sells, Marley spread the men out in a tight perimeter for security. In about ten minutes, the medevac dustoff arrived, the downblast from the rotors causing a miniature sandstorm. When the litter carriers got to me, Spaag grabbed me under the armpits, Marley supported my body, and Don Cripps had hold of my legs to load me onto the litter. They loaded me and the other wounded onto the chopper and we were gone. Marley said later it was always strange to him how one minute we were all together and the next minute men you had spent months with day and night, like you were brothers, would be whisked away in a chopper, never to be seen or heard of again. You never got a chance to say good-bye.

Captain Sells reached the perimeter just as the chopper lifted off. The men who remained behind were on ragged edge, so Sells took over the platoon and laagered them into a secure position for the rest of the day. Once that was done, he called the other two platoon leaders, Platoon Sergeant Paul Archambo, acting Delta Two-six, and Second Lieutenant William Ordway, Delta Three-six, who were on separate patrols one to two kilometers away. Sells ordered them to join up with him with so he could laager the entire company into a defensive perimeter for the night.

The next day the battalion commander, Colonel George E. Wear, flew out from LZ Uptight in his command helicopter to the area where Delta Company was laagered. He asked Captain Sells to come with him to visit Delta One-six and his men in the Second Surgical Hospital at Chu Lai. I vaguely remember Colonel Wear and Captain Sells walking into the intensive care ward where those with the most traumatic wounds were located. They talked with me for a short while before I drifted off in a drugged stupor. The sight of us so shocked Captain Sells that when he returned to the company he told the platoon leaders and sergeants he would never visit such a ward again.

War stops only for those soldiers killed or so badly wounded they can no longer conduct it. As traumatized as Delta One-six's men were from the day's events, there was no time in a combat platoon for men to mourn. The mission must be carried out. Captain Sells transferred the Fourth Platoon leader, Lieutenant Steve Weeks, to take over my platoon and become the new Delta One-six. After the day of rest, Captain Sells sent the platoons out to continue patrolling, searching for the Viet Cong or NVA who clearly controlled the area.

A few nights later, as Lieutenant Weeks and Sergeant Marley placed the men in their three-man positions, Marley stepped on what appeared to be a punji pit. Luckily the matting covering the hole was thick enough to hold Marley's weight, and he quickly hopped off before it caved in. Lieutenant Weeks was about to stomp the matting in until the men held him back, thinking it could be a booby trap. As they peeled back the covering, they saw a wire going through the middle of the hole. Using a knife to carve around the outside of the hole, they uncovered a booby-trapped 105 artillery round. They left the booby-trapped shell alone that night and in the morning tied a string on the wire, took cover, and jerked the string. The 105 round exploded, blasting a three-foot hole in the ground and throwing shrapnel in all directions.

Offensive Operations

The First of the Fourteenth Golden Dragons continued operations on the Bataganian Peninsula in the Quang Ngai Province, with four rifle companies (Alpha, Bravo, Charlie, and Delta), one cavalry platoon, and one reconnaissance platoon. The combat on the peninsula was unrelenting: no quarter was given and none was taken. Quang Ngai Province was one of five provinces in South Vietnam never pacified, and American soldiers entered at their peril.

18 January 1968

Seven days after I had been wounded, Bill Ordway (Delta One-three), my good friend and the Third Platoon leader, triggered a booby-trapped grenade hidden on one of the innumerable sandy trails connecting the villages spread throughout the peninsula. A piece of shrapnel severed his jugular vein, and he bled to death within a few minutes. One of his men, "Money" Johnson, who was standing next to him, lost an eye to a piece of shrapnel from the explosion. Two other men from the Third Platoon were also wounded.

19 January 1968

Nearly one week after I stepped on the Bouncing Betty in Phu Nhieu, Delta One-six was ordered back to the same village, located on the sandy dunes along the South China Sea. Captain Sells called Lieutenant Weeks and told him to take half the platoon into the village and to have Sergeant Marley take the other half five hundred meters down to the beach and set up an ambush.

Marley told me that by this time no one was walking down any trails. The loss of six men and the loss of Lieutenant Bill Ordway had proven the folly of going along any well-marked trail. The whole area had proved to be heavily mined and booby-trapped. In an attempt to counter these weapons, Captain Sells had requested a scout dog from battalion headquarters. HQ sent out a dog handler with a German shepherd that was supposed to be able to detect any buried mines or booby traps.

Marley split off two squads and moved to the low jungle growth along the beach, arranging his men in an ambush position. Lieutenant Weeks took two squads and went in search of a spot to enter the village without using a trail or path. Finally the point squad found an opening in one of the hedgerows surrounding the village. It looked as if no one had been through the hole in a couple of months, but Lieutenant Weeks, not taking any chances, found an old man outside the village and decided to run him through the hedge first. The old man went through with no problem. Then the dog and his trainer went through without raising any indication of danger.

Marley's men were in position by then. Walking out onto the beach, he looked back toward the village just in time to see the last couple of men going through the hedgerow. As he turned to go back to his position he heard a loud explosion and knew immediately that someone had triggered another Bouncing Betty. Marley ordered his men to saddle up and they all went running down the beach toward the village. Marley thought the beach would be an unlikely place to mine and he was in a hurry to rejoin the platoon, to offer assistance and to guard against attack.

When they arrived, the survivors in the two squads were attending to the wounded. The capriciousness of war had trumped all precautions that day. One old man, a dog, his trainer, and eleven men had passed through the hedgerow, walking right over the Bouncing Betty. The twelfth man, PFC Leonard Sparks, had stepped on it. The mine had come out of the ground and exploded waist high, shearing Sparks's legs off just below his butt. The thirteenth man, newly assigned to the platoon and standing immediately behind Sparks, was killed instantly. He took the blast from the front, which detonated a light antitank weapon (LAW) he had been carrying across his chest. The explosion blew him in half, scattering blood and pieces of his body over the other men. Another three men were also wounded by the blast. Lieutenant Weeks quickly got the men in order and called in a dustoff. Marley helped to load the wounded onto the chopper. Marley said later that the incident was a repeat of the horror of the week before when I had triggered a Bouncing Betty. As he gathered the shocked remainder of the platoon together, he could see that they were demoralized.

In the span of less then two weeks, the platoon had lost twelve wounded and one killed, about half the operating platoon. Most of the infantry combat platoons of the four infantry companies of the First Battalion, Fourteenth Infantry had been patrolling and fighting continuously during the eight months they had been in Vietnam. Each infantry company was composed of three infantry platoons and one heavy weapons platoon. Each infantry platoon was composed of forty-three men and an officer. At this point in the war, attrition rates had risen to the point the platoons could not field a full complement of forty men and an officer. Replacements from the States were slow in coming, and there were never enough of them. Consequently, Delta One-six and the other platoons worked at a little over half strength. Obviously, the loss of thirteen men seriously hampered the platoon's combat efficiency.

They were soldiers, however, and soldiers must stay on mission patrol, find the enemy, and engage him until reinforcements arrived. Delta One-six had taken the most casualties, so Captain Sells attached himself and his own five-man command group to Delta One-six, adding more firepower and strength.

A few days later, Captain Sells sent Sergeant Marley back to the First Cav base camp, LZ Baldy, just south of Da Nang, to get information about the layout of the firebase. In a week, the First Battalion of the Fourteenth Infantry would be replacing the First Cav in a leapfrog maneuver toward the DMZ.

25 January 1968

The Golden Dragons turned control of LZ Uptight over to Task Force Barker, part of the Eleventh Brigade, who had relieved the First of the Fourteenth when we left Duc Pho. Now they were again relieving the First of the Fourteenth. Members of that task force would be accused later of slaughtering hundreds of Vietnamese civilians at the village of My Lai on 16 March 1968, in what would become known as the My Lai Massacre. My Lai was only ten kilometers to the south of where I was wounded.

26 January 1968

The First of the Fourteenth was ordered to establish firebase Hardcore approximately twenty-five kilometers south of Da Nang in order to block elements of the Second NVA Division as they streamed toward Da Nang. Intelligence reports indicated something big was in the making, but they assumed it was just another large battle shaping up. In reality, the NVA division was maneuvering in preparation for the Tet Offensive. Consequently, there were large concentrations of NVA units in the area chosen for the LZ, but no one realized that until Alpha and Delta Companies made combat air assaults into the LZ. The LZ at Hardcore was "hot," laced by heavy enemy fire. One gunship from the 7/17 Air Cavalry was hit by 12.62 mm ground fire and crashed. Alpha Company led the helicopter combat assault on the landing zone, followed by Delta Company. Two men from the Delta Two-six were wounded. Captain Sells, who had survived nine months in the field, was rewarded by being ordered out of the field to take a job back in Battalion HQ. In an ironic twist of fate, Captain Charles L. Cosand, who had been my Fort Benning OCS Ninety-second Company commander, replaced Captain Sells.

31 January 1968

At 0300 hours, eighty-four thousand NVA and Viet Cong soldiers launched the Tet Offensive, attacking thirty-six of the forty-four provincial capitals. All hell broke loose. Fierce fighting raged throughout South Vietnam, and American military units, surprised by the offensive, were moved to support each other as the hundreds of battles and firefights spread across the countryside.

4 February 1968

Bravo Company, patrolling out from LZ Hardcore, fought a six-hour battle at the village of Tho Son, suffering a number of wounded. Under intense enemy fire, Warrant Officers Norman Shanahan and Gregory Shuntz flew in to pick up the wounded. Bravo Company withdrew from the village. Meanwhile, Delta Company moved into position to attack Tho Son in the morning. After they were in position, Spaag, the M-60 machine gunner, was bitten on the neck by a scorpion and developed a fever of 105 degrees. The company commander did not want to risk bringing in a medevac, nor did he want to lose his machine gunner. Spaag's friend Jim Hahn nursed him through the night, so Spaag could carry his M-60 machine gun in the attack scheduled for dawn.

5 February 1968

Delta Company was ordered to attack Tho Son village from the south at first light in concert with Bravo Company. Delta Company moved in the premorning darkness to a position behind a railroad embankment. The plan was to attack on a line across the rice paddies to the village where they would trap the NVA against a river on the other side. The plan called for a marine unit to fire an artillery barrage ahead of the men of Delta Company as they advanced across the open rice paddy, but bad luck continued to dog Delta One-six. They were on the gun-target line.

One marine artillery gun had been set up inaccurately so that when the artillery barrage began, the first shell fell close to Delta One-six. All the infantrymen immediately knew the danger they were in as the shell exploded, sending shrapnel whizzing through the air. Lieutenant Weeks and the other RTO in the platoon, Pete Peterson, made frantic calls to get the marine unit to cease fire, but five shells from that gun were already in the air. Two rounds of 105 mm howitzer high explosive shells landed on the company command group and Delta One-six, wounding nine men. Captain Cosand suffered hits in the face and leg. Eight men from Delta One-six were wounded, including Lieutenant Weeks, whose left arm was severely mangled and would later be amputated above the elbow.

Steve Spaag, the M-60 machine gunner, and Pete Peterson, the RTO, were also hurt. They and the other wounded were lifted out by dustoffs. The first platoon sergeant, Sergeant Glass, was promoted temporarily to first platoon leader. Once the wounded were clear, the remaining men returned to their positions and the attack proceeded across the rice paddy into the village. Spaag, Peterson, Cosand, Weeks, and the other five wounded men were sent to the Sixty-seventh Evacuation Hospital. When the nine bloody, bedraggled men were brought into the operating room, one of the nurses, Lieutenant Sederic, noticed the men were from Delta Company. She asked Spaag if he had known a Lieutenant Bill Ordway in Delta Company who had been killed. Spaag replied he did know him. She told Spaag that she and Lieutenant Ordway were engaged to be married, and she burst into tears.

6 February 1968

Both Delta and Bravo Companies crossed the Bong Song River in pursuit of the NVA they had forced out of the village the day before. The enemy fought back and heavy fighting lasted throughout the day.

7 February 1968

The First of the Fourteenth encountered heavy enemy fighting all day. Two helicopters were shot down. Delta and Bravo Companies set up blocking positions across the northern fork of the Song Chiem Son River.

8 February 1968

The enemy attacked LZ Hardcore with mortar and rocket fire. Fighting continued throughout the day, with all companies engaging the enemy.

9 February 1968

Companies A, B, C, and D were engaged in firefights and battles throughout the day, with all companies taking casualties. One helicopter was shot down and another came under intense fire when it tried to bring in ammunition to Charlie One-six. In the middle of the afternoon, after a bloody battle, Delta linked up with Bravo Company and they laagered in for the night. Eleven wounded men had to be evacuated before dark, but the enemy fire was so intense that one gunship was shot down and the dustoff was hit while trying to liftoff with the wounded. Mortar shells and automatic rifle fire continuously swept both companies. A mortar shell landed in the middle of Delta One-six, wounding Greg Iding and James Garrett Miller. Cries of "Medic" sounded out, and Charlie "Doc" Hoffman and Norman Charles Kissinger rushed to the two men. While they were tending to the wounded, more mortar shells dropped on their position, killing all four men and wounding sixteen others in Delta One-six, including Jim Hahn.

10 February 1968

At 0825 hours Delta Company requested a dustoff for twenty-two WIAs and four KIAs.

After four weeks, First Platoon, Delta One-six had taken so many causalities it had ceased to be an operational combat unit. It had been an especially bad time for the platoon leaders. Of the four second lieutenants who started combat operations with Delta Company, Weeks and I had lost limbs and Bill Ordway was dead. The second platoon leader, Lieutenant Dennis W. Cohoon, Delta Two-six, had left the field, and the acting Delta Two-six platoon sergeant, Paul G. Archmbo, had been wounded in a mortar attack.

25 February 1968

Private Cliff Torrey was wounded when Delta Company was attempting to replace a unit under heavy fire. He had just unloaded from a combat assault helicopter and was running from the chopper when he was hit by shrapnel from mortar rounds landing in the LZ.

26 February 1968

Delta Company command group lost one KIA and six WIA when an American fighter pilot turned too close to the target on his fourth pass and accidentally punched out a 500-pound Mark 82 bomb short of the target. The bomb exploded twenty meters from the Delta Company command post and Delta One-six Platoon, wounding a number of men. The officer writing the after-action report stated, "Another adverse effect of a 'short' bomb, in addition to the causalities, is the deterioration of confidence in air support." As I read that I thought, "No shit."

27 February 1968

Hard fighting continued around LZ Hardcore until the First of the Fourteenth Golden Dragons were relieved by the Fourth Battalion, Thirty-first Infantry. The month of February 1968 had been the toughest single period of combat for the battalion. During the Tet Offensive, from 3 February to 27 February, the Golden Dragons suffered 40 killed and 153 wounded. Ten aircraft were shot down.

After the War

The reader knows what happened to some of my men. What of the others?

Sergeant Schaldenbrand returned to his hometown of Pittsburgh, where he worked in the steel mills.

SP4 Bob Ruto, my faithful radio telephone operator (RTO), was walking behind me, carrying the radio, and saw the blur of the Bouncing Betty as it popped out of the ground. He was severely wounded from the waist down. Two weeks later we caught up with each other briefly in the 249th General Hospital in Japan, before he was sent to Walter Reed Army Hospital to be treated by a famous vascular surgeon in an attempt to save his legs, which, give thanks, were saved after months of reconstructive surgery. One day in the fall of 1968 the surgeon told Ruto he was well enough to go home; Ruto went home, but he never came back. Years later he was arrested by army investigators as a deserter. Ruto had served a year of combat in Vietnam, been severely wounded, and spent nearly a year in an army hospital, only to be arrested as a deserter just as President Carter granted amnesty to those deserters who had fled to Canada. The irony was thick. An army review board exonerated Ruto, but the episode was terribly embarrassing. The government was wrong to treat him in this way. He contacted me in the 1980s, and I had a number of wonderful visits with him and his splendidly supportive wife.

Private Jim Hahn, the rifleman on point when I stepped on the land mine, was wounded on 9 February 1968. Hahn was sent to Okinawa for three months to heal from his wounds, after which he was sent back to Vietnam, where he rejoined Delta One-six at Firebase Brillo Pad. He finished his tour of duty and was sent back to the States in September 1968, where he finished the remainder of his time in the army. Hahn later moved back to Shelbyville, Kentucky. He and his wife, Patricia, had three children: Gina, Lee, and Daniel. After Patricia died, Jim remarried. He and his current wife, Bonnie, have two children: Greg and Gretchen. Jim is currently in the construction business, building houses.

Steven Spaag was wounded on 5 February 1968 by friendly fire that also wounded Peterson, Captain Cosand, Lieutenant Weeks, and five other men. Spaag's right leg was torn by shrapnel and he was sent to the Sixty-seventh Evacuation Hospital, where he met the nurse, Lieutenant Sederic, who had been engaged to marry Lieutenant Ordway. After his hospital stay, Spaag returned to the States to serve out his army time. Spaag and I had always talked of becoming farmers when we got back, but his older sister bought the family farm. Spaag returned to Minnesota, where he worked in a salvage yard for twenty years. When that company went out of business, Spaag went to work in another salvage yard for a number of years, until its business declined and he was let go. After leaving the salvage yard, Spaag started his own bulldozer business, which he still operates today. He was married soon after he returned from Vietnam and has six children and twelve grandchildren.

Clarence Johnson, an American Indian, who was our second M-60 machine gunner and nicknamed Indian's Gun, returned to his home state of Oklahoma.

Sergeant Brad Marley returned to his hometown of Carlin, Nevada, after the war and went to work at the local phone company. He transferred to Salem, Oregon, in 1969 and married Kathy Parkin. They had a son named Chad, but in 1975 he and Kathy divorced. In 1976 he married Cassie Cooper, and they remain happily married today. Sergeant Marley returned to Vietnam in 1995 when he went to Hanoi on a business trip. When he got there, it was as if nothing had changed at all: there were the same rice paddies, the same water buffalo, and most of all the same smells. He worked for the phone company until 2002, when he retired after thirty-six years.

Captain Harold Sells, disheartened after writing letters to the parents of the thirty-five Delta Company men killed during his time as company commander, decided to leave the army, ending his nine-year career. He went on to work as an executive for various fabric mills, and we have maintained loose contact over years. He went through a couple of divorces and is now in Florida caring for his mother.

Private Leon Sparks, who lost both legs to a Bouncing Betty, ended up at Fitzsimmons Army Hospital. He was given a medical disability discharge from the army and returned to his wife and home in Indiana, where he was given a desk job at the auto repair shop he had been working for when he was drafted.

Lieutenant Steve Weeks also ended up at Fitzsimmons Army Hospital, and we were in the same room for a number of weeks. We were known in the hospital as the lieutenants who had both lost their left arms above the elbow while leading the same platoon. The bets were that the lieutenant who took over Delta One-six after Steve had a jinx on his left arm. Steve's wife, Elizabeth, who went by the nickname Buffy, moved west from their home in Chicago and rented an apartment outside the hospital gate. Steve and Buffy treated me like a brother, and we became such good friends that he agreed to be best man at my wedding later that year. They had a daughter, Jennifer, and unfortunately were later divorced. Steve remarried, moved to Colorado Springs, Colorado, and started several businesses. He sold the businesses a couple of years ago and, after passing a special test to receive a license allowing him to drive a truck using one arm, bought an eighteen-wheeler, which he uses to haul freight all over the country. Steve is also a champion horseman, competing in riding contests around the West.

PFC Greg Iding's mother contacted me in 1987, ten years after *The Killing Zone* was published. Greg, from Ohio, was one of the four men killed in a mortar attack on 9 February 1968, along with Charles "Doc" Hoffman, Norman Kissinger, and James Miller. One of Mrs. Iding's friends had read the *The Killing Zone* and mentioned that Greg was in the book. She wrote me a letter asking me to tell her about her son's life in Vietnam and how he had died. It was the first letter I had received from a parent of one of the men in my platoon who had been killed. I had thought that these parents might hold me responsible for their sons' deaths. Quite to the contrary, I found I was their last connection to their sons. The army conveys little information to families about the circumstances of a soldier's death, beyond the bare fact that they had been killed due to enemy action. So I wrote to tell her about Greg's life in the platoon—the friends he had made, what a good soldier he was, and how his platoon mates and I held him in high regard because of his willingness to "hump the boonies," or carry his weight on all the dirty, dangerous jobs a combat infantryman must do in war. I described to her how her son's reliability and steadfastness was so important to me in managing the problems of running a combat platoon. I needed good men like him to carry out our mission. I told her that Greg was killed immediately, with no suffering, and that he had died among friends who loved him like a brother. We continue to correspond: I send her pictures of our children and we exchange Christmas cards.

Lieutenant Bill Ordway's mother contacted me the same way. Bill had been killed when shrapnel from a booby-trapped grenade pierced his jugular vein on 18 January 1968. Like Mrs. Iding, Mrs. Ordway wished to know more about her son. A friend of hers had read an excerpt from a letter of mine that talked about Bill's death and had been published in the book *Dear America: Letters Home from Vietnam*. Until she died in a nursing home years later, we maintained contact through Christmas cards and letters. She always seemed to delight in reading information about our two daughters' school functions and activities. Bill was an only son, and I often think she took pleasure from our reports about our children. Maybe they reminded her of the children who would have been her grandchildren if Bill had survived the war. She wrote in one of her letters that her husband died within a year after receiving the news about their son's death. She thought he died of a broken heart.

Private Cliff Torrey was a good friend of Greg Iding's and one of the platoon members I remembered well. Cliff was on a three-day R and R the day I was wounded. He had put in for helicopter gunner and had gone in for the physical. He returned after I was wounded and was with the platoon through most of the heavy fighting in the first weeks of the Tet Offensive. After he was wounded on 25 February 1968, Torrey was sent from the hospital back to the States, where he finished out his time. He got married and has four children: three girls and a boy whom he named after his good friend Jim Yoder, who was killed in November 1967 when our platoon was ambushed. Today, Cliff sells industrial hardware.

Jim Brown, who was assigned to the platoon in mid-February during the Tet Offensive, was placed in Sergeant Muto's squad with "old timers" Clifford Torry and Jessie Vesquez. Jim was wounded in a fire-fight on 28 April 1968 at the same time William Harff of First Platoon, and Lewis Nelson, the Second Platoon medic, were killed by enemy mortars. Jim was sent back to the States to recuperate. He went into manufacturing, married his wife, Carol, and they have a daughter named Kelly.

Private James Yoder, a point man and one of eighteen children in a family from Tennessee, died when the platoon was ambushed and encircled a few days before Thanksgiving 1967. Someone in his family read The Killing Zone, and some of his many cousins, nephews, and nieces have been in touch with me over the years by letter and e-mail, asking the same heartrending questions that Mrs. Iding and Mrs. Ordway asked about their sons. The nephews have wanted to know about James's personality, what he endured, his bravery, and everything I can remember about him. They have issued a standing invitation for me to visit Tennessee, but I have not yet done so. Visiting them will be my next duty before the year is out.

Don Cripps, one of the men who carried me to the dustoff, was wounded during a mortar attack near the end of February 1968. He was sent back to the States, where he recovered and was discharged. He was one of the men who attended our First Platoon reunion in 2004. Sadly, he was killed three weeks later in a car accident.

Basil Peterson, a rifleman who also carried a radio from time to time, was wounded three times. On 5 February 1968 he was hit by friendly fire from artillery, and in late March he was wounded by friendly fire yet again. On his twenty-first birthday, 28 April 1968, he was wounded by enemy fire. Later he received an Article 15, a "nonjudicial punishment," for missing a flight back from R and R. Even though he had hitched a ride back on a C-130 and arrived before the flight he had missed, he was still punished for missing the flight.

The 498th Medical Company provided the air ambulance that supported our unit whenever we called for a dustoff to pick up the wounded. On page 34 of *The Killing Zone*, I describe an episode on 19 September 1968, where a couple of feet were torn off the rotor blades of a dustoff as the helicopter, carrying three seriously wounded men, lifted out of a rice paddy and hit a tree. The pilot managed to keep the helicopter flying and made it back to base with the wounded. On 14 February 1980, I received a letter from Platoon Sergeant Jimmy D. Coln, who was a senior flight medic with the unit at that time. He had read *The Killing Zone*, and he wrote to tell me the two pilots who lost twenty-three inches of rotor blade that day were twenty-year-old warrant officers John Shelton and Jack Sloniyer. Jack Sloniyer was killed five months later in a crash south of Qui Nhon.

***

As for me, my plans to make a career of the army ended with the Bouncing Betty. Having only one arm forced me to take a new path. While stationed at Fitzsimmons, I remarried and decided to make a new home in Denver. After the army retired me under a medical discharge, I returned to college, receiving an undergraduate and master's degree in business administration from the University of Denver. When I got sufficiently up and about, I worked in my cousin Andy Anderson's real estate company and for my wife's family business for a few years. But something nagged at me, and one day, pretty suddenly, I decided to go to work for the Veterans Administration. It was 1974, and my family, well settled in Denver, was disappointed. They wanted me to stay in business, but I wanted to serve my country again.

For thirty-three years, I have not regretted that decision. I worked in

Veterans Benefits for seven years and at the age of thirty-five was fortu-
nate to be appointed as the Veterans Administration's national director of
the Prosthetic and Sensory Aids Service, working at the VA Central
Office in Washington, D.C. The service provides all the prosthetic
devices used by disabled veterans throughout their life; the disabled are
dependent on these devices for mobility and independence. When I was
appointed, the service was in disarray and lacked leadership. Disabled
veterans and Congress were complaining that veterans were not getting
the wheelchairs, artificial limbs, and other prosthetic devices they needed
in a timely manner, nor were they receiving high-quality prosthetics. The
undersecretary for health wanted a disabled Vietnam veteran to come
into Washington, step into the high-profile job, and straighten out the
disorganized, dysfunctional service. Upon arriving in Washington, I took
immediate action and began to implement management changes and
provide leadership for the national program.

Today approximately a thousand people work for Prosthetic and
Sensory Aids Service at the VA hospitals and outpatient clinics throughout America, Puerto Rico, the Virgin Islands, and Guam. In 2005 we
provided prosthetic devices and services to 1.5 million disabled veterans at a cost of 1.1 billion dollars. This included approximately 8,000
artificial limbs, 77,000 wheelchairs, 229,000 surgical implants, 755,000
eyeglasses, plus hundreds of thousands of other devices. I have had the
same passion for this job I had for combat command. I get to take care
of the men and women who have been hurt in the service of their country. I have been in charge of the service for twenty-seven years and I love
it. The position is the perfect place to be to make sure the country's vets
are provided with the best prosthetics in the world. Another bonus of
working in Washington, D.C., is that I am only six miles from Walter
Reed, the army hospital where the traumatically injured or wounded are
sent from their theaters around the world. I consider it part of my duty
as an amputee and a former soldier to visit the men and women
amputees so they can see that I function as a normal person. I tell the
amputee and his family that his life is not over; he is taking another path
that will lead to a life just as full and rich as any other path. It has been

most gratifying to have the amputee or his family tell me months later that my entrance into the hospital room bolstered their spirits and gave them a sense of relief seeing me function with an artificial arm and a hook. They often tell me that when they met me, they realized that things were going to work out ok.

My Return to Vietnam

My job at the VA has a fascinating international facet—to help foreign countries fabricate and distribute limbs to those soldiers and citizens wounded in war or civil strife. I have traveled to Laos, El Salvador, Egypt, Sri Lanka, and Cambodia, but all of those experiences pale compared to 1988 when, twenty years after Delta One-six's disaster, I went back to Vietnam.

When I was a soldier, my job had been to kill Vietnamese. Now I was sent to help the Vietnamese, but more, I was to learn something about myself that put the war into perspective.

For some years after the war, America had been trying to account for its MIAs and POWs. Animosity between the two countries had grown so great that by 1987, America and Vietnam had stopped talking to each other. In an attempt to break the deadlock, President Reagan appointed a former chairman of the Joint Chiefs of Staff, U.S. Army General Jack Vessey, as presidential emissary to Vietnam on MIA and POW issues. General Vessey quickly flew to Hanoi, seeking a way to renew talks, and returning with an agreement that untangled the political and economic issues from the humanitarian ones. The Vietnamese would address the latter—for instance, POWs and MIAs—if America would address the huge Vietnamese issue of 300,000 amputees from the war.

Reagan told Vessey to proceed, and soon I became part of a three-man team bound for Hanoi to assess Vietnam's means of developing an amputee program. No U.S. airlines were allowed to fly into Vietnam, so we went to Bangkok, where we received our visas at the Vietnamese embassy and bought tickets to Hanoi on the Vietnamese airline, Hang Khong Vietnam. My emotions seesawed as we touched down at the airport. It all seemed so surreal to return to Vietnam, my hated enemy. But if successful, our mission would benefit the families of America MIAs and POWs, and I was determined to carry on.

On our second day in Hanoi, when we broke for lunch, I went for a walk around the Lake of the Restored Sword in the middle of Hanoi. Halfway around, I noticed a young Vietnamese soldier, clad in a green army uniform and wearing a green pith helmet, pushing his bicycle toward me. A boy of four or so, obviously his son, perched on the bike's seat. Both were oblivious to me as they enjoyed their walk. They had about them a look of love that gave me pause. These were human beings—of course, they were—and yet for twenty years I had hated them, all of them, as an enemy less than human.

A soldier is taught to kill. The training starts within a day or two of entering the army or marines. In order to kill, the soldier is taught to dehumanize the enemy, to kill targets. Any hesitation, any thought that he is killing someone's father, son, or brother, and the soldier may be slow to pull the trigger. Soldiers kill French Frogs, German Krauts, slanty-eyed Japs, Rebs, Yanks, Pepper Bellies, Dinks, Onion Eaters, Chinks, Ragheads, and so it continues: an endless list throughout time. And at the end of the day, the soldier is assured the killing is justified. When he comes home he will be welcomed as a hero, receive forgiveness, and be absolved of his sins.

But it never worked that way for the Vietnam veteran. He carried with him all the horrible tragedy of war and yet, at home, was held to blame. No forgiveness, therefore no resolution and no absolution. The Vietnam War gave birth to a generation of anger and bitterness. Truly a lost generation. And for me, a lost platoon, my brothers killed and wounded. I'd had, I thought, reason to hate.

Few of us had thought so deeply back then, but something had been moving in me. I now realized that they, the "dinks"—this man, his son, all—were one of us. I completed my walk around the lake, knowing that a burden had been lifted from my spirit. No, I had not suddenly come to love the Vietnamese, but I had come to see them as people.

I flew to Vietnam fourteen more times as part of General Vessey's team, and I traveled from one end to another—North and South—met many of their veterans from the war, and exchanged many war stories, as old soldiers do. One afternoon, after visiting a children's hospital at Hai Phong Harbor, we asked the driver to stop somewhere for a bite to eat. Our companions from the Vietnamese Foreign Affairs Office were the same ones always assigned to escort us. They spoke English very well and knew our personal history from talks on our previous trips.

The sun was brutally hot as we drove slowly along the noisy, dusty street looking for a restaurant. In the middle of one block, a faded white French colonial building stood out. A thin, dignified Vietnamese man in a white suit stood with folded arms in the open doorway. A sign advertising noodles hung between the open floor-to-ceiling windows next to the doorway. Our two-car caravan pulled up in front as the man in the white suit looked at us. One of the Foreign Affairs men got out of our car and walked up to the man to explain who we were and to ask if there was room for all of us in his restaurant. He nodded yes, waved his arm at us to come along, and went inside to prepare our tables.

Inside, the gentleman in the white suit directed his staff as they prepared two large round tables for us near the front. The door and windows were wide open to allow the humid air to circulate as much as possible. The five of us who were Americans were drenched in sweat and welcomed the restaurant's shade.

Eight men sat at a large round table next to ours. All our age or older, they wore the scruffy dark slacks, shirts, and berets typical of veterans. Smoke drifted in a cloud from their cigarettes. Large beer bottles sat in the middle of the table. They looked at us with interest, their hard-lined, sun-darkened faces void of expression. As we sat down, they asked a question of one of the foreign officers, who quickly provided an answer. The Vietnamese we met were always direct in wanting to know who we were, where we came from, and had we been in the war. The foreign officers had answered those questions so many times they seldom translated the questions to us, and simply proceeded to answer.

Suddenly one of the Vietnamese vets smiled broadly and approached our table, stopping by my chair. When I stood up, he grabbed my hand in both of his and shook it, talking excitedly. Understanding nothing, I stood mute, smiling and looking toward a Foreign Service officer for an explanation. Both groups were in a kind of staring standoff until the Foreign Service officer came to our rescue. As the two Vietnamese talked back and forth, the Foreign Service officer glanced my way, uncertain as to how I might take what was going on.

Finally, all became clear. They had learned that I had been a soldier and had fought near Phu Nhieu, Vietnam, on the Bataganian Peninsula in 1968. The soldier shaking my hand had been in the North Vietnamese Army fighting in the same area at the same time. He was excited to have met an old enemy. I grinned, looked at him, and said, "If you fought in the same area I was at the same time, maybe you are the one who planted the land mine that blew my arm off." He replied, "Maybe I did, so let me buy you a beer," releasing my hand to wave the waitress over. The moment of tension dissolved as I laughed and told him that was a hell of a good idea. As we drank, I spoke of my wife and two small daughters at home and he suddenly rose from his chair to run next door, returning with three small blue-and-white vases, presents for my loved ones. He told me it was good the war was over. I agreed it was better to drink beer together than to kill one another.

The Killing Zone tells a story nearly forty years old, through the eyes of a twenty-three-year-old lieutenant. My second book, *Aftermath*, tells the story of rehabilitation and healing in an army hospital where I turned twenty-four. At the age of forty-four, twenty years later, the U.S. government sent me back to Vietnam on a humanitarian mission. I'm now sixty-one and have had a rich, full life with family, friends, job, church, travel, and much else. I often think back to that day in Vietnam when I stepped on the Bouncing Betty and my life changed forever. It has been a good life.

Full Circle

The Killing Zone plays a part in that life. Ed Barber, an editor at W. W. Norton, read my manuscript and liked what I had written.

Published in fall of 1978, *The Killing Zone* has been in print ever since. Twice a year, a check from W. W. Norton arrives at our home, along with a report listing the number of books sold. I expected each year that like some old soldier, the book would simply fade away. I was pleasantly surprised when Ed called in the fall of 2005 to say that Norton would reissue *The Killing Zone* in 2007, and that he wanted me to write an afterword. There were no rules. I could write what I wanted. A new generation had grown to maturity and wanted to know about Vietnam, the war their fathers, grandfathers, uncles, and granduncles had fought that so divided the country.

My dad had served in the Pacific Theater in WW II. I had not paid much attention to his war stories until it was too late. How I yearned to have his stories to understand better what he had endured. In much the same way, the Vietnam veteran has war stories to tell, but very few Americans were willing to listen until it was nearly too late. I am pleased that Ed Barber and W. W. Norton realized in 1977 that even unpleasant truths need to be recorded.

The book has long stood on the reading list at West Point and at many other colleges that teach leadership and military history. I have spoken at West Point and to dozens of other military groups plus innumerable colleges and universities over the years. I have written many articles for magazines and Outlook pieces for the *Washington Post*. Such is the odd and unexpected power of publishing of a book.

In writing *The Killing Zone*, I had two goals. I wanted to show future generations that the American soldier in Vietnam was a good soldier. In 1978, the antiwar, antimilitary feeling in the United States was pervasive in newspapers, on television, among writers, in movies, and in colleges. I had started college at the University of Denver in the fall of 1968, while I was still on active duty in the military. The Students for a Democratic Society (SDS), the Weathermen, and other antiwar groups on campus targeted anyone in the military as fair game for their antiwar stance. Such hostility was not pleasant for me or other Vietnam veterans. It was hard to be denigrated for serving our country. Many veterans never admitted they were in the service for years after Vietnam. Angry at the antiwar faction, I wanted to set the record straight by proving that the men I served with had fought and died with honor.

I also wanted future young infantry lieutenants and noncommissioned officers to learn from my experiences, both good and bad. Some actions I took as a combat officer had worked out well and some had not. The time had come to deal with both. Perhaps some would learn from my mistakes, especially the lesson that combat does not go by the book.

Most surprising—and pleasing—of all, I get a great deal of mail and a good reception wherever I go on behalf of the book. Both lead me to hope that I have come close to my goals. I thank all in my life for that.

—Fort Washington, Maryland
December 2006